Secure Love Scripts

Secure Love Scripts

What to Say When You Need Closeness Without Clinging

Kaia Solander

Mindful Pages

Published in 2026

ISBN: 9789309332630 (PB)
ISBN: 9789309337758 (eBook)

Published by

Mindful Pages
Imprint of Alpha Editions LLC
312 W. 2nd St #1834
Casper, WY 82601, USA

This book was developed using advanced writing tools to support the drafting and ideation process. All content has been thoughtfully curated, refined, and reviewed to ensure quality and relevance.

Content

Introduction

In 1952, inside a London hospital ward, James Robertson pointed a camera at a two-year-old girl called Laura and recorded a form of distress that polite institutions had learned not to see. The room was clean, the sheets stiff, the air carrying that sharp hospital smell of soap and boiled linen. Laura had not been neglected. She was fed, bathed, and medically observed. Yet over several days, separated from her mother under the visiting restrictions of the time, she moved from protest to despair to a withdrawn composure that looked, to an untrained eye, like improvement. Her cry became a thread pulled through cloth: small, repeated, almost unbearable.

Robertson's film, *A Two-Year-Old Goes to Hospital*, did not discover attachment, but it made separation visible. Alongside the work of John Bowlby at the Tavistock Clinic and the 1951 World Health Organization report on maternal care and mental health, it helped disturb an old professional confidence: the belief that children merely needed competent physical care and would soon "settle" if adults did not indulge their distress. The camera showed something more exacting. A human being can be warm, fed, safe from obvious harm, and still suffer when connection becomes uncertain. Love is not sentiment alone. It is a nervous system event.

The adult version is less cinematic, but no less real. A message sits unread. A partner's voice sounds flat. Someone says, "I'm just tired," and the words land as weather before they land as meaning. There may be no hospital ward, no institutional rule, no dramatic abandonment; only a phone face-down on a kitchen table, the hum of the refrigerator, and the mind beginning its private investigation. Has something changed? Was that goodbye colder than usual? Should another message be sent, or would that make things worse? The body often answers before language does. The stomach tightens. The chest narrows. The thumb hovers. Then speech, when it arrives, comes out disguised.

The paradox of reassurance is that the moment a person most needs it is often the moment they become least capable of asking for it clearly. Need rushes ahead; language limps behind. A request for closeness becomes a complaint. A bid for comfort becomes a cross-examination. A fear of disconnection dresses itself as sarcasm, accusation, silence, apology, or a flurry of texts that do not quite say the one honest thing: I want to know we are still connected. That sentence is not childish. It is not weak. It is one of the central facts of human life, though adults often spend great energy trying to make it look more sophisticated.

Attachment theory gave the twentieth century a language for this fact, but language can harden into labels when handled carelessly. "Anxious", "avoidant", "secure", "dysregulated": these words can clarify patterns, yet they can also turn living people into case notes. The more useful question is not, "What category am I?" but "What happens to my speech when closeness feels uncertain?" One person pursues, sending three messages where one would do. Another retreats, not because they do not care, but because care itself feels like pressure. One raises their voice to force contact; another becomes impeccably reasonable while disappearing behind a wall of calm. These are not merely personality traits. They are strategies, and strategies are often old solutions trying to survive in new rooms.

The distinction matters because needs and strategies are easily confused. Closeness is a need; repeated checking is a strategy. Safety is a need; controlling the other person's response time is a strategy. Understanding is a need; interrogating tone, punctuation, and facial expression until the room goes brittle is a strategy. When the two collapse into one another, couples argue about the surface behaviour while the deeper hunger goes unnamed. The argument becomes, "You text too much," or "You never answer properly," when the quieter truth is more vulnerable: one person is trying to soothe fear, and the other is trying not to be swallowed by it.

Both may be sincere. Both may be clumsy. Sincerity alone does not make communication safe.

Ainsworth's Strange Situation studies, developed in Baltimore in the late 1960s and 1970s, placed infants and caregivers into brief separations and reunions, then watched what the reunion revealed. The genius of the work was not that babies disliked separation; everyone already knew that. The revelation was in the pattern of return. Some children reached, were comforted, and resumed exploration. Some clung and could not settle. Some looked indifferent while their bodies told a different story. The lesson, translated cautiously into adult life, is not that lovers become infants when anxious. It is that reunion is a test of trust. The question is not simply whether closeness exists, but whether it can be found again after interruption.

Modern intimacy is full of interruptions. The old village did not have read receipts. Marriage in 1880 did not involve interpreting a partner's silence through a glowing rectangle at midnight. The devices are new; the fear is ancient. Digital contact has made access feel like evidence. A quick reply can seem like proof of love; a delay can feel like a verdict. Yet the same technology that carries tenderness also magnifies ambiguity. Three dots appear, vanish, reappear. A message is seen but unanswered. A voice note is played twice, searching for warmth in the pause before the second sentence. What used to be a gap is now measurable. The mind treats the measurement as meaning.

Still, not every unmet need should be dignified as attachment pain, and not every request for space is a wound in disguise. There are limits to what better phrases can repair. Some relationships are marked by contempt, coercion, chronic dismissal, or danger; in such cases, clear wording may reveal the problem more sharply rather than resolve it. A script is not a spell. It cannot make an unavailable person generous, or turn repeated disrespect into care. Its power is more modest and, for that reason, more trustworthy: it helps a person tell the truth without throwing the truth like a weapon.

That modest power is not small. Consider the difference between "Do you even care about me?" and "I am feeling unsure after earlier; could you reassure me that we are all right?" The first sentence asks for comfort while preparing for battle. The second risks directness. It does not guarantee the desired response, but it gives the relationship a cleaner chance. Or take the difference between "Fine, do whatever you want" and "I am disappointed, and I need a little time before I can respond kindly." One punishes through fog; the other marks a boundary without turning the boundary into exile. The words do not erase emotion. They give emotion a handle.

This is where secure language earns its name. Security is often mistaken for not needing much. That misunderstanding has done quiet damage. The secure person is imagined as self-contained, low-maintenance, serene under all conditions, never needing to ask whether love is still present. But secure attachment is not the absence of need; it is the ability to bring need into relationship without disguising it as threat. It is the capacity to say, "Come closer," without demanding captivity; "Give me space," without implying abandonment; "That hurt," without prosecuting the whole character of the person who hurt you. Security is not emotional minimalism. It is honest dependence with dignity.

The phrases that support this dignity tend to be plain. They do not dazzle. They do not sound like theatre. "I miss you." "Can we try that again?" "I am getting overwhelmed and I still want to stay connected." "I need twenty minutes, then I will come back." Their plainness is part of their strength. Under stress, the mind does not reach for elegant essays; it reaches for practised sentences. A firefighter does not invent a protocol in the burning building. A musician does not wait until the concert to learn scales. The body needs language that has already been made available, language worn smooth enough to hold when the pulse is high.

The need for such language becomes clearest in the small domestic scenes that rarely appear in public accounts of love. Someone has had a brutal day and cannot bear to be touched at the door. Someone else has waited all evening for that touch and hears the refusal as rejection. A partner asks for reassurance three times; by the fourth, the answer has lost tenderness and become labour. One person wants a call before bed because silence feels like falling; the other wants one quiet hour because constant availability feels like being watched. Nobody is monstrous here. Yet without clear speech, each becomes the villain in the other's nervous system.

The hidden work is to separate immediacy from importance. An anxious feeling may be urgent without being accurate. A need may be real without requiring instant satisfaction. A boundary may be loving even when it disappoints. These distinctions are not cold; they are merciful. They allow a person to ask, "What am I trying to soothe?" before turning discomfort into accusation. They allow a couple to decide whether the moment calls for reassurance, planning, repair, silence, touch, or a scheduled return. They also protect the person being asked. Love cannot remain generous if it is treated as an emergency service with no closing hours.

Reassurance, in particular, has to be rescued from both shame and excess. It is possible to ask for too much of it, especially when each answer becomes obsolete within minutes. It is also possible to ask for too little and grow secretly resentful, performing independence while collecting evidence of neglect. The healthiest reassurance is neither endless nor forbidden. It has a shape: one sentence, one hug, one small plan, one clear return time. A person might say, "Could you tell me we are okay, and then I am going to take a walk to settle myself?" That sentence does something sophisticated. It receives comfort without outsourcing the whole task of regulation.

Boundaries belong in the same conversation as closeness because they are not opposites. A boundary is not a wall built against love; it is a door with a handle. It tells another person how contact can continue without injury. "I cannot keep texting about this tonight" becomes very different when paired with "I care about us, and I can talk at nine tomorrow." The first half protects capacity; the second protects connection. Without the second half, space may sound like disappearance. Without the first, closeness may become a demand with no respect for limits. Secure love requires both: the courage to reach and the discipline not to grab.

Conflict tests these skills most sharply because arousal edits the dictionary. A person who can speak beautifully over coffee may become primitive in a quarrel. Words shorten. Tone hardens. History floods the present. "You were late" becomes "You never think of me." "I need a break" becomes "You always run away." The thread pulls again, this time through both people at once. De-escalation is not the same as surrender. It is the decision to slow the damage so the real issue can survive the conversation. "I want to get this right; I am getting activated" is not a decorative sentence. It is a hand placed on the brake before the car leaves the road.

Repair is the place where many relationships reveal their true culture. Harm happens in all close relationships, but repair does not happen automatically. Some people apologise by collapsing into shame, forcing the injured person to comfort them. Others apologise by explaining until the apology disappears beneath evidence. A clean repair is more disciplined. It names the behaviour. It names the impact. It offers a believable next step. "I raised my voice; that was frightening and unfair. Next time I will ask for a pause before I get to that point." This is not self-punishment. It is moral clarity made practical.

The same clarity is needed in the digital spaces where modern attachment often performs its most anxious theatre. Protest texting has a recognisable sound: the baiting question, the dramatic "never mind", the cold "k", the message sent not to communicate but to provoke pursuit. Such messages are rarely born from indifference. They are born from longing that has lost its nerve. The alternative is not to become perfectly composed. It is to become more legible. "I am feeling anxious and I do not want to spiral, so I am going to put my phone down. Can we talk later?" That sentence refuses both performance and punishment. It leaves a lamp on.

There is a counter-example worth taking seriously. Some people have learned secure-sounding language and use it to varnish control. "I am just stating my needs" can become a polished way to demand compliance. "I am setting a boundary" can become a refined announcement that only one person's comfort matters. The vocabulary of emotional health is not immune to misuse. This is why the test of a script is not whether it sounds mature, but whether it respects reality on both sides. Does it leave room for the other person's capacity? Does it distinguish a request from a command? Does it allow disappointment without retaliation? Does it protect dignity, including the dignity of hearing "not now"?

The deeper aim is not to manufacture faultless communication. Faultless lovers would be intolerable, if they existed. The aim is to make the next sentence less damaging and more true. Human beings do not become secure by never feeling the old panic. They become more secure when panic no longer gets sole authorship of the message. A late reply can still sting. A tired voice can still unsettle. A request for space can still awaken old fears. But between sensation and speech, a small room can be built. In that room, one can choose whether to accuse, disappear, plead, test, or ask.

The old attachment experiments showed the importance of return, but adult love asks for something more complex than reunion after separation. It asks for negotiated closeness between two people with histories, jobs, habits, wounds, temperaments, phones, families, fatigue, and pride. It asks people to hold the thread without yanking it. That is a harder art than romantic culture admits. Grand declarations are easy compared with the sentence spoken at 10.43 p.m. when both people are tired and one feels unwanted. Fidelity is often made not in vows but in these ordinary moments of translation: fear into request, pressure into timing, hurt into repair.

Every intimate relationship eventually presents the same diagnostic question, though it arrives in different clothing: can need be spoken here without either person becoming smaller? If the answer is always no, the relationship is asking too high a price. If the answer is sometimes yes, then language becomes a place to practise courage. The trade-off is real. To ask clearly is to risk hearing the truth. To set a boundary is to risk disappointing someone. To receive reassurance without clinging is to accept that love can comfort us without completing every unfinished place within us.

The work begins where the next conversation begins: at the point where instinct reaches for its old script and the self, with some effort, chooses another. Not a perfect sentence. Not a performance of serenity. Just a cleaner one. A sentence with room for closeness and room for breath. A sentence that can hold the thread without turning it into a leash.

Chapter 1
Name What You Need

The message has been sent, and now the room has changed. Nothing visible has happened. The cup is still on the table, the chair still holds the weight of the body, the phone still lies there with its blank, dark face. Yet inside, something has begun moving quickly. The last reply was shorter than usual. The goodbye sounded distracted. A small silence opens, and into it rushes a crowd of interpretations: they are annoyed, they are pulling away, they are tired of this, they have finally seen too much.

The next impulse may feel like clarity, but it is often urgency wearing a convincing mask. Send another text. Ask whether everything is all right. Make a joke with an edge in it. Withdraw before being rejected. Say nothing, but make the silence loud. What looks, from the outside, like overreacting is often an attempt to regain contact with the ground. The person does not necessarily want drama. They want the phone to stop feeling like a locked door.

The trouble is that the first available words are rarely the truest ones. "Why are you being weird?" may mean, "I am frightened by the distance I think I can feel." "Are we okay?" may mean, "I need to know I still matter to you." "Fine, forget it" may mean, "I wanted you to come closer, and I am ashamed that I wanted that." Human beings often speak from the strategy before they have found the need. By then, the conversation has already stepped onto the wrong path.

The central tension is simple and difficult: the need is usually tender, but the strategy often arrives armoured. Closeness may come dressed as interrogation. Safety may come dressed as control. Understanding may come dressed as criticism so detailed that the other person feels put on trial. The more urgent the longing, the more likely it is to be expressed in a way that makes fulfilment harder. That is the cruel little twist. The person reaches for connection with a hand shaped like defence.

This matters because relationships do not only suffer from what people need; they suffer from the forms those needs take when they remain unnamed. A need can be met, negotiated, postponed, or held with care. A strategy, once mistaken for the need itself, becomes a battlefield. One person argues against the repeated texts, the sharp tone, the sudden withdrawal, or the restless checking. The other hears the argument as rejection of the underlying longing. Both begin defending the wrong thing. The cup stays on the table. The phone becomes the whole weather.

The stakes extend beyond a single awkward exchange. When a person repeatedly hides need inside protest, they may start to believe that their need is the problem. When a partner repeatedly encounters need only as pressure, they may begin to brace before tenderness has a chance to appear. Over time, the relationship develops habits of anticipation. One expects to be disappointed; the other expects to be accused. What began as a moment of uncertainty becomes a choreography: pursuit, defence, apology, resentment, quiet, repeat.

There is dignity in becoming more exact. Not colder. Not less affected. Exact. A person who can separate the ache from the action gains a small but decisive freedom. They no longer have to treat every surge of feeling as an instruction. They can notice the body tightening, the story forming, the old sentence rising, and ask what is actually being sought beneath it. Sometimes the answer is reassurance. Sometimes it is rest, repair, information, touch, space, or the comfort of knowing when reconnection will happen. The difference is not cosmetic. It changes what can be asked for.

The path begins by distinguishing the living need from the strategy that has been trying, sometimes badly, to serve it.

Then comes the brief inward pause: enough time to register the body, name the emotion, and find the smallest honest ask that can be spoken without escalation. From there, the work narrows further, because intimacy cannot respond well to a heap of accumulated complaints disguised as one conversation. One clear request has more force than a crowded catalogue of grievances.

There will be resistance to this simplicity. A part of the mind may insist that naming the need plainly is too exposed, too generous, too likely to be refused. It may prefer the sideways sentence, the protective accusation, the message that tests rather than asks. Yet the old strategy has a cost, and the cost is often paid by the very closeness it was meant to protect. Before the next words leave the mouth, or the next message leaves the thumb, the sharper question waits: what am I really asking for, and am I brave enough to ask for that instead?

Needs versus strategies

In 1951, the World Health Organization published John Bowlby's report *Maternal Care and Mental Health*, written in the aftermath of wartime separations and institutional childcare across Europe. Bowlby, working from London, argued that the child's need for a continuous, responsive bond could not be reduced to food, shelter, and hygiene. The claim unsettled a tidy assumption: if the body was cared for, distress should settle. Yet children separated from familiar caregivers often showed something more exacting than ordinary sadness. They protested, searched, clung, withdrew. The behaviour was visible. The need underneath it was easier to misunderstand.

That distinction remains one of the most useful in adult love. A child crying at the door is not "asking" for a door; the door is only the place where absence has become visible. The need is contact. The strategy is protest. Adults are more eloquent, but not always clearer. A person may send five messages, ask three versions of "Are we okay?", become icy at the table, or dissect a partner's tone until the conversation has no oxygen left. The surface behaviour looks demanding. Beneath it may be something simpler and more human: *I do not know whether I am safe with you right now*. That is the handle.

The mistake begins when the strategy is treated as the need itself. "I need you to text me back immediately" may feel true in the moment, but immediacy is usually not the deepest need. It is the chosen route to relief. The need may be reassurance, predictability, emotional presence, or a sense that absence has not become abandonment. When this distinction collapses, couples start negotiating the wrong object. One person defends their right not to be glued to a phone; the other defends their right to feel cared for. Both may be defending something legitimate. Neither may be naming the centre.

A need has moral simplicity. It can be received without being obeyed in exactly the form requested. Closeness, safety, understanding, rest, dignity, repair: these are not crimes against another person's freedom. A strategy is more complicated, because it is a behaviour placed into the shared space. Texting repeatedly at midnight, demanding certainty during a work meeting, refusing to speak until the other person guesses what is wrong, or asking "Do you even love me?" in a tone that punishes any answer; these strategies have effects. They create decisions for the other person. They alter the room. They may even make the original need harder to meet.

Mary Ainsworth's observational work in Baltimore in the late 1960s and early 1970s sharpened this point. In the Strange Situation procedure, brief separations and reunions between infants and caregivers revealed patterns of protest, avoidance, clinging, and recovery. The importance of that research for adult relationships is not that adults become infants when distressed; that would be too crude. The value lies in what reunion shows. When contact is disrupted, behaviour becomes diagnostic. Some people reach directly and can be soothed. Some reach and cannot take in the answer. Some appear distant while carrying stress beneath the surface. The visible action is not random. It is an attempt to manage uncertainty.

In adult intimacy, uncertainty often arrives in tiny packages. A partner turns away while answering a question. A reply changes from warm paragraphs to a clipped sentence. Someone forgets to mention a plan until the last minute. The anxious mind does not merely notice these details; it begins to assign meaning. The feeling may be fear, but the strategy may appear as investigation. "Why did you say it like that?" "You used to care more." "So I suppose I am just not important." The person is trying to locate the handle, to find the place where the fear can be opened and answered. Yet the other person experiences not a request for comfort, but an accusation with no safe reply.

The repair begins with a precise question: what feeling am I trying to soothe, and what would actually help? The question is small enough to remember, but it changes the architecture of the exchange. It asks the distressed person to step beneath the first impulse. Repeated texting may be trying to soothe panic. Asking "Are we okay?" may be trying to soothe uncertainty. Criticising a partner's tone may be trying to soothe the humiliation of feeling unchosen. Going silent may be trying to soothe the fear of saying too much and being rejected for it. Once the feeling is named, the strategy loses some of its authority. It becomes one option, not a command.

The difference can be heard in the sentences themselves. "Why are you ignoring me?" points outward and assumes guilt. "I am feeling disconnected and would like to know when we can talk" points to the emotional fact and makes a workable request. "You never reassure me properly" condemns the whole history of the relationship. "Could you tell me we are still all right after earlier?" asks for a specific act in the present.

"Fine, do whatever you want" hides pain inside punishment. "I am disappointed and need a little reassurance before I can settle" gives pain a recognisable shape. The need becomes visible enough to respond to.

This is not the same as making every emotion polite. Politeness can become another disguise, especially for people trained to make their needs convenient. A person may say, "No, it is fine," while their body keeps the score: tightened jaw, shallow breathing, a quick change of subject, a small private withdrawal that later hardens into resentment. The aim is not prettiness. The aim is accuracy. A clean request may still tremble. It may still sound tender, embarrassed, or unfinished. What matters is that it does not force the other person to decode pain from smoke.

One reason strategies become so convincing is that they often work for a moment. The extra message may get a reply. The sharp question may force attention. The sulk may make the other person pursue. The accusation may produce an apology, even if the apology is frightened rather than sincere. Short-term relief teaches the nervous system to repeat the manoeuvre. Yet the longer pattern is costly. The partner begins to associate need with pressure. The anxious person begins to associate closeness with performance. Both become less free. One cannot ask without panic; the other cannot respond without bracing.

There is a useful severity in admitting that a strategy can be understandable and still harmful. The origin of a behaviour does not erase its impact. A person who grew up with emotional inconsistency may have excellent reasons for scanning tone and timing. A person whose previous relationship ended through slow withdrawal may have excellent reasons for fearing distance. But those reasons do not make interrogation gentle, nor do they make repeated checking harmless. Understanding explains the smoke; it does not require anyone to breathe it indefinitely. The more adult task is to honour the need while revising the method.

This distinction also protects the person receiving the request. Without it, every boundary can feel like cruelty. If the stated "need" is immediate access, constant availability, or endless reassurance, then any limit appears as rejection. But if the deeper need is connection, the form can be negotiated. A partner may not be able to answer every message during the day, yet may be willing to send a predictable check-in. They may not be able to process a heavy conversation at midnight, yet may agree to speak in the morning. They may not have the right words on demand, yet may offer touch, presence, or a clear return time. The need remains respected; the strategy becomes flexible.

A credible limitation has to be named: some relationships do not become safe simply because one person learns cleaner language. If a partner routinely mocks vulnerability, withholds contact as punishment, lies about consequential matters, or turns every request into evidence of defect, the problem is not merely poor wording. Secure phrasing cannot compensate for chronic disrespect. There are also moments when a person is too flooded to translate need into graceful speech. Human beings do not always access their best language under pressure. The distinction between need and strategy is not a purity test. It is a tool for seeing what is happening, including when the surrounding relationship cannot meet it.

The limitation does not weaken the distinction; it makes it more honest. Clear language reveals reality. When someone says, "I need to know we are still connected," the answer, or the lack of one, gives information. When someone says, "I cannot do repeated reassurance texts, but I can talk at seven," the response shows whether a boundary can coexist with care. Vague distress keeps both people trapped in interpretation. Specificity measures something. It tests whether the relationship can hold a need without turning it into a courtroom.

The most common confusion appears around reassurance. "I need reassurance" often sounds like a demand for emotional rescue, because it is broad enough to have no edges. "I need to know we are still connected" is narrower, and therefore kinder. It asks for a signal rather than a performance. The reply might be one sentence, a hand on the shoulder, a brief call, or a plan to return to the conversation. The form matters less than the clarity of the emotional target. Without that target, reassurance becomes a bucket with no bottom. With it, reassurance can become a bridge.

Understanding works the same way. "You need to understand how much you hurt me" may be true, but it can also arrive as a sentence with a hidden trial inside it. What kind of understanding is being sought? Is it an acknowledgement of impact? A changed behaviour? A chance to tell the whole story without interruption? A concrete agreement for next time? If the need is not named, the conversation circles. The hurt person keeps adding evidence; the other person keeps defending intent. Both mistake more words for more clarity. The handle is still missing.

Safety is perhaps the most delicate of the three because it is easily confused with control. "I need to feel safe" can be used with sincerity, but it can also become so broad that the other person is made responsible for removing every discomfort. Emotional safety does not mean never being disappointed, never waiting, never hearing "not now", or never tolerating ambiguity. It means the relationship has enough respect, honesty, repair, and predictability that discomfort can be spoken without humiliation. A request for safety must therefore be attached to visible behaviours: speak more softly, tell me when you need space, do not leave during conflict without a return time, be clear when plans change. Safety becomes real when it can be practised.

The quiet discipline is to translate from strategy back to need before the strategy takes the microphone. "I want to send another message" becomes "I am trying to soothe uncertainty." "I want to accuse" becomes "I am trying to protect myself from feeling foolish for needing them." "I want to disappear" becomes "I am trying to avoid the shame of asking." This translation does not make the feeling vanish. It gives the feeling a handle. It allows the next sentence to be chosen rather than inherited.

The forward test is rarely dramatic. It happens in the small pause before the second text, the half-second before the sarcastic reply, the breath before "Are we okay?" becomes the only sentence available. A person can cling to the strategy because it promises relief, or risk naming the need because it gives closeness a cleaner chance. The question is not whether the need is acceptable. The question is whether the chosen strategy is actually helping anyone meet it.

The 30-second self-check

Why can thirty seconds feel extravagant when the wrong sentence may cost an evening? In a kitchen at the end of a long day, a person hears their partner say, "I forgot to reply," and the room seems to tilt. The kettle clicks off. Steam touches the cupboard door. A phone lies on the counter, its screen bright with the message that arrived too late. The answer that rises first is not a sentence so much as a flare: "You always do this." It is fast. It feels earned. It may also be inaccurate.

The cost of that first flare is not theoretical. A vague ache, when rushed into language, often hardens into a vague accusation. The body knows something has happened before the mind has sorted what it means. Shoulders lift. Breathing shortens. Heat rises behind the face. The body keeps time. Yet a bodily signal is not a complete interpretation. A tightened chest can mean fear, anger, shame, exhaustion, grief, or the old memory of not being chosen. If the signal is treated as a verdict, the next words are likely to prosecute rather than reveal.

A short pause interrupts that prosecution. It is not silence used as punishment, nor is it the polished restraint of a person pretending not to care. It is a small act of orientation: what is happening in my body, what emotion is most present, and what is the smallest workable ask I can make without turning this moment into a trial? The pause is modest because under pressure grand self-analysis usually fails. Distress does not wait politely while a person conducts an inner seminar. It needs a handle close enough to reach.

Antonio Damasio's work on emotion and decision-making, including the somatic marker hypothesis developed in the 1990s at the University of Iowa, offers one useful frame for this. His research argued that bodily feeling is not a primitive nuisance standing in the way of reason; it helps guide judgement by marking possible choices with felt significance. In intimate conflict, that insight cuts both ways. The body may alert a person that something matters. It may also over-mark an old danger as if it belongs fully to the present. A racing pulse can say, "Pay attention." It cannot, by itself, say, "Your partner does not love you."

This distinction gives the self-check its discipline. The first move is not to dismiss the body, but to read it more carefully. Where is the sensation? Tight throat, clenched jaw, hollow stomach, hot face, heavy limbs, restless hands. The location matters because it draws attention away from the story and back to the signal. "My chest is tight" is more workable than "You are abandoning me." "My jaw is clenched" is more precise than "You never listen." Such sentences do not yet solve the relational problem. They prevent the first bodily alarm from becoming a moral accusation too soon.

From sensation comes emotion, and emotion benefits from being named without ceremony. Anger may be on top, but embarrassment may be beneath it. Fear may arrive disguised as irritation. Loneliness may speak in the grammar of contempt. Naming the emotion does not require perfect psychological accuracy; it requires enough truth to reduce confusion. "I feel scared and embarrassed" opens a different door from "You made me look stupid." "I feel disconnected" creates a different atmosphere from "You clearly do not care." The words are still strong, but they are no longer throwing furniture around the room.

James Gross's process model of emotion regulation, developed at Stanford University in the late 1990s, is often associated with the idea that emotions can be shaped at several points: by the situation one enters, the attention one gives, the interpretation one forms, and the response one chooses. In the domestic scale of a tense exchange, this means the decisive moment may be very small. Before the second text. Before the raised voice. Before the old sentence. A person may not be able to stop distress from arriving, but may still alter what distress is allowed to drive. That is the hinge.

The self-check then turns towards the smallest workable ask. Smallness is not weakness; it is design. A distressed person may want the whole relationship restored, the whole history understood, the whole fear erased. But a conversation cannot usually carry all that at once. The smallest ask translates distress into an action the other person can actually consider. "Can you tell me when you can talk?" "Can you sit beside me for a minute?" "Can you say whether you are upset with me or just tired?" "Can we pause and come back after dinner?" These requests do not solve every underlying pattern. They create enough footing for the next step.

This is where many people lose their way. They wait to speak until the request is emotionally comprehensive, and because no single sentence can contain the whole ache, they speak in a flood. Yesterday's tone, last week's cancelled plan, the message from earlier, the old disappointment, the fear of being too much, the private ledger of who tried harder: all of it arrives together. The other person, faced with a storm rather than a request, begins to defend, correct, or shut down. The original need disappears beneath evidence. The room becomes crowded.

A useful self-check refuses the crowd. It asks for one sentence that can be repeated without escalation. This condition matters. If the sentence becomes harsher each time it is spoken, it was not yet clean. "I need you to stop making me beg for basic care" may be emotionally understandable, but it cannot be repeated calmly without deepening the wound. "I need a clear time when we can reconnect" has more stability. It can be said once. It can be said again. It carries feeling without turning the other person into the enemy.

The repeated sentence is not a script in the theatrical sense. It is more like a handrail. Under stress, people reach for what is available, and if only accusation is available, accusation will do the work. A handrail sentence gives the body somewhere else to place its weight. "I am feeling wobbly and I want to stay kind." "I need reassurance, not a debate." "I am too activated to discuss this well, and I want to come back." These phrases are not magic. They do not guarantee a generous response. They make it less likely that the first panic will write the whole exchange.

A credible limitation deserves attention: a pause can be misused. Some people retreat into "processing" as a refined form of avoidance. Others demand that a distressed partner regulate alone before they are deemed worthy of response. The self-check is not a requirement to become perfectly calm before asking for care, nor is it a licence for someone else to withdraw indefinitely from responsibility. It is a brief act of translation, not a long exile. When the pause becomes disappearance, it stops serving clarity. It becomes another strategy.

The same limitation applies when distress is overwhelming. There are moments when the body is too flooded for elegant language. The throat closes; the mind blanks; every sentence feels either dangerous or false. In such moments, the smallest workable ask may be extremely plain: "I cannot speak well yet." "I need a minute." "Please do not leave without saying when you will come back." These are not polished sentences. They are honest enough to preserve contact. That is the standard. Not perfection. Contact with less harm.

The self-check also protects against the false glamour of intensity. Many people mistake emotional force for emotional truth. If a feeling is huge, they assume the claim attached to it must be huge as well. But scale and accuracy are different things. A panic may be large because it is old, not because the present offence is large. A feeling may deserve compassion without being allowed to dictate the charge. "I feel terrified" is not the same as "You are terrifying me." "I feel abandoned" is not the same as "You abandoned me." One names the inner weather; the other assigns blame. The difference can save a conversation.

Psychologist Susan David, writing in *Emotional Agility* in 2016, popularised a related distinction between being overwhelmed by an emotion and noticing it as an experience one is having. The value here is not a fashionable vocabulary of self-management, but the simple grammatical shift. "I am anxious" can become "I am noticing anxiety." In intimate language, the shift softens certainty. A person can say, "I am noticing I am reading your quietness as distance," which leaves room for correction. Compare that with "You are being distant," which leaves the other person only the options of denial, defence, or confession. The first sentence invites information. The second demands a verdict.

The thirty-second self-check earns its place because it sits between impulse and suppression. It does not say, "Do not feel that." It says, "Do not hand the microphone to the first interpretation." This is especially important for people who were taught to doubt their needs. They may fear that pausing means talking themselves out of asking. But the pause is not there to shrink the need. It is there to make the need legible. A clear ask is often braver than an explosive one because it has fewer hiding places. It cannot rely on volume, guilt, or drama. It has to stand on its own.

In practical terms, the check measures three things that are otherwise easily confused: body, emotion, request. Body: the physical alarm. Emotion: the meaning moving through the alarm. Request: the next visible act that might help. The sequence matters. Without the body, speech becomes detached and performative. Without emotion, the request can sound oddly managerial. Without the request, the other person is left holding a description with no door out of it. "My chest is tight, I feel unsure, and I would like a clear goodnight before we sleep" is not ornate. It is usable. The handle has appeared.

The smallest ask must also respect capacity. This is where clarity becomes ethical. "Tell me we will never have this problem again" is not workable. "Promise you will always reply quickly" collapses reassurance into control. "Can you send a message when you know you will be offline for the evening?" is measurable. "Can we agree to pause this and return after breakfast?" gives time a boundary. "Can you reassure me once, and then I will take a walk?" shares responsibility. A workable ask does not pretend the other person has infinite emotional supply. It asks for something a real person might do.

There is an austerity in this, but not coldness. The austerity lies in refusing to inflate the moment beyond what it can bear. Not every unsettled feeling needs a tribunal. Not every missed cue needs a full relational audit. Some moments need a hand on the shoulder, a return time, a slower tone, a sentence of reassurance, a decision to sleep before discussing logistics.

The self-check helps identify which one is being sought. Without it, the mind may drag the entire relationship to the counter and demand that it answer for a single bruise.

The quiet motif returns here: the body keeps time, but language chooses the hour. A quick pulse may announce that something feels urgent; the self-check asks whether the next sentence must be urgent too. Often, the most consequential relational skill is not knowing the perfect thing to say. It is noticing the split second in which several possible selves become available: the self that accuses, the self that disappears, the self that pleads, the self that asks plainly. The pause does not make the choice easy. It makes the choice visible.

The forward test is stark and ordinary. When distress rises, will the next sentence carry the whole storm, or only the part that can be met now? A person cannot always control the alarm. They can often choose whether to turn it into a charge, a silence, or a request with a handle. That choice, made in the brief space before speech, is where secure language begins to become more than an idea.

Choosing one clear request

Why can a request that would take ten seconds to speak become a quarrel that consumes the whole evening? The surface answer is usually content: the message was late, the tone was off, the plan changed, the apology felt thin. Yet the deeper answer is structure. One person does not ask for one thing. They arrive carrying the whole drawer: reassurance, explanation, apology, planning, evidence, justice, perhaps a quiet wish to be held before any of it is discussed. The drawer opens. Everything spills.

A partner stands by the sink, still wearing their coat, and hears, "Can we talk?" The words sound simple, but the air behind them is crowded. Within minutes, the conversation contains last weekend, the missed call, the way they speak when tired, the unanswered message, the cancelled dinner, the old promise to "try harder", and the urgent question of whether love still feels safe. None of these concerns may be false. That is what makes the moment so difficult. The problem is not that the feelings are invented; the problem is that they have entered through the same narrow door. The room cannot hold them.

The discipline of one clear request begins where the previous self-check leaves off. The body has signalled. The emotion has been named. The need has become more visible. Now comes the question that separates secure communication from emotional unloading: what is the next ask that matters most? Not the truest ask in the grand philosophical sense. Not the ask that would settle every wound in the relationship. The next ask. The one that can be heard, considered, and answered without requiring the other person to solve the entire history of the bond in a single sitting.

This is not restraint for the sake of neatness. It is an act of relational accuracy. When several requests are stacked together, each one contaminates the others. A request for reassurance becomes mixed with a request for behavioural change. A request for a hug becomes entangled with a complaint about household labour. A request to discuss weekend plans becomes charged with the question of whether one person feels valued at all. The other person may respond to the easiest item and miss the emotional centre, or respond defensively to the sharpest item and miss the tender one. Either way, the true priority goes unheld.

George A. Miller's 1956 paper, "The Magical Number Seven, Plus or Minus Two", published in *Psychological Review*, is often simplified in popular memory, but its larger point about cognitive limits remains useful: the human mind can hold only so much at once before it begins to group, drop, or distort information. Intimate conflict adds heat to that limit. A person under emotional pressure does not receive a crowded complaint as a carefully indexed archive. They hear threat, failure, demand, disappointment. They start triaging. The smallest request is not small because the relationship is small; it is small because attention is finite, especially when shame or fear has entered the room.

One clear request, by contrast, gives the other person a visible handle. "Can you hold me for two minutes, then we can talk logistics?" is different from "You never make me feel important, and now I suppose we still have to sort the weekend because I am the only one who plans anything." The first sentence names sequence. The body needs contact before the calendar can be discussed. The second sentence may contain genuine pain, but it makes the listener answer love, history, character, fairness, and scheduling all at once. A person can respond to a handle. They cannot easily respond to a flood.

The clearest request is often the one closest to regulation. If the nervous system is alarmed, reassurance may need to come before analysis. If the conversation is confused, information may need to come before apology. If the timing is poor, a return plan may need to come before content. If both people are tired, rest may need to come before repair. This ordering is not avoidance. It is sequencing. A surgeon does not begin with the most delicate work while the room is still chaotic. A couple, in their ordinary and unsterile kitchen, must learn a similar respect for conditions.

Sequencing protects both people from the trap of the "while we are here" list. The phrase is familiar because it sounds efficient. While we are here, there is something else. While we are here, I have also been meaning to say. While we are here, you did this last week too. The list promises thoroughness, but often produces collapse. The first issue is no longer being addressed; it has become the opening exhibit in a wider case. The listener feels ambushed. The speaker feels newly frustrated because, once again, the important points are not being received. The drawer opens wider.

The force behind the list is understandable. People stack requests when they fear they will not get another chance. They gather evidence because they worry a single need will be dismissed. They attach old injuries to current moments because the old injuries never received a clean hearing. The list says, in its distressed way, *please understand the size of this*. Yet size is not the same as sequence. A need may be large and still require one doorway at a time. Indeed, the larger the pain, the more carefully it must be carried.

John Gottman and Robert Levenson's observational research on couples, conducted across decades and associated with the University of Washington in Seattle, gave close attention to the behaviours that unfold during conflict: criticism, defensiveness, contempt, withdrawal, repair attempts, physiological arousal. Whatever one makes of any single model of couple interaction, the observational emphasis is instructive. Relationships are not shaped by inner feeling alone. They are shaped by visible moves: turning towards, interrupting, softening tone, refusing eye contact, changing subject, making a repair, escalating the charge. A stacked request is not merely a private intensity. It is a move in the room, and it invites counter-moves.

Choosing one request therefore requires a brief act of prioritisation that may feel almost brutal at first. What matters now: closeness, clarity, repair, timing, or change? If the answer is closeness, the sentence may be, "Can you sit with me for a moment before we discuss this?" If the answer is clarity, it may be, "Can you tell me whether you are upset or just exhausted?" If the answer is repair, it may be, "Can you acknowledge that the way you said that landed painfully?" If the answer is timing, it may be, "Can we agree when to talk, rather than trying to solve it now?" If the answer is change, it may be, "Can we make a specific plan for next time?" Each request opens a different door. Confusion often begins when a person tries to open all of them with one sentence.

There is dignity in postponing what is real. Many people hear postponement as dismissal because they have known too much avoidance masquerading as patience. But postponement, when named honestly, is not erasure. It says: this matters, and it deserves a better container than the one available right now. "I want to talk about the pattern, but tonight I need reassurance first." "I do want to discuss the plans, but I am too raw to do logistics before we reconnect." "The bigger issue matters; can we set a time for it tomorrow?" These sentences do not minimise the wider concern. They prevent it from being mishandled.

A clear request also makes consent possible. That word is often used in narrower contexts, but its relational meaning is wider: the other person must be able to understand what is being asked in order to answer honestly. A foggy demand leaves little room for a clean yes, a clean no, or a workable later. "Be more present" may be emotionally meaningful, but it is difficult to accept or decline because it has no edge. "Put your phone away for the first fifteen minutes of dinner" is concrete enough to meet, negotiate, or refuse. "Care about me properly" leaves the other person in the dock. "Tell me one thing you appreciate about us before we go to sleep" gives them an action.

The credible limitation is that one clear request can be misused by someone who wants to shrink the relationship's problems into manageable fragments forever. There are patterns that require more than a single ask: repeated dishonesty, chronic emotional absence, contempt during conflict, broken agreements that have become routine. A person should not be asked to keep reducing a serious pattern to one polite sentence so the other person never has to face its scale. Precision is not self-silencing. The art lies in distinguishing between the request that belongs to this moment and the larger reckoning that requires protected time, steadier conditions, and a willingness from both people to look at the pattern without flinching.

That limitation matters because secure language must not become a cage. Some situations deserve a fuller conversation. Some injuries deserve sustained repair. Some boundaries require more than a gentle phrase. But even then, one clear request remains useful because it marks the next accountable step. "I need us to set aside time to talk about this pattern" is still one request. "I need us to decide whether we are both willing to work on this" is still one request. "I need a pause tonight, and I need the conversation not to disappear" is still one request. The scale may be serious; the next step can still be defined.

The most important request is not always the most dramatic one. It is often the one that prevents damage. A hug before logistics may save the logistics from becoming a loyalty test. A return time before space may save space from feeling like abandonment. A single reassurance before problem-solving may save the conversation from becoming a courtroom. A boundary before explanation may save explanation from turning into pleading. To choose clearly is to ask what would keep connection possible while still respecting the truth of the issue.

This is why "Can you hold me for two minutes, then we can talk logistics?" is more than a sweet phrase. It contains an order of operations. Touch first. Planning later. It does not pretend the practical matter has vanished. It recognises that the practical matter will be handled better once the body is less alone. The sentence also respects the other person's capacity by limiting the request. Not "fix me". Not "prove everything". Two minutes. Then the next task. The handle is visible, and the drawer stays closed.

The same principle applies when reassurance and change are both needed. A person may feel tempted to say, "You need to reassure me and stop doing this because I cannot keep feeling so unimportant." The emotional truth may be strong, but the ask is tangled. It may be cleaner to say, "Right now I need reassurance that we are okay. Later I want to talk about how we handle late replies." That sentence does something mature: it refuses to sacrifice the future pattern, but it does not force the pattern conversation to carry the immediate panic. It trusts sequence without surrendering substance.

Choosing one request also reveals whether the speaker is asking or testing. A test hides the desired answer and punishes the other person for not finding it. "Do whatever you want" is often a test. "I guess I will just deal with it myself" is often a test. "Are you sure you are not annoyed?" may become a test when asked repeatedly after an answer has been given. A request does not hide the target. It says what would help. That exposure can feel risky because it gives the other person a real choice. Yet intimacy cannot mature where every need is smuggled in as an exam.

There is a quiet moral courage in asking for one thing plainly. The person gives up the temporary power of overwhelm. They stop burying the tender need under a pile of supporting evidence. They risk the embarrassment of being simple. "I miss you." "I need a definite time." "I want a softer tone." "I need you to acknowledge the impact." These sentences can feel almost too bare. But bare language is often where repair begins, because there is less for the other person to fight and more for them to hold.

The forward test comes at the moment the list begins to form. The mind will argue that everything is connected, and it may be right. The missed reply may connect to the old wound; the old wound may connect to the larger pattern; the larger pattern may deserve a serious conversation. But connection is not permission to say everything at once. The question is sharper than that: what single request, if answered now, would make the next honest conversation more possible rather than less?

Chapter 2
Timing, Tone, and Delivery

Why can the right sentence become the wrong one when it arrives too quickly? A person can name the need with care, choose one clear request, and still lose the moment by delivering it like an alarm. The words themselves may be reasonable: "I need reassurance," "Can we talk?", "I want to reconnect." Yet if they arrive in a rush, one after another, pressed against the other person's silence, they may no longer sound like invitations. They sound like pursuit. The doorbell rings again.

Imagine a partner who has not replied for a while. The first message is gentle. The next is tighter. The third carries the bruise: "Are you ignoring me?" By the time a reply comes, both people are already inside a conflict that has not been spoken aloud. One has been waiting with a tightening chest; the other arrives to find that the delay has been turned into evidence. Nothing dramatic may have happened, and yet the exchange now has a temperature. Timing has become part of the message.

The same is true in the room rather than on the phone. A person walks in tired, distracted, still half inside the demands of the day. The one waiting has rehearsed a careful sentence, but the rehearsal collapses on contact with the other person's absent face. The request comes out sharpened. "Can you at least act like you want to be here?" Beneath it may be a legitimate longing for warmth. What lands is criticism. The voice has carried what the words were trying not to carry.

This is the central trade-off: closeness often feels most urgent precisely when the conditions for being heard are poorest. The nervous system wants immediate soothing, but another human being may not be available at the exact second anxiety demands proof. A follow-up can be caring; pursuit can become pressure. A direct tone can be honest; an intensified tone can make honesty harder to receive. The work is not to become less truthful. It is to stop confusing emotional force with emotional clarity.

Timing matters because urgency is contagious. When one person approaches with panic in the body, the other person may not hear only the content; they may feel the demand embedded in the pace. A message sent too soon after another message may say, without meaning to, "Regulate me now." A question asked at the doorway, before shoes are off and breath has returned, may say, "Prove your love before you have arrived." A conversation begun at the edge of sleep may say, "This cannot wait," even when waiting would preserve the tenderness of the issue. The body reads tempo before it studies vocabulary.

Tone matters because intimate speech can slip, almost invisibly, into old hierarchies. Pleading places one person below, begging for scraps of proof. Scolding places one person above, judging the other into compliance. Performing places the relationship before an imaginary audience, where the speaker sounds wounded, noble, or dramatic rather than available. These tones may emerge from pain, not malice, but they distort the request. The listener is no longer being invited into closeness; they are being cast in a role. Parent, culprit, rescuer, audience, judge. None of these roles makes love more spacious.

The lasting cost is not only the single quarrel. Over time, timing and tone teach the relationship what to expect. If requests arrive mainly as emergencies, the other person may begin to brace before tenderness has a chance to appear. If boundaries arrive mainly as punishment, space begins to smell like rejection. If reassurance is asked for only in the language of accusation, comfort starts to feel like a cross-examination. A couple then inherits a dangerous pattern: one person increases intensity to feel safer, while the other retreats to feel less controlled. Both moves make sense from inside. Together, they tighten the knot.

There is a quieter possibility. A person can follow up without chasing. They can seek reassurance without demanding an instant emotional performance. They can speak with steadiness while remaining visibly affected. "When you have ten minutes, can we reconnect?" carries a different posture from "Why are you not answering me?" "I am feeling wobbly; I would like a bit of reassurance" does not pretend to be invulnerable, yet it does not hand the other person a script in which they must soothe, confess, and apologise before understanding what has happened. Such sentences do not reduce the need. They give it better manners without making it false.

The path now moves from the choice of request to the conditions under which that request can be received. The question of when to ask is really the question of whether the moment can hold the need without turning it into pursuit. The question of tone is whether honesty can remain adult when the body is frightened, disappointed, or ashamed. Together, timing and delivery determine whether the sentence becomes a bridge or another locked doorbell pressed too hard.

The unresolved friction is plain: if the need feels urgent, waiting can feel like self-abandonment; if the request arrives with too much urgency, the other person may experience it as threat. Somewhere between silence and pursuit lies a sentence that can stand upright. The next test is whether closeness can be asked for at a pace the relationship can actually bear.

When to ask, not chase

Why can a message sent after ten anxious minutes feel less like communication and more like pursuit? A person looks at the phone, sees no reply, and feels the silence thicken. The first follow-up may be reasonable: "Just checking you saw this." The second carries strain: "Are you busy or upset?" The third has already begun arguing with an absence. By then the phone is no longer a tool. It has become a doorbell being pressed too hard.

The problem is not the wish to reconnect. That wish may be entirely legitimate. A late reply, a changed tone, or an unfinished exchange can leave the body searching for a signal of safety. The problem begins when the request for contact loses its shape and becomes pressure. The person chasing may feel they are merely trying to settle their own alarm; the person being chased may feel they are being dragged into an emotional emergency they did not consent to enter. Two experiences occupy the same moment, and both feel persuasive from the inside.

Timing is never neutral in intimate speech. A sentence spoken at the right moment can land as tenderness; the same sentence delivered too quickly, too often, or too close to another person's limit can land as demand. "Can we reconnect?" is not the same sentence at breakfast, during a work call, after three unanswered messages, or at midnight when both people are exhausted. Context edits language before either person has interpreted it. The nervous system reads pace, repetition, and pressure before it studies grammar.

John Bowlby's attachment work, developed in London across the mid-twentieth century and brought into wider professional view through his 1951 World Health Organization report, helps explain why separation cues can feel disproportionate to the visible facts. The original scene may be small: a delayed response, a distracted goodbye, a partner turning towards a screen. Yet the attachment system does not measure only the event; it measures access. Is the person reachable? Are they emotionally with me? If I call, will someone answer? When access feels uncertain, the body may treat delay as danger long before reason has finished gathering evidence.

That does not mean every urgent feeling deserves urgent expression. It means urgent feeling needs better timing than panic prefers. Chasing attempts to close distance immediately. Asking recognises distance and proposes a bridge. The difference can be heard in the verb hidden beneath the words. "Why are you ignoring me?" corners. "When you have ten minutes, can we reconnect?" invites. "Answer me, please" grips. "Could you let me know when you are free to talk?" locates the next possible moment. Both may arise from the same ache. Only one preserves room for the other person's capacity.

The doorbell motif matters because it captures the relational effect of repetition. Pressed once, it communicates: someone is here. Pressed again and again, it changes the atmosphere. The person inside may not open faster; they may move more cautiously towards the door. Repeated texts, repeated reassurance questions, repeated "just checking" messages can work the same way. They may be meant to soothe uncertainty, but they often increase it. The sender watches for signs of avoidance. The receiver feels crowded. The silence that follows becomes more charged than the original delay.

Mary Ainsworth's Strange Situation research in Baltimore in the late 1960s and 1970s offers a second useful anchor, not because adult love should be reduced to infant behaviour, but because the reunion moment reveals something enduring about human bonds. Separation is not the whole test; the return is. Some distress escalates when reassurance is uncertain or inconsistent. Some distance increases when bids for closeness arrive with pressure attached. In adult relationships, the central question becomes whether a person can signal need in a way that makes return more possible, not less.

An appropriate follow-up has edges. It gives information, asks for a measurable next step, or names a time frame without demanding immediate emotional labour. "I am guessing you are busy; could you let me know when you can talk?" has edges. "I am feeling unsettled after earlier; can we check in later tonight?" has edges. "When you have ten minutes, can we reconnect?" has edges. These sentences do not pretend the need has vanished. They simply refuse to convert need into pursuit. The other person can answer them without first defending their character.

Chasing, by contrast, tends to blur the ask. It often begins with a real question and then adds interpretation faster than reality can answer. "Did you see my message?" becomes "Are you avoiding me?" then "I suppose this tells me everything." The person is no longer asking for contact; they are building a case. The visible behaviours are familiar: stacked messages, escalating punctuation, baiting remarks, dramatic withdrawals, or a sudden change from warmth to frost. Each move tries to pull reassurance from the other person, yet each also makes genuine reassurance more difficult to offer freely.

There is a painful intelligence inside chasing. It often develops in people who have learned that quiet needs are missed. If a person grew up around inconsistent attention, or has been in relationships where distance signalled punishment, their system may have learned to act quickly before absence becomes abandonment. The chase says, in its own distressed language, "Do not leave me alone with uncertainty." That history deserves respect. It does not, however, make pursuit an effective form of contact. A strategy can be understandable and still misfire.

The key difference lies in whether the message makes a request or creates a debt. "Please reassure me right now" may be honest, but it can also place the other person under emotional command. "I am feeling wobbly; could we check in when you have space?" tells the truth while allowing timing to be shared. This distinction protects both people. The anxious person is not forced into false self-sufficiency. The other person is not treated as an emergency service whose availability must expand whenever fear appears. Care remains care because it has not been coerced.

Stephen Porges's polyvagal theory, introduced in the 1990s and widely discussed in clinical and relational fields, has influenced how many practitioners describe the body's responses to threat, connection, and shutdown. The theory itself is debated in parts, as serious theories often are, but the everyday observation is difficult to deny: tone, pacing, facial expression, and predictability affect whether a person experiences a conversation as safe or threatening. A message that arrives with pressure can recruit defence even when its content is reasonable. A request that includes a return time or a choice can reduce the sense of alarm. The body listens for danger in the delivery.

The credible limitation is important. There are relationships where "do not chase" can be weaponised by the person who disappears. If one partner routinely ignores messages, refuses to define availability, cancels conversations without returning to them, or treats every request for contact as unreasonable, then the issue is not simply anxious timing. A person cannot build security alone with perfect phrasing while the other person offers chronic ambiguity. In such cases, a clear follow-up may reveal the lack of reciprocity rather than repair it. The distinction between asking and chasing should never become an instruction to tolerate neglect quietly.

The reconciliation is found in mutual measurability. An anxious partner can make a request with edges; a distancing partner can offer a reliable point of return. "I cannot talk now, but I can call after dinner" is a small sentence with large consequences. "I saw this and will reply properly tomorrow" changes silence into information. "I need space tonight, and I want us to reconnect in the morning" separates withdrawal from abandonment. These statements do not give endless access. They give orientation. The door may stay closed for a while, but the person outside knows it has not been bricked over.

Asking rather than chasing often requires tolerating the uncomfortable middle. The message has been sent. The need is real. The answer has not yet arrived. This middle space can feel humiliating to people who equate waiting with powerlessness. It may tempt them to regain agency through action: another message, a sharper question, a visible withdrawal, a social post designed to be seen. Yet not all action is agency. Some action merely transfers anxiety into the relationship and asks the other person to carry it. Waiting with a clear request already made is not passivity. It is discipline under emotional weather.

A well-timed request includes three quiet recognitions. The need matters. The other person has a life beyond the moment of need. The relationship deserves language that does not make either person smaller. These recognitions can live inside ordinary sentences: "I would like to talk, but I do not want to rush you." "Can you tell me when you are available, so I do not keep guessing?" "I am going to step away from my phone for a bit; please send me a time when you can reconnect." Such lines do not sparkle. They work because they reduce unnecessary ambiguity.

There is also a distinction between frequency and reliability. Some people seek security by increasing frequency: more messages, more check-ins, more immediate replies. But frequency without reliability can still feel unstable, while reliability with modest frequency can feel deeply steady. A partner who sends a thoughtful message at a predictable time may create more safety than one who responds constantly for a week and then vanishes for a day. The visible behaviour matters: a return time kept, a check-in honoured, a delayed reply explained without contempt. Trust grows around kept rhythms, not frantic volume.

The same principle applies to difficult conversations. An urgent issue may not need to be discussed at the instant it is felt. If the other person is driving, working, exhausted, caring for someone else, or visibly flooded, the demand for immediate processing may damage the very subject that needs care. "This matters, and I want to talk when we can both do it well" is not avoidance when it is paired with a real time. Without a return point, delay becomes fog. With one, delay becomes preparation.

The person who tends to chase may fear that softer timing will make the need disappear from view. That fear is understandable. Many people have watched their needs evaporate once they stopped pressing. But secure asking is not vague patience. It is specific and accountable. "Can we talk sometime?" may drift. "Can we talk after dinner for ten minutes?" has a shape. "I need reassurance" may be too broad to hold. "Can you tell me we are okay before you go offline?" gives the other person a concrete act. Clarity prevents patience from becoming self-erasure.

The person who tends to withdraw may need to recognise that silence is also a message. Not replying, not setting a time, not acknowledging a tender request, not returning after asking for space: these are not neutral absences in an intimate bond. They are visible behaviours that the other person must interpret. A return time is not a concession to neediness; it is relational hygiene. It keeps space from becoming a threat. It keeps autonomy from smelling like punishment.

The unresolved test is ordinary and exacting. When the urge comes to press the doorbell again, what is truly needed: more contact at any cost, or a clearer path to contact that someone else can actually walk? The answer will not always soothe immediately. It may require the humility of waiting, the courage of specificity, or the disappointment of learning that the other person cannot meet even a clean request. But the distinction remains: chasing tries to force the door open; asking names the door, the need, and the next possible knock.

Tone that stays adult

In 1964, the psychiatrist Eric Berne published *Games People Play* in New York and gave popular language to a pattern that many couples recognise long before they can name it: adults speaking to one another from roles that do not feel adult at all. Berne's transactional analysis distinguished, in broad strokes, between Parent, Adult, and Child states of communication. The framework has been debated, revised, and outgrown in places, yet its central observation remains piercingly useful at the kitchen table: the words may be spoken by grown people, but the tone can smuggle in a hierarchy.

One person says, "I just wanted to know when you'd be home," but the voice lands as pleading, small and watchful, already afraid of being too much. Another says, "It would be nice if you could think of someone other than yourself," and the voice lands as scolding, upright and punitive, as if issuing a moral inspection. Someone else sighs, smiles too brightly, and says, "No, honestly, it's fine," while every syllable performs injury for an invisible audience. The content may contain truth. The tone may distort it. Tone carries the weather.

The danger is not simply that a partner may misunderstand. The deeper danger is that tone assigns roles before the real request has a chance to appear. Pleading casts one person as powerless and the other as gatekeeper. Scolding casts one person as deficient and the other as examiner. Performing casts the relationship as a stage, where sincerity gives way to effect. Once those roles are active, the conversation is no longer only about reassurance, timing, or closeness. It becomes a struggle over dignity. The original need waits at the side, still unfed.

Adult tone is not cold tone. This distinction matters. Many people imagine that maturity means sounding smooth, neutral, and emotionally economical, as though feeling itself were a breach of form. But an adult sentence can tremble. It can carry grief, disappointment, desire, embarrassment, or fear. What makes it adult is not the absence of intensity; it is the refusal to turn intensity into rank. "I am feeling wobbly; I would like a bit of reassurance" is emotionally exposed, but it does not kneel, accuse, or perform. It stands upright. It asks without shrinking.

A pleading tone often begins with a real fear: if I ask plainly, I may be refused; if I am refused, I may feel foolish for needing anything. So the sentence bends before it is even spoken. "Sorry, I know this is stupid, but could you maybe just, I don't know, tell me we're okay?" The speaker tries to make the need lighter by apologising for its existence. Yet the apology places extra weight on the listener. Now they are not simply being asked for reassurance; they are being asked to rescue the speaker from shame about needing reassurance. The visible behaviour is smallness: hedging, over-explaining, self-erasure, a voice that rises at the end as if asking permission to exist.

The adult alternative is not entitlement. It is proportion. "I am feeling unsure after earlier. Could you reassure me that we are okay?" That sentence does not pretend the need is trivial, and it does not insist that the other person must respond in exactly one way. It gives the other person something clean to answer. A yes can be genuine. A later can be negotiated. Even a no becomes information rather than a wound buried under layers of self-abandonment. The speaker has not made themselves small to earn care.

A scolding tone often begins with a different fear: if I ask gently, I will not be taken seriously. So the sentence arrives wearing authority. "You need to learn how to communicate." "I should not have to explain basic respect to you." "Any decent partner would know this." Scolding may feel powerful because it reduces vulnerability. The speaker no longer has to say, "I felt lonely when I did not hear from you." They can say, "You failed." Yet scolding changes the task. The other person is no longer invited to understand impact; they are pushed to defend character. The tone turns a request into a verdict.

John Gottman and Robert Levenson's observational research on couple conflict, associated with the University of Washington in Seattle across decades, made careful study of the visible behaviours that predict whether conflict becomes repairable or corrosive: criticism, defensiveness, contempt, withdrawal, and attempts at repair. One does not need to treat any single model as sacred to recognise the practical truth. A sentence that attacks character tends to summon defence. A sentence that names impact creates more room for response. "You are selfish" and "I felt alone when I did not know when you were coming back" may spring from the same disappointment, but they do not build the same room.

Performance is subtler and often more socially acceptable. It can look controlled, articulate, even elegant. The performing person may sound wounded in a way designed to be witnessed: "No, don't worry, I'm used to it." The words appear restrained, but the tone asks to be pursued, contradicted, or admired for endurance. Performance hides the request while increasing the penalty for missing it. The partner is meant to understand that "I'm fine" means "come closer", that "do what you want" means "choose me", that "I'll manage" means "notice how much I am carrying." This is not clarity. It is theatre born from fear.

The adult sentence removes the audience. It speaks to the person present, not to an imagined jury. "I wanted you to choose the evening with me, and I feel hurt that you did not." "I am not fine yet, but I do not want to punish you." "I need a little reassurance before I can soften." These sentences may feel embarrassingly direct to someone accustomed to indirect bids. That embarrassment is part of the work. Directness takes away the drama that once protected the tender wish from refusal. It also gives closeness a fairer chance.

Tone becomes adult when it can invite a "yes" or a "later" without punishment. That phrase deserves weight. Many requests are technically phrased as questions while emotionally allowing only one acceptable answer. "Can we talk now?" may sound innocent, but if "not now" is met with coldness, accusation, or collapse, the question was not truly a question. It was a demand dressed in softer clothes. Adult tone leaves room for capacity. "I would like to talk. If now is not possible, please tell me when" preserves the need while acknowledging the other person's limits. It asks for contact without demanding instant surrender.

This does not mean every "later" should be accepted indefinitely. A later without a return point becomes fog. A partner who repeatedly postpones without coming back is not offering capacity; they are creating uncertainty. Adult tone belongs on both sides. The person asking can avoid pursuit; the person delaying can give a real time, a real condition, or a real alternative. "I cannot do this before work, but I can talk after dinner" is adult because it contains both boundary and return. It does not leave the other person standing outside a closed door with no handle.

Virginia Satir, whose family therapy work gained influence in California during the twentieth century, described communication patterns such as placating, blaming, computing, and distracting. The terminology belongs to its own therapeutic tradition, and not every term needs to be carried intact into ordinary life. Still, the core insight travels well: under stress, people often abandon congruence. They become smaller than they are, larger than they are, colder than they are, or more theatrical than they are. Adult tone is congruent tone. It lets the inner reality and the outer sentence resemble each other closely enough that another person does not have to decode the distortion.

Lowering intensity is therefore not the same as lowering honesty. It may mean changing "You never care" into "I am scared you are less engaged with me tonight." It may mean changing "Please, please don't be annoyed with me" into "I am worried you are annoyed, and I would like to check." It may mean changing "Fine, I'll just stop asking" into "I am disappointed, and I need a minute before I can respond kindly." The truth remains. The pressure decreases. The sentence stops trying to control the other person's emotional position and starts revealing the speaker's own.

There is a bodily component to this. A sentence does not travel only through vocabulary; it travels through pace, volume, facial expression, and the space allowed after speaking. A steady tone gives the other person time to register the request. A rushed tone can make even gentle words feel cornering. A flat tone may communicate contempt when the speaker means self-protection. A singsong tone may communicate mockery when the speaker means to keep things light. The mouth may be saying, "I want to be close," while the delivery says, "You are in trouble." The listener responds to both.

The credible limitation is that tone can be unfairly policed. People who are hurt, exhausted, neurodivergent, traumatised, culturally expressive, or simply less practised in polished speech may be told to "watch their tone" by someone who wants to avoid the content. A demand for perfect delivery can become a way of dismissing legitimate pain. "I would hear you if you said it differently" can be true, but it can also be evasive. Adult communication cannot require that the wounded person sound serene before their hurt counts. The question is not whether the tone is flawless. The question is whether it leaves room for dignity on both sides.

Reconciliation lies in mutual accountability. The speaker can own the delivery without surrendering the message: "I sounded sharper than I wanted. The issue still matters." The listener can name the impact of tone without erasing the need:

"I want to hear this, and I am finding the scolding hard to take in." These sentences preserve two truths at once. Tone matters. Content matters. Neither gets to cancel the other.

The most adult tone often sounds almost plain. "I miss you." "I felt dismissed." "I need a clearer time." "I am not ready to talk gently yet." "I can hear that you care, and I still need reassurance." Plainness can feel underpowered to someone used to intensity, but it has a hidden strength: it reduces the amount of translation required. The other person does not have to peel away sarcasm, guilt, performance, or collapse to locate the request. The sentence arrives with its hands visible.

Adult tone also refuses the false bargain between being honest and being kind. Many people think honesty must come with force or kindness must come with dilution. Neither is true. A steady sentence can be severe. "I cannot keep having this conversation by text" is kind if it prevents escalation. "I care about you, and I will not be spoken to with contempt" is honest without becoming cruel. "I want reassurance, not an argument" is direct without being punitive. The measure is not softness alone; it is whether the sentence respects both the need and the person hearing it.

There is an old satisfaction in scolding, a desperate sweetness in pleading, and a strange protection in performing. Each offers a temporary escape from the exposure of a clean request. But each also asks the relationship to organise itself around a role rather than a reality. Adult tone does not promise comfort. It offers contact without costume. It lets the speaker be affected without becoming helpless, firm without becoming superior, expressive without becoming theatrical.

The forward test is deceptively simple. When the next need rises to the mouth, what role is trying to speak: child at the locked door, parent with the raised finger, actor under the lamp, or adult in the room with another adult? The answer may be audible before the sentence is complete. Tone carries the weather; it also tells the relationship whether shelter is possible.

Chapter 3
Scripts for Asking for Closeness

Why can asking to be held feel more dangerous than starting an argument? The argument offers armour. It gives the body something to do with fear: sharpen the voice, gather evidence, make the other person answer for the distance. A clean request has no such protection. "Can we sit together for a few minutes? I miss you." The sentence is brief, almost unbearably plain. It does not accuse. It does not build a case. It places the wish on the table like a cup of tea cooling between two people.

A person may long for closeness while behaving as though closeness must be extracted. They stand at the edge of the room, waiting to be noticed, and grow colder with every passing second. They want an arm around them but say, "You seem busy." They want a softer goodbye but say, "Never mind." They want the ordinary reassurance of a body beside theirs, yet what comes out is a complaint about effort, priorities, or tone. The longing is not false. The delivery has lost the door.

The most difficult requests are often the simplest because they leave so little room to hide. To ask directly for closeness is to risk discovering the other person's actual capacity. That risk can feel intolerable when the need is tender. It may seem safer to hint, test, sulk, or criticise, because indirectness preserves a private defence: if they do not come closer, perhaps the request was never truly made. Yet the price of that defence is high. The other person is asked to read a signal that has been disguised as something else, then blamed for misreading it.

The central tension is therefore not whether closeness is allowed. It is whether closeness can be asked for without making the other person responsible for proving love on command. A secure request has two qualities that must live together: clarity and freedom. Clarity says, "This is what I want." Freedom says, "You may answer honestly." Without clarity, the relationship becomes a guessing game. Without freedom, the request becomes pressure. The work is to let desire speak without turning desire into a test.

This matters because closeness is not merely a romantic ornament added after the serious business of a relationship is complete. It is one of the ways human beings regulate distance, repair small ruptures, and remember that the bond is more than a schedule of tasks. A hand on the back, a few quiet minutes on the sofa, a shared cup before returning to the day, a message that says "I miss you" without demanding immediate proof in return: these visible acts carry meaning precisely because they are modest. They tell the body that connection has not vanished beneath logistics.

Yet closeness cannot remain nourishing if it is forced. A hug demanded as evidence stops feeling like tenderness. A conversation extracted from an exhausted person may produce words, but not presence. A bid for warmth that punishes a "not right now" teaches both people to fear the next bid. One becomes afraid to ask because refusal feels unbearable; the other becomes afraid to receive the question because any limit may be treated as rejection. The relationship then loses the ease of small approaches. The sofa becomes a courtroom. The cup cools untouched.

A gentler art is possible: asking in a way that leaves the invitation breathable. Sometimes the sentence can be direct, because the need is clear and the moment can hold it. Sometimes it must be lighter, because the other person's capacity is uncertain or the speaker can feel their own intensity rising. Sometimes the answer will be no, or not yet, and the next task is to keep that refusal from becoming a verdict on the whole relationship. The path moves through these moments carefully, not to make desire timid, but to make it more trustworthy.

The quiet power of a low-pressure invitation is that it allows closeness to approach without a spotlight. "Want a quick cup of tea together before we dive back in?" asks for contact, but it does not make the answer carry the entire weight of the relationship. A time limit can be merciful. A small invitation can honour both people's nervous systems. It says, in effect, I would like to meet you here, briefly and kindly, if you have room. The cup of tea matters because it gives closeness a human scale.

The unresolved friction is that love needs both courage and consent. To ask too indirectly is to abandon oneself before the other person has had a chance to respond. To ask too forcefully is to crowd the very closeness one hopes to receive. Somewhere between hinting and demanding sits the sentence that can be heard: clear enough to be known, light enough to be answered freely. The next question is whether the heart can ask for nearness without turning the answer into a trial.

Direct closeness requests

In 1952, at the Tavistock Clinic in London, James Robertson's film *A Two-Year-Old Goes to Hospital* gave professional observers an uncomfortable image of separation: a young child, cared for in the practical sense, became visibly distressed when cut off from the person whose presence meant safety. The film's force did not lie in melodrama. It lay in detail. A small body searched, protested, quietened, and withdrew. The bed was clean. The need remained.

That historical scene belongs to childhood, yet its adult echo is unmistakable. A person can be sitting beside someone they love and still feel the ache of distance. The distance may not be dramatic. One body turns towards a laptop. One answer comes without eye contact. One evening becomes a series of practical exchanges about food, errands, children, work, money, laundry, tomorrow. Nobody has done anything cruel. Still, the hand wants another hand. The voice wants warmth. The body wants evidence that the bond is not merely functional.

The vulnerable move is to ask directly. "Can we sit together for a few minutes? I miss you." There is nowhere to hide inside that sentence. It does not accuse the other person of neglect. It does not disguise longing as irritation. It does not make a small courtroom out of the sofa. It simply places the wish where both people can see it. This is why direct closeness requests feel both mature and strangely exposing: they remove the protective fog around desire.

Indirectness often feels safer because it preserves deniability. A person who wants closeness may say, "You're very busy tonight," and wait for the other to hear the concealed plea. They may tidy loudly, sigh at the doorway, or answer in clipped syllables. They may make a joke with a small blade in it: "Nice to know I live with your phone." The need is not false; the signal is distorted. The other person now has to guess whether the issue is attention, affection, resentment, boredom, fatigue, or something older than the evening itself. Mind-reading becomes the tax charged on unclear longing.

Direct requests reduce that tax. They convert atmosphere into language. "Come and sit with me for a bit?" is easier to answer than a silence full of accusation. "I would like a hug before we talk about the bills" is easier to hold than "You never notice when I'm upset." "Can we have ten minutes with no screens?" is more workable than "You care more about that thing than me." Directness does not guarantee generosity, but it gives generosity a cleaner route. The other person is no longer being asked to solve a puzzle before offering comfort.

The request must carry both desire and permission. Without desire, it becomes vague. Without permission, it becomes pressure. "Can we sit together for a few minutes? I miss you" works because it names the wish and leaves room for an answer. It is not the same as "If you loved me, you would sit with me." The first invites closeness. The second makes closeness a test of character. A direct closeness request should not contain a hidden verdict, because verdicts produce defence where tenderness might have been possible.

Mary Ainsworth's Strange Situation research in Baltimore in the late 1960s and early 1970s made separation and reunion observable in a controlled setting. Its relevance here is not that adult partners are infants, nor that every moment of distance should be treated as a crisis. The useful point is subtler: reunion matters. Human beings seek signs that connection can be restored after interruption. In adult relationships, those signs are often ordinary and physical: sitting side by side, turning the body towards the other, softening the voice, touching a shoulder, lingering before leaving the room. Closeness becomes real through visible behaviours.

Physical closeness has a particular honesty because the body cannot be fully argued into ease. A debate may continue for an hour while both people remain lonely inside it. A hand offered at the right moment may communicate what several paragraphs cannot. Yet physical closeness must remain chosen. A request for touch is not a claim of ownership. "Would a hug feel okay?" respects the other person's body as much as one's own longing. "Can I sit next to you?" leaves space for capacity. "I would like to hold your hand while we talk, if that feels all right" makes tenderness cooperative rather than compulsory.

Emotional closeness can be asked for just as directly, though many people find it even more difficult than asking for touch. "Can you be with me for a moment before you try to solve it?" is an emotional closeness request. "Could you listen without fixing for a few minutes?" asks for presence, not performance. "Can you tell me what you heard me say?" asks for attunement. "I want to feel like we are on the same side" names the relational position being sought. These sentences help because they translate the misty word *connection* into behaviour: listening, reflecting, staying, softening, turning towards.

John Gottman's later popular writing about "bids for connection", based on his long observational work with couples in Seattle, gave a useful name to something lovers recognise without terminology. A bid may be small: a comment about the sky, a glance from across the room, a hand reaching in the dark, a quiet "come here". Partners are not tested by grand declarations alone; they are shaped by these ordinary bids and responses. Direct closeness requests are a more explicit form of the same movement. They say, without drama, "Here is my bid. Can you meet me?"

The risk is that some people will use directness as a way to intensify demand. "I am being clear" can become a polished version of "you must comply." That is the credible limitation. Direct language is not automatically secure language. A sentence can be grammatically clean and emotionally coercive. "I need you to hug me now" may sound honest, but if refusal leads to punishment, the request was not truly a request. Closeness cannot be extracted and still remain closeness. The test is whether the other person can say "not right now" without being made to pay.

This is where secure phrasing requires restraint. The request should be specific enough to answer and light enough to decline. "Can we sit together for five minutes before you start work?" has a clear shape. "Can you give me some affection?" may be too vague under strain. "Could you put your arm around me while we watch this?" gives the other person a visible action. "Can we have a quiet goodnight, even if we are not ready to discuss everything?" asks for a small piece of connection without pretending the whole conflict is solved. Specificity lowers the emotional noise around the ask.

There is a difference between asking for closeness and asking another person to erase discomfort. "Can we cuddle so I can stop feeling anxious?" may be honest, but it risks turning the other person into a sedative. "I am feeling anxious and would like a cuddle if you have room" carries more dignity on both sides. The anxiety is named. The wish is named. The other person's capacity remains real. The body may still want immediate soothing, but the sentence does not make immediate soothing the price of love.

Directness also protects against the slow corrosion of resentment. Unasked needs do not disappear; they often become evidence. The person who never says "I want more affection" may begin to count every missed opportunity. The person who wants to sit together after dinner but only hints may become quietly furious when the hint is missed. The inner ledger grows detailed: who reached first, who looked up, who moved closer, who noticed the sadness in the room. By the time the need is spoken, it may arrive not as a request but as a prosecution. A direct request made early can prevent tenderness from hardening into a case file.

The tone of the request matters as much as the wording. "Can we sit together for a few minutes?" can be warm, brittle, sarcastic, pleading, accusatory, or calm. The words provide the structure; the tone supplies the emotional climate. A secure closeness request should sound as though a "yes" would be welcome and a "not now" would be disappointing but survivable. This does not require pretending not to care. It requires signalling that the other person is being invited, not trapped. The sofa cannot become a witness stand if it is to remain a place of rest.

When a request is refused, the meaning of the original ask is tested. If "Can we sit together?" is followed by "Fine, forget it, you clearly don't care" when the answer is no, then the request contained a hidden threat. If the response is "Okay, I feel disappointed; can we find a time later?" then the request remains relational. This difference is enormous. It tells both people whether closeness is being asked for as a shared act or demanded as proof. Love needs enough freedom to breathe, even when the longing is intense.

The most useful direct requests often begin with a small admission and end with a concrete invitation. "I miss you; can we sit together?" "I feel far away from you; could we have a few quiet minutes?" "I want to be close, but I do not want to pressure you; would a hug be welcome?" "I am tender after earlier; can we hold hands while we talk?" The admission prevents the request from sounding mechanical. The concrete invitation prevents the admission from becoming a vague emotional burden. Together, they give the other person a door rather than a maze.

There is also skill in matching the request to the moment. A partner rushing out of the door may not be able to offer a long conversation, but may be able to pause for one embrace. Someone exhausted after work may not be able to process relational nuance, but may be able to sit quietly nearby. Someone overwhelmed by conflict may not be able to offer touch, but may be able to say, "I care, and I need a little space first." A good request does not ignore conditions. It reads the room without abandoning the need.

This is not emotional minimalism. It is emotional precision. The direct request refuses both extremes: the dramatic demand that makes closeness compulsory and the silent hope that asks the other person to guess. It allows longing to become visible in a form that can be received. The dignity lies in saying enough. Not everything. Not the whole history of feeling unwanted. Not the full archive of every missed bid. Enough for the present moment to know what is being asked.

The quiet motif returns: the sofa, the cup, the hand, the few minutes. Secure closeness is often built at this scale. Not through grand proof, but through ordinary invitations answered with ordinary care. A person asks to sit. Another person turns. A hand is offered, or a later time is named. The moment may look small from the outside. Inside the bond, it can change the weather.

The forward test is painfully simple. When the wish for closeness rises, will it be hidden inside complaint, hinted through silence, sharpened into a test, or spoken as a request another person can freely answer? The difference is not only in the words. It is in the courage to let desire stand plainly, without disguise and without force.

Low-pressure invitations

Why can five quiet minutes feel safer than a long emotional conversation? A person stands at the kitchen counter, spoon tapping the side of a mug, watching steam rise from tea neither of them has yet touched. The day has been crowded. There is a tender subject nearby, but not yet speakable. The direct request for closeness might feel too exposed; the full conversation would be too much. So the invitation comes gently: "Want a quick cup of tea together before we dive back in?" Nothing grand is demanded. The door is opened a little.

A low-pressure invitation is not a disguised plea. It is not a test with a trapdoor underneath. Its strength lies in its scale. It asks for a small, specific piece of contact that another person can realistically consider: a cup of tea, a short walk, a few minutes on the sofa, a hand held during the first part of a conversation, a shared pause before returning to the demands of the day. The invitation does not pretend there is no longing. It simply refuses to make the entire relationship stand trial at the threshold of a single answer.

The emotional intelligence of this approach is easily underestimated. Many people reach for either dramatic directness or wounded silence, as though the only choices are full exposure or no exposure at all. But intimacy often needs a middle register. There are moments when "I need to feel close to you" is true, yet too intense for the available conditions. There are moments when the other person looks tired, distracted, or internally crowded, and a heavy request may invite defence rather than warmth. There are also moments when the speaker distrusts their own intensity and wisely chooses a smaller door. The cup matters.

John Bowlby's attachment work, developed in London across the middle of the twentieth century and brought into formal circulation through his 1951 World Health Organization report, gave enduring language to the human need for accessible bonds. Yet accessibility is not the same as unlimited emotional availability. A partner can be loving and still tired. A person can care deeply and still need a transition between work and home, conflict and repair, solitude and contact. A low-pressure invitation respects this complexity. It says, in effect, "I would like to reach you, and I do not want to overwhelm you in the reaching."

That balance matters because closeness can be crowded by the very hunger that seeks it. A person who feels starved for warmth may unknowingly ask in a way that makes warmth difficult to offer freely. "We need to talk about why we have been so distant" may be true, but if it lands on someone who has just walked through the door, it may feel like being pulled into deep water without warning. "Come and have tea with me for a few minutes?" has a different emotional texture. It offers contact before analysis. It gives the nervous system a smaller task.

The time limit is not a gimmick. It is an act of mercy. "For a few minutes" changes the invitation because it gives the other person an edge. A request without edges can feel endless: if they sit down, are they now entering an hour-long conversation, an emotional audit, a demand for reassurance, or a conflict they did not know had begun? A bounded invitation reduces that uncertainty. "Want to take a ten-minute walk?" "Can we sit together until the kettle boils?" "Could we have a quiet five minutes before we talk about the practical stuff?" The limit helps the other person say yes without fearing capture.

Mary Ainsworth's Strange Situation research in Baltimore in the late 1960s and early 1970s showed, in controlled observations of separation and reunion, how meaningful the return to contact can be. The adult lesson is not that lovers should behave like children, but that reunion is often built from small recognisable signals. The person comes back. The body turns. The voice softens. A hand is offered. A low-pressure invitation creates such a signal without turning it into an examination. It makes contact available at a size the moment can bear.

Smallness has its own authority. A shared cup of tea may seem trivial beside the large abstractions people use when they feel threatened: trust, commitment, respect, priority, safety. Yet each abstraction must eventually become visible or it remains mist. Trust may look like keeping a promised return time. Respect may look like putting the phone face-down during a short conversation. Priority may look like stepping away from a task long enough to sit beside someone. Safety may look like being allowed to say, "Not right now, but after dinner." The low-pressure invitation tests these realities gently. It does not require a speech. It asks for a behaviour.

This is why low-pressure bids are especially useful when the speaker is unsure of the other person's capacity. Capacity is not character. Someone may not have the space for a difficult conversation but may have room for a brief moment of shared warmth. Someone may not be able to offer physical affection because their body is tired or touched-out, but may be able to sit nearby. Someone may not be able to produce elegant reassurance on demand, but may be able to say, "I am here." A smaller invitation discovers what is possible without assuming that a smaller answer means smaller love.

It is also useful when the speaker is unsure of their own intensity. There are moments when the hunger for closeness has sharp edges. The person can feel the temptation to make the request too loaded, to ask for a hug while secretly requiring proof, to suggest a conversation while silently demanding repair, to invite tea while preparing to punish refusal. A low-pressure invitation, honestly made, helps regulate the ask itself. It narrows the request to something the speaker can offer without ambush. "Would you like to sit with me for a few minutes?" is easier to keep clean than "Can you make me feel like I matter?"

The distinction between invitation and test is decisive. A test hides the desired answer and treats any other answer as failure. "I suppose you're too busy for me" is not an invitation. "Do you even want to spend time with me?" may contain a real wound, but it asks the other person to defend their love before any closeness can occur. "Never mind, forget it" after a pause turns the request into a trap. A genuine invitation can tolerate a real response. It may feel disappointed, but it does not retaliate. It keeps dignity intact on both sides.

John Gottman's language of "bids for connection", developed through his long programme of observational work with couples in Seattle, remains useful here because it dignifies the small approach. A bid is not always a major disclosure. It may be a comment, a glance, a joke, a request for attention, a move closer on the sofa. Low-pressure invitations are conscious bids. They make the bid legible without inflating it. "Come look at the sky for a minute" can be a bid. "Want to make tea together?" can be a bid. "Can we pause and breathe before we carry on?" can be a bid. The point is not the activity itself, but the turn towards.

The credible limitation is that low-pressure invitations can become too low-pressure if they are used to avoid honest need. Some people soften every request until nothing clear remains. They ask, "Fancy hanging out?" when they mean, "I have missed you all week and need to feel chosen." They say, "No worries if not," so quickly that the request disappears before the other person can take it seriously. They keep the stakes hidden because being easygoing feels safer than being known. Over time, this can breed the very resentment low-pressure language is meant to prevent. A gentle invitation is not the same as self-erasure.

The reconciliation lies in making the bid light without making it false. "Want a quick cup of tea?" may be enough when the need is simply for a warm moment of contact. If the hidden truth is larger, the invitation can carry a small admission without becoming heavy: "I have missed you today; want a quick cup of tea before we get back to things?" "I am feeling a bit far away from you; could we take a short walk?" "I do not want a big conversation right now, but I would like to sit close for a few minutes." The softness remains. The need is not smuggled out of sight.

A low-pressure invitation also protects consent because it does not confuse closeness with compliance. It allows the other person to answer according to their real capacity. "Not right now" may hurt, but it is not automatically rejection. It may mean tiredness, concentration, overstimulation, urgency, or the need to finish a task before turning fully towards the relationship. The invitation should leave space for this distinction. "No problem; could we do it after you finish?" keeps the thread intact. "Forget it, I should not have asked" cuts the thread and blames the other person for not catching it fast enough.

The most elegant low-pressure invitations often contain four quiet features: warmth, specificity, brevity, and a visible exit. "Want to sit with me until the kettle boils?" is warm and specific; it is brief, and it ends naturally. "Fancy a ten-minute walk before we carry on?" gives the body movement and the mind a limit. "Could we share a quiet coffee before the day starts?" names the invitation without asking the other person to solve a problem. Such sentences work because they are not overloaded. The cup returns as a small container for a larger wish.

There is a particular usefulness in pairing connection with ordinary rituals. Tea, a walk, washing up together, sitting on the step, watering plants, folding laundry, driving without the radio for a few minutes: these are not sentimental props. They lower the stakes because they give closeness something to do. Many people find face-to-face emotional intensity difficult, especially when the relationship already feels strained. A side-by-side invitation can make contact less exposing. The body shares space before the mouth has to carry everything.

This does not mean difficult subjects should be endlessly postponed into cosy rituals. The low-pressure invitation is not a way to domesticate every conflict into pleasant avoidance. It is a way to re-establish enough human connection for the next conversation to become less adversarial. "Can we have tea first?" should not become "Can we never speak about the pattern?" The distinction is visible in what follows. If the invitation creates warmth and then the necessary conversation is honoured, it serves the relationship. If it becomes a permanent detour, it serves fear.

Low-pressure invitations work best when they are offered before resentment has hardened. The earlier the bid, the lighter it can be. A person who says, "I miss you; want to sit together for a few minutes?" gives the relationship an easier task than a person who waits until the loneliness has fermented into accusation. By the time the sentence becomes "You never want to spend time with me," the other person must respond not only to the need but to the charge. Early bids are often kinder because they ask for a small course correction rather than a dramatic rescue.

The person receiving the invitation has responsibility too. Small bids are easy to miss because they rarely announce themselves as important. A cup of tea may be just a cup of tea, but it may also be a hand extended without fanfare. Turning towards does not always require deep emotional availability. Sometimes it requires only a brief, honest answer: "Yes, five minutes," "I would like that after I send this," or "I cannot right now, but I do want to later." A clear "later" is often far kinder than a vague half-attention that leaves the asker feeling foolish for having reached.

The deeper skill is recognising that closeness need not always arrive as intensity. It can arrive as a modest invitation made at the right scale. There is profound steadiness in a relationship where both people can ask for small contact without suspicion, and refuse or delay it without punishment. The atmosphere changes when bids are allowed to be ordinary. Love stops requiring a crisis to justify its requests.

The forward test is quiet and exact. When the wish for closeness is present but the moment feels delicate, what size of invitation can the relationship honestly hold? Too vague, and the need goes unseen. Too loaded, and the other person may brace. Somewhere between the unsent wish and the heavy demand sits the small door: a cup of tea, a short walk, a few minutes, an answer that can be freely given.

If closeness is declined

Why can one small "not right now" feel as though the whole relationship has spoken? A person reaches across the sofa and asks for a cuddle. The other person, tired from the day and already inwardly elsewhere, says, "I cannot just now." Nothing cruel has been said. No door has slammed. Yet the body of the person who asked may hear a much larger sentence: *I do not want you. You should not have asked. Your need has made you foolish.* The room goes quiet. The cup sits untouched.

The next few seconds matter. One path turns disappointment into protest: "Fine, forget it," or "You never want to be close." Another path turns disappointment into disappearance: a stiff smile, a sudden errand, a private vow not to ask again. Both are understandable. Both are costly. Protest makes the refusal bigger than it was; shutdown makes the need smaller than it is. A declined bid for closeness is not easy to receive, because the body may register it before the mind can interpret it. The no lands first.

The central task is to separate refusal from rejection. Refusal is an answer to a particular request at a particular moment. Rejection is a broader meaning attached to the self or the bond. "I cannot cuddle right now" may mean tiredness, sensory overload, distraction, resentment, illness, preoccupation, or the need for a transition. It may also, in some relationships, signal deeper distance. The difficulty is that anxiety wants to decide immediately. It does not like ambiguity. It would rather convert a small no into a final verdict than remain in the discomfort of not yet knowing what the no means.

Attachment research helps explain the force of that reaction. Mary Ainsworth's Strange Situation observations in Baltimore in the late 1960s and early 1970s showed how strongly separation and reunion shape behaviour, not because every moment of adult disappointment mirrors childhood, but because contact and its interruption carry bodily significance. When closeness has been requested and not received, the attachment system may read the moment as a rupture requiring urgent repair. The hand reaches; the hand is not met. Even when the reason is innocent, the nervous system may begin searching for evidence that the bond is unsafe.

This is why the response to a declined request must do two things at once: acknowledge the disappointment and preserve the next bridge. "Okay, I feel disappointed, but I understand you are not up for it. Can we aim for a cuddle after dinner?" That sentence is not passive. It does not pretend the no feels pleasant. It also refuses to punish the no. The structure matters. The disappointment is named, the other person's capacity is respected, and a future point of contact is requested. The moment is allowed to hurt without being allowed to define the whole relationship.

The small bridge is crucial. Without a next step, a refusal can feel like open water. "Not now" may be tolerable if it is paired with "after I finish this," "when I have had a shower," or "tomorrow morning before work." The future point need not be dramatic. It may be a cuddle after dinner, a walk later, a quieter goodnight, a hand held during the next conversation. What matters is not the grandeur of the gesture, but the conversion of refusal into orientation. The no is still a no. It is no longer a void.

John Bowlby's work in London across the mid-twentieth century placed emphasis on the importance of accessible attachment figures: not constant presence, but reliable availability. That distinction is essential here. Secure love does not require every bid for closeness to be met immediately. Immediate availability is not the same as reliability. A partner who can say, "I cannot now, but I do want to later," may offer more security than one who says yes resentfully and goes emotionally absent inside the hug. The visible behaviour to look for is not perfect compliance; it is whether care returns.

There is a temptation, when closeness is declined, to litigate the meaning at once. "Why not?" may be a real question, but in the charged moment it can become an interrogation. "Are you annoyed with me?" may be reasonable once; repeated several times, it can turn the other person's limit into evidence they must disprove. "You used to want to" drags history into a moment that may only require timing. The mind wants certainty. The relationship may need sequencing. A better sentence might be, "I am noticing I am taking this personally. Is this about needing space, or are you upset with me?" Such phrasing asks for context without making the other person stand trial.

A declined bid can also uncover the speaker's hidden contract. The request may have sounded optional, but internally it may have carried a private condition: if you love me, you will say yes. When the answer is no, the contract is exposed. This is painful because the person who asked may feel deceived by their own vulnerability. They thought they were making a request; their nervous system was seeking proof. The difference is not moral failure. It is information. A request can survive refusal. A test cannot. When a no arrives, the relationship discovers which one was actually made.

There are cleaner ways to keep dignity intact. "Okay. I wanted closeness, so I feel a bit tender. Could you tell me when would be better?" "I hear that you need space. I am going to take a few minutes so I do not make that mean more than it means." "Thanks for being clear. I am disappointed, and I would like us to reconnect later." These sentences do not require the speaker to be serene. They require enough steadiness not to weaponise pain. The person remains visible without becoming punitive.

The person declining closeness has equal responsibility. A bare no, especially in a tender moment, can bruise more than necessary. "No" may be honest, but honesty can still be considerate. "I cannot cuddle right now; I am overstimulated, but I love you and I can sit near you later" is different from "Not now." "I do want to be close, but my body needs space for a bit" is different from turning away without explanation. A declined request lands better when it contains reassurance, reason, or return. Not all three are always possible, but some signal of care prevents the no from sounding like exile.

Virginia Satir's twentieth-century family therapy work in California drew attention to incongruent communication patterns: placating, blaming, over-rationalising, distracting. The language belongs to a particular therapeutic tradition, yet the observation is useful when closeness is declined. One person may placate and accept a hug they do not want, creating quiet resentment. Another may blame and make the request itself seem unreasonable. Another may retreat into cool explanation while the other person is visibly hurt. Congruence asks for something more demanding: the courage to say what is true without making the other person wrong for having a different truth.

Consent is the ethical heart of closeness. Physical affection, emotional attention, conversation, listening, and repair all lose their tenderness when extracted. A hug given under pressure is not the same as a hug freely offered. A conversation forced from someone who has already said they are beyond capacity may produce words, but not trust. This does not mean the disappointed person must swallow their hurt. It means the hurt must be spoken without converting the other person's limit into an offence. "I wanted that, and I am sad you are not available" is honest. "You clearly do not care" is a sentence built from injury and guesswork.

The credible limitation is that repeated refusal changes the meaning of refusal. If every request for closeness is declined, postponed, minimised, mocked, or met with irritation, the issue is no longer a single no. A pattern has emerged. A person should not be trained to reinterpret chronic emotional absence as mere timing. Secure language does not require endless generosity towards persistent unavailability. There is a difference between "not now" and "not really, not ever, but do not complain about it." The first can be handled with a return time. The second requires a more serious reckoning.

Reconciliation lies in pattern recognition without instant catastrophising. One declined cuddle after a difficult day is not the same as months of avoided touch. One request for space after conflict is not the same as a relationship where all bids are treated as burdens. The disciplined response asks: is this a moment, or is this a pattern? The answer should be measured through visible behaviours, not fear alone. Does the person return later? Do they offer another form of warmth? Do they acknowledge the disappointment? Do they make space for closeness at other times? Does the relationship have a rhythm of repair, or only excuses dressed as boundaries?

The time between a no and the next point of contact is psychologically important. It can become a breeding ground for stories. The mind replays the request, edits the tone, interprets the facial expression, searches memory for similar moments. If nothing is named, the story grows in the dark. A next step interrupts that growth. "Okay, can we aim for after dinner?" is not a demand for certainty about the whole bond. It is a practical marker. It gives the disappointed person a place to put the feeling while respecting the other person's present limit.

There is also grace in offering oneself an immediate alternative without using it as punishment. "I am going to make tea and settle myself for a bit" is different from storming out. "I will read in the other room for half an hour, then I would like to check in" is different from cold withdrawal. The visible behaviour matters: tone, pace, whether the door is slammed, whether the phone becomes a weapon, whether the return is kept. Self-soothing after refusal is not the same as going solo forever. It is the temporary holding of oneself while the bridge remains intact.

The scripts that work best after declined closeness tend to be brief because the moment is already tender. "Okay, thanks for telling me. I am disappointed, but I can handle it. Could we reconnect later?" "I hear your no. I do not want to pressure you. Can we find another time?" "I am going to remind myself this is about now, not everything." "I wanted closeness, and I still want us to be gentle with each other." These sentences protect the no, protect the need, and protect the future. They do not make disappointment disappear. They keep disappointment from becoming a weapon.

The quiet motif returns: the cup sits untouched, but it need not stay that way. A declined invitation may pause connection without ending it. The question is whether both people can keep the table set. One does not punish the refusal; the other does not vanish inside it. One acknowledges the ache; the other offers a return. This is a demanding form of tenderness because it refuses the childish fantasy that love always says yes and the hardened fantasy that needing a yes is shameful.

The next test comes the moment the answer is not the one hoped for. Will the no become a verdict, a performance, a retreat, or a bridge to the next possible yes? The difference may be held in a single sentence: "Okay - can we aim for later?" Beneath its simplicity is an adult wager: closeness can survive delay if both people refuse to turn delay into abandonment.

Chapter 4
Scripts for Reassurance Without Pressure

Why can one sentence of reassurance calm a person for a moment, while the tenth version begins to damage the very trust it is meant to protect? The question appears in ordinary rooms, not dramatic ones. Someone goes quiet after dinner. Someone else notices the shift and feels the old alarm rise. The first question may be gentle: "Are you okay?" The second is tighter: "Are you sure?" By the third, the request has changed shape. It is no longer seeking comfort. It is cross-examining the bond.

Reassurance has a strange reputation. People are often ashamed to need it, as though mature love should operate without confirmation, without warmth, without the occasional spoken reminder that the relationship still has ground beneath it. Yet the opposite problem is just as real. Reassurance can become a ritual of temporary relief, repeated so often that each answer weakens instead of steadies. The person asking feels soothed for a few minutes, then uncertain again. The person answering begins to feel not trusted but tested. The lamp keeps being switched on and off.

The difficulty is not reassurance itself. Reassurance is one of the ordinary currencies of attachment: a kind word after tension, a hand offered after distance, a brief sentence that says the rupture has not become abandonment. The difficulty begins when reassurance is asked for in a way that makes the other person defend their care rather than offer it. "Do you even care?" sounds like a question, but it contains an accusation. "Are you going to leave me?" may express fear, but it can make the listener responsible for disproving a future they have not chosen. The need is real. The method tightens the room.

The central tension is therefore precision. A clean reassurance request names a present need without turning the other person into a suspect. It asks for comfort, not a confession. It seeks a signal, not a lifetime guarantee. "Could you tell me something you appreciate about us right now?" is very different from "Why do I always have to ask whether you still want me?" The first gives the other person a doorway into tenderness. The second hands them a file of charges. Both may come from the same ache. Only one leaves the bond with room to breathe.

This matters because repeated checking can imitate closeness while quietly eroding it. The anxious person may feel they are preserving connection by monitoring tone, timing, facial expression, punctuation, and silence. The other person may experience the same behaviour as a loss of goodwill: every pause interpreted, every tired answer weighed, every neutral expression treated as evidence. Over time, the relationship begins to feel less like a place of rest and more like a room full of sensors. Nothing can simply be what it is. Quietness must explain itself. Tiredness must prove it is not rejection.

There is also a future cost. When reassurance has no edges, both people become trapped in a cycle that neither truly wants. One person asks because they are afraid; the other answers because they care, then answers again because the first answer did not hold, then answers again with a trace of irritation that confirms the fear. The lamp flickers. What was meant to soothe now creates new material for anxiety. This is how love can become exhausting without anyone intending harm: the need remains unnamed in its precise form, and the strategy expands until it crowds the relationship.

The more useful movement is from accusation to present-moment comfort, from checking to context, from endless reassurance to a dose that can actually be received. A person may ask for one sentence, one hug, one clear plan, one piece of information that turns guessing into reality. "Your quietness is landing as distance for me - are you tired or upset?" is not a demand for emotional certainty; it is a request for context. "Can you reassure me once, then I will take a walk to settle?" does not make the other person the sole keeper of calm. It allows care to be given without requiring care to become infinite.

This distinction protects tenderness from becoming labour. Reassurance is most nourishing when it is specific enough to meet and bounded enough to remain generous. If every answer must be repeated until fear disappears completely, reassurance becomes a bucket lowered into a well with no bottom. If reassurance is forbidden because needing it is treated as weakness, the relationship becomes dry and unnecessarily proud. The adult task sits between these errors: to ask for comfort plainly, receive it honestly, and recognise the point at which another sentence will not answer what the body is really asking.

The unresolved friction is intimate and exacting. When uncertainty rises, will the next words invite reassurance or put love on trial? Will the question seek information, or demand impossible certainty? Will comfort be allowed to help, or must it be consumed until both people are depleted? The first script begins at the threshold where fear wants to cross-examine and the self must decide whether to ask, cleanly, for warmth.

Ask for reassurance cleanly

Why can one sentence of reassurance feel like oxygen, while the question that asks for it sounds like an accusation? A person sits across the table after a tense evening, watching the other rinse a plate too carefully. The room is ordinary: tap water, ceramic clink, the low yellow light above the sink. The anxious question rises quickly: "Do you even care?" It has the shape of inquiry, but not the spirit of one. The answer has already been cornered.

The need underneath may be simple. "I feel frightened that we are not all right." "I want to know you still see something good between us." "I need a small sign that this distance is not the whole story." But the sentence that escapes first often carries the heat of prosecution. "Do you even care?" does not merely ask for comfort. It asks the other person to defend their moral character while the speaker waits for relief. The lamp flickers again.

Clean reassurance begins with refusing to cross-examine the bond. This does not mean asking timidly, or pretending the need is smaller than it is. It means shaping the request so the other person can offer comfort without first climbing out of a pit of accusation. "Could you tell me something you appreciate about us right now?" is specific, present, and answerable. It does not ask for an eternal guarantee. It asks for a piece of warmth that can be given in the moment.

John Bowlby's attachment work, developed in London across the mid-twentieth century and formalised for wider professional attention through his 1951 World Health Organization report, helps explain why reassurance can matter so deeply. Human beings do not only need practical reliability; they need signals of emotional access. A partner may pay bills, share chores, attend events, and still leave the other feeling uncertain if affection, warmth, and repair are rarely spoken or shown. The visible behaviour matters: a returned look, a softening of voice, a sentence that says the relationship has not vanished beneath stress.

Yet reassurance becomes strained when it is asked for as proof against fear rather than as comfort within fear. The difference is subtle but decisive. "Tell me you love me" may be clean in one context and loaded in another. If it means, "I am tender and would like to hear it," it can be a beautiful request. If it means, "Convince me beyond doubt, and I will interrogate the answer if it does not land perfectly," the request becomes impossible. No sentence can bear that burden for long.

A trap question hides accusation inside grammar. "Do you even care?" implies that perhaps the other person does not. "Are you still attracted to me, or are you just pretending?" offers two answers, both poisoned. "Why am I always the one who needs closeness?" may contain a legitimate pattern, but in the moment it demands confession rather than connection. Such questions create defensive labour. The listener must prove innocence before tenderness can enter. By then, the original longing has already been made harder to meet.

A clean request removes the courtroom. "I am feeling unsure after earlier; could you reassure me that we are okay?" "I am reading your quietness as distance, and I could use a kind sentence." "Could you remind me of something steady between us?" "I know we are tired, but I would like to hear that you still want to work this through." These sentences do not pretend to be neutral. They are emotionally honest. Their strength is that they name the present need without making the other person answer for every fear the moment has awakened.

Mary Ainsworth's Strange Situation research in Baltimore in the late 1960s and early 1970s remains useful here because it showed how much meaning gathers around separation and reunion. The adult equivalent is not a laboratory episode, but a relational interruption: an argument, a delay, a distracted tone, a cold goodbye, a long silence at the end of the sofa. Reassurance marks the return. It says, through words or behaviour, that distance has not become abandonment. The lamp is turned back on.

The present-moment frame is crucial. "Right now" protects the request from becoming too vast. "Could you tell me something you appreciate about us right now?" is different from "Do you still think this relationship is worth it?" The latter may be a necessary conversation in some circumstances, but it is not always the right request when the body simply needs a small sign of connection. The present-moment frame keeps reassurance from becoming a referendum. It asks for one visible act: a sentence, a look, a touch, a clear statement of care.

This kind of wording also helps the speaker discover what is actually needed. "Reassure me" can be too broad to satisfy. It may invite a partner to guess: affection, apology, desire, commitment, context, gratitude, physical closeness, future planning. When the request becomes more precise, the other person has a real chance. "Can you tell me you are not angry with me?" is different from "Can you tell me you still want to be close?" "Can you say one thing you appreciate about how we handled that?" is different from "Can you promise we will never argue like that again?" Precision reduces the emotional noise around the need.

The cleaner question is often more vulnerable because it gives up the protection of blame. "Do you even care?" has a shield built into it. If the other person responds poorly, the speaker can retreat into accusation: there, proof. "Could you tell me something you appreciate about us?" has less armour. It risks a real answer, perhaps even a clumsy one. This is why secure communication often feels more exposed than conflict. Conflict allows the person to feel powerful while asking indirectly for comfort. Clean reassurance asks plainly and waits.

There is a risk in asking too cleanly in a relationship that repeatedly refuses tenderness. The language may be careful, but the response may still be cold, mocking, evasive, or chronically unavailable. This limitation matters. Better phrasing cannot manufacture goodwill where there is none. A person should not conclude that every unmet reassurance request is their fault for wording it imperfectly. Clean language is not a bargain with reality; it is a way of revealing reality. If a simple, respectful request for comfort is repeatedly treated as a burden or a defect, that information belongs in the assessment of the relationship.

The reconciliation is to distinguish a poor moment from a poor pattern. A partner may be tired, distracted, or emotionally clumsy on one evening and still be fundamentally responsive. They may need a clearer request before they can offer useful reassurance. They may need a moment to understand what is being asked. But if the response is consistently contemptuous, dismissive, or punishing, the issue has moved beyond phrasing. The visible pattern must be measured: do they return to the conversation, offer warmth later, acknowledge the need, repair missed moments, or only criticise the need itself?

Clean reassurance also requires the speaker to receive what was requested. This is harder than it sounds. An anxious mind may ask for one sentence, receive it, and immediately test it for flaws. Was the tone warm enough? Did they hesitate? Would they have said more if they meant it? Why did they use that word and not another? The reassurance is consumed and then doubted, leaving both people more tired. A clean request asks for a specific dose; receiving it cleanly means allowing that dose to count, even if the body has not fully settled.

This does not mean pretending that one sentence cures fear. It means not making the other person repeat the sentence until the fear disappears completely. There is a difference between comfort and compulsion. "Could you say that once more, slowly?" may be tender and useful. "But do you really mean it?" asked again and again turns reassurance into a trial. The first seeks contact. The second seeks certainty, and certainty is often the wrong object. Love can offer signals, patterns, actions, repair, and presence. It cannot offer absolute immunity from doubt.

A clean request usually contains ownership, specificity, and a reachable action. Ownership sounds like, "I am feeling unsure," not "You are making me insecure." Specificity sounds like, "Could you tell me something you appreciate?" not "Make me feel better." A reachable action sounds like one sentence, one hug, one check-in, one clear answer, not an open-ended demand to remove all distress. The structure is not mechanical; it is respectful. It treats the speaker's need as real and the other person's capacity as real too.

The distinction becomes clear in ordinary sentences. "Do you even want to be with me?" may be the cry of someone frightened, but it asks the other person to disprove abandonment at scale. "I am feeling shaky; could you tell me you want to be here tonight?" narrows the ask. "Why are you acting so distant?" can sound like accusation. "Your quietness is making me feel uncertain; could you tell me whether you are tired or upset?" asks for context. "You never say anything nice anymore" attacks a pattern in a moment of need. "Could you tell me one thing you like about us?" gives the moment a possible repair.

There is an ethical dimension here. The way reassurance is requested affects whether it can remain generous. If comfort is repeatedly extracted through panic, accusation, or collapse, the other person may begin to experience reassurance as a duty performed under surveillance. Warmth thins when it is forced. But if comfort is requested clearly and received without endless challenge, it can remain voluntary. The difference shows up in the body: one partner turns towards rather than braces; the other asks without flinching at their own need.

Clean reassurance should not be confused with emotional minimalism. Some people have learned to make their requests so small that they almost vanish. "Sorry, this is silly, but maybe could you possibly..." Such phrasing may seem considerate, but it often carries shame. The other person is asked not only to reassure, but to contradict the speaker's self-erasure. A steadier sentence has more dignity. "I would like reassurance." "I need a kind word." "Could you tell me we are okay?" The need is not inflated. It is not apologised out of existence. It simply stands.

The quiet motif returns in the lamp. Reassurance is not daylight that abolishes every shadow; it is a lamp switched on where two people are actually standing. It lights a specific patch of floor: after the argument, before sleep, during the silence, at the edge of a difficult conversation. When the request tries to illuminate the entire future, the lamp fails. When it lights the next step, it can be enough.

The forward test arrives when the frightened question forms. Before it becomes "Do you even care?", can it be translated into the comfort being sought? Before it becomes "Are you going to leave?", can it become "I need to hear that we are still connected tonight"? Before the cross-examination begins, can the need be placed on the table without accusation? The answer will decide whether reassurance becomes a bridge or another room where love is asked to defend itself.

Replace checking with clarity

Why can the same question asked three times make a person feel less secure than asking once and receiving an imperfect answer? A partner is quiet in the car. The road hums beneath the tyres, the dashboard glows, and the silence begins to gather meaning. "Are you okay?" gets a brief "Yes." A minute later: "Are you sure?" Another mile passes. "You seem annoyed." By the fourth question, the silence is no longer the only issue. The checking has become part of the tension.

Checking feels like an attempt to gather evidence. It watches the other person's face, tone, timing, punctuation, posture, appetite, sighs, pauses, and pace of reply. It asks, again and again, for the same reassurance in slightly altered form, hoping one answer will finally land deeply enough to quiet the alarm. The relief may come, but it rarely lasts. The anxious mind soon finds a flaw in the data: the voice was flat, the answer too quick, the hug too brief, the word choice too careful. The lamp flickers.

Clarity works differently. Checking asks for certainty. Clarity asks for information. Certainty wants the other person to remove doubt from the body; information helps the mind stop inventing explanations in the dark. "Are you upset with me?" may be a clean question if asked once with openness. Repeated several times, it becomes a demand for emotional proof. "Your quietness is landing as distance for me - are you tired or upset?" is different. It names the speaker's interpretation while leaving room for reality to correct it. The question does not accuse the quietness. It asks what the quietness means.

The distinction matters because checking often begins as an understandable response to ambiguity. A person detects a change and wants to know whether connection is still intact. The other person may genuinely be tired, preoccupied, hungry, overstimulated, ashamed, irritated, or simply quiet. Without context, the anxious mind selects from its own archive. If past distance meant punishment, quietness may read as withdrawal. If affection has been inconsistent, a delayed reply may read as loss. If conflict has gone unresolved before, a neutral face may read as danger. Checking tries to reduce this uncertainty by repeatedly sampling the bond.

Yet repeated sampling changes what is being measured. The first question may find out whether someone is upset. The fifth may find out whether they are now irritated by being questioned. This is the tragedy of checking: it can create the very evidence it feared. A partner who was merely tired may become defensive. A partner who was thinking about work may begin to feel scrutinised. A partner who answered honestly may feel that honesty was not accepted. The checker then notices the defensiveness, the irritation, the withdrawal, and thinks, *There it is*. The pattern confirms itself.

John Bowlby's attachment work in London across the mid-twentieth century, including his 1951 World Health Organization report, helps illuminate why access to another person can feel so emotionally charged. Attachment is not a decorative theory about affection; it concerns the felt availability of a trusted figure. In adult relationships, availability is often inferred through small behaviours: a reply, a softened tone, a returned glance, a willingness to explain. When those behaviours become ambiguous, the body may begin to seek repeated confirmation. The need for access is real. The method of repeated checking can still become costly.

Clarity respects the need for access without making the relationship submit to endless verification. It asks for context at the level where context can be given. "You seem quiet. Is this a tired quiet or an upset quiet?" "I am noticing I am reading your short replies as distance. Is something wrong between us, or are you busy?" "When you looked away earlier, I felt unsure. Did I misread that?" These sentences do not pretend the speaker has no anxiety. They simply refuse to treat anxiety as proof. They bring the interpretation into the open as an interpretation, not a verdict.

The grammar matters. "You are being distant" closes the door. "I am reading this as distance" opens one. The first sentence declares reality; the second names perception. This does not make the speaker weak. It makes the exchange more accurate. Perception is allowed to be strong, but it is not allowed to impersonate fact before the other person has spoken. "Your quietness is landing as distance for me" is emotionally honest. "Are you tired or upset?" asks for information. The sentence carries feeling and humility at once.

Mary Ainsworth's Strange Situation research in Baltimore in the late 1960s and early 1970s observed how separation and reunion reveal patterns of seeking, avoidance, protest, and settling. The adult relevance is not literal imitation, but the pattern of response under uncertainty. Some people pursue more intensely when they cannot read the other person. Some appear indifferent while monitoring every cue. Some can ask once, receive context, and settle enough to continue. Replacing checking with clarity strengthens that last capacity: the ability to seek information without turning the whole bond into an emergency.

Repetitive checking often confuses two different questions. One is factual: "Are you upset?" The other is existential: "Am I safe with you?" The factual question can sometimes be answered. The existential one cannot be fully settled by repeating the factual question. A partner may say, "I am not upset," and mean it. If the deeper fear is "I am not secure unless I feel completely certain," the answer will never be enough for long. Clarity asks the factual question cleanly, then notices whether the remaining distress belongs to the present conversation or to the body's difficulty tolerating uncertainty.

This is where checking becomes exhausting for both people. The person asking feels needy and ashamed, yet compelled to continue. The person answering feels mistrusted, even when they are telling the truth. Trust, in this context, is not an abstract virtue; it shows up as the decision not to keep interrogating after a clear answer has been given, the decision to ask for context rather than certainty, the decision to let a tired face be a tired face unless other evidence suggests otherwise. Trust is measured in behaviours. It is built in these small refusals to over-test.

There is a credible limitation. Some relationships have taught the checker to check. If a partner often says "I am fine" while punishing later, denies obvious anger, hides important information, or changes the story after being asked directly, then repeated checking is not merely an anxious habit; it may be a response to unreliable communication. In such conditions, the problem cannot be solved by asking more elegantly. Clarity requires a reasonably honest environment. Without that, a cleaner question may reveal the absence of trustworthiness rather than repair the pattern.

The reconciliation lies in separating present clarity from historical suspicion. If the other person has generally shown reliability, then repeated checking may be more about the asker's alarm than the partner's behaviour. If the other person has repeatedly made plain answers unsafe to trust, then the relationship needs a more serious conversation about honesty, follow-through, and emotional consistency. The test is behavioural: when asked a clear question, does the person answer directly, return to unfinished matters, repair misleading signals, and keep agreements? Or do they use ambiguity as a place to hide? Clarity does not demand blind trust. It asks reality to show itself.

Replacing checking with clarity also means choosing questions that can actually be answered. "Do you still care?" is difficult because care is too large and too easily doubted. "Are you annoyed with me about the conversation earlier?" has edges. "Is your quietness about me, or are you in your own thoughts?" offers a clean distinction. "Would it help if I gave you space, or would you rather talk?" invites context and choice. Good questions reduce the number of possible interpretations. They do not eliminate all uncertainty; they narrow the fog enough for the next step.

A clear question should usually be asked once, then followed by either reception, a request for a next step, or self-regulation. If the answer is, "I am tired, not upset," the response might be, "Thank you. I am going to remind myself not to make your tiredness about me." If the answer is, "I am upset, but not ready to talk," the next move might be, "Okay. Can you tell me when we can return to it?" If the answer is vague, the request can become more specific: "I do not need the whole conversation now; I just need to know whether we are okay for tonight." Each move asks for usable information rather than endless reassurance.

The body may not settle immediately after receiving clarity. That is not failure. The purpose of the clear question is not to abolish every anxious sensation; it is to stop feeding the anxiety with fresh uncertainty created by the conversation itself. A person may still feel unsettled after hearing, "I am tired, not upset." They may still need a walk, a shower, a written reminder, a hand on the chest, or a private sentence such as, "I have asked clearly, and I have received an answer." The relationship has done its part for that moment. The remaining work may belong partly inside the self.

This distinction protects reassurance from becoming a compulsion. A compulsion asks again because doubt has returned. Clarity asks again only when new information is needed. The difference is visible in the behaviour. Asking, "You said you are tired; do you want quiet or company?" seeks practical context. Asking, "Are you sure you are not upset?" after the answer has already been given seeks relief from doubt. The first helps the next decision. The second tries to drain anxiety from a bucket with no bottom. The lamp flickers because the hand keeps touching the switch.

Clarity also improves kindness. A person who asks for context rather than certainty is less likely to assign hostile meanings too quickly. "Your message sounded short - were you rushing?" is kinder than "Why are you being cold?" "When you cancelled, I felt unimportant; was there something urgent, or did you forget?" is more factual than "You never prioritise me." "I noticed you pulled away when I moved closer; did you need space?" is gentler than "You do not want me anymore." These questions keep reality available. They leave space for explanations the anxious mind may not have considered.

The person being asked has responsibilities as well. Clarity cannot thrive if answers are cryptic, contemptuous, or evasive. "Nothing" said with obvious hostility is not clarity. "I do not know, stop asking" may be honest about overwhelm, but it still needs a return point if the issue matters. "I am quiet because I am tired, not because of us" is a gift of context. "I am upset, but I need half an hour before I can talk" is a boundary with a bridge. "I do not know what I feel yet; can we check in after dinner?" gives uncertainty a shape. The answer need not be perfect. It needs to reduce unnecessary guessing.

The scripts that replace checking often begin with a careful admission: "I am noticing I am reading..." This phrase is useful because it distinguishes perception from accusation. "I am noticing I am reading your silence as anger." "I am noticing I am making the late reply mean distance." "I am noticing I am tempted to ask again, and I do not want to pressure you." Such admissions lower the temperature because they show the speaker is observing their own mind, not simply handing the other person a charge sheet. They invite collaboration rather than defence.

There is also dignity in asking for the kind of clarity that prevents future checking. "If you are quiet because you are tired, could you tell me that early so I do not guess?" "When you need space, could you give me a return time?" "If you are upset but not ready to speak, could you say that directly?" These requests turn recurring ambiguity into practical agreements. They do not require constant reassurance. They ask for signals. Signals are visible behaviours: a text before going offline, a sentence before withdrawing, a named time for return, a distinction between tiredness and anger.

The deeper movement is from surveillance to contact. Checking watches the other person for evidence. Clarity turns towards them for information. Surveillance makes the relationship feel inspected. Contact makes it feel inhabited. The difference may be quiet, but it changes the atmosphere. A person can look across the room and say, "I am unsure what your quietness means. Can you help me read it?" That sentence still contains vulnerability. It also contains respect. It assumes the other person is not merely an object to be monitored, but a subject who can speak.

The forward test comes when the urge to ask again feels irresistible. Is there new information to seek, or only old doubt asking for another serving? If there is new information, the question can be made concrete and kind. If there is only doubt, the next act may be to let the answer already given remain on the table long enough to matter. Reassurance becomes secure not when uncertainty disappears, but when uncertainty no longer gets to turn every quiet moment into an interrogation.

Reassurance with a limit

Why can one sentence steady the room while the tenth begins to empty it of warmth? A person sits on the edge of the bed after a difficult exchange, asking, "Are we okay?" The answer comes gently: "Yes, we are okay." For a moment, the body softens. Then doubt returns through another door. "But are you sure?" The second answer is still kind, though thinner. A third question follows. The lamp flickers again.

The need is not absurd. Reassurance can be a deeply sane request after conflict, distance, uncertainty, or an awkward silence. A bond sometimes needs to be named in order to be felt. Yet reassurance without a boundary can become strangely unhelpful. The person asking receives comfort, but cannot keep it. The person answering offers care, then finds that care has not counted. What began as tenderness becomes labour. What began as relief becomes a loop.

The limit is what keeps reassurance human. A limit does not make the need illegitimate; it gives the need a container. "Can you reassure me once, then I will take a walk to settle?" is not a refusal of comfort. It is comfort with a handrail. The sentence asks for one clear act of care and then returns some responsibility to the person who is distressed. That combination matters. Reassurance works best when it is received as support, not assigned the impossible task of abolishing every trace of fear.

John Bowlby's attachment work in London across the mid-twentieth century, including his 1951 World Health Organization report, gave durable language to the importance of accessible emotional bonds. Accessibility, however, was never meant to mean endless availability on command. In adult relationships, reliable connection must coexist with finite capacity. A partner may be willing to say, "I love you and we are okay," but may not be able to repeat it until anxiety finally exhausts itself. The visible behaviour that builds trust is not infinite repetition; it is a clear signal of care followed by a pattern of return.

A useful dose of reassurance is specific enough to be recognised. One sentence. One hug. One plan. One clear distinction between tiredness and anger. One return time. These small forms are not emotionally small. They work because they can be given, received, and remembered. "Tell me one thing that still feels good between us." "Can you hold my hand for a minute?" "Can we agree to talk after breakfast?" "Could you say plainly that this argument has not changed your care for me?" Each request has an edge. The edge protects the generosity inside it.

Without an edge, reassurance can become a bucket lowered into a well with no bottom. The first answer soothes. The second checks whether the first was real. The third checks whether the second contained irritation. The fourth asks the other person to reassure not only the original fear, but the fear created by their growing fatigue. The loop begins to manufacture its own evidence. The anxious person detects strain and thinks, *They are pulling away*. The other person feels mistrusted and thinks, *Nothing I say matters*. Both interpretations contain a sliver of truth by the time the loop has done its work.

James Gross's process model of emotion regulation, developed at Stanford University in the late 1990s, is useful here because it treats emotion not as a single event but as a sequence shaped by attention, interpretation, and response. In relational terms, this means reassurance is one part of regulation, not the whole of it. The other person may help mark safety, but the distressed person still has choices about where attention goes next, what story is repeated privately, and whether another request would genuinely add information or merely feed the cycle. The limit is not punishment. It is a decision point.

The sentence "Can you reassure me once, then I will take a walk to settle?" contains a quiet ethic. It does not deny dependency. It also does not outsource the entire storm. The speaker asks for contact and then names a self-regulating next step. A walk, a shower, a journal note, a few minutes of breathing, making tea, lying down with a hand on the chest: the particular action matters less than the shift in responsibility. The reassurance is allowed to help. It is not made responsible for doing everything.

This protects the person giving reassurance from resentment. Resentment often grows when care is repeatedly offered but never allowed to land. Someone may begin with tenderness and end with a clipped tone, not because they lack love, but because every answer seems to dissolve on contact. A bounded request gives the answer a fair chance to count. "Please say it once, and I will practise believing you for the next half-hour" is different from "Keep saying it until I feel certain." Certainty is a poor demand to place on another person. Care can be given. Certainty cannot be manufactured to order.

There is also protection for the person receiving reassurance. Endless reassurance can quietly teach a person that their own inner ground is irrelevant. The anxious body learns to reach outward every time doubt appears, even after a clear answer has already been offered. Over time, this can make waiting feel impossible and solitude feel threatening. A limit interrupts that training. It says: receive the signal, then carry it for a while. The practice is not heroic independence. It is shared regulation with a boundary.

The limit must be realistic. A person in genuine distress may not be able to receive a single sentence and instantly become composed. The point is not to perform calm. The point is to avoid using the other person as the only instrument of calm. A more workable version might be, "Could you tell me we are okay, and then sit near me while I settle myself?" or "Could you reassure me once, then I am going to step away from my phone so I do not keep asking?" The limit should fit the moment. Too severe a limit becomes self-abandonment. No limit becomes pursuit.

Mary Ainsworth's Strange Situation research in Baltimore in the late 1960s and early 1970s remains relevant because it showed that reunion is not merely about contact; it is also about whether contact can be used. Some forms of distress cannot easily take in comfort, even when comfort is present. Adult relationships show a gentler version of the same difficulty. A partner may offer a kind answer, and the anxious person may still feel unconvinced. The issue then is not only the availability of reassurance, but the capacity to metabolise it. A bounded dose encourages that capacity without shaming the need.

A credible limitation has to be kept in view. Some people invoke "limits around reassurance" to avoid giving any reassurance at all. They treat every request for comfort as dependency, every need for confirmation as weakness, every desire for warmth as emotional excess. That is not maturity. It is distance wearing the costume of boundaries. A relationship in which reassurance is consistently withheld, mocked, or rationed as punishment is not practising health; it is creating scarcity. The limit must protect care, not replace it.

The reconciliation lies in reciprocity. The person asking for reassurance can make the request specific and bounded. The person offering reassurance can make the response sincere and not grudging. "Yes, we are okay. I am tired, but I love you and want to talk tomorrow" gives more safety than a resentful "I already told you." The anxious person then has something solid to hold. The reassuring person is not trapped in endless repetition. Both make a visible move towards trust: one offers warmth, the other lets it count.

One sentence can be enough when the sentence is chosen well. "I am upset, but I am not leaving." "I still want us." "This argument matters, but it has not erased my care." "I need space tonight, and I want to reconnect in the morning." These are not grand declarations. They are relational markers. They tell the body where it is standing. A hug can serve the same function if freely offered. So can a plan. "Let us sleep now and talk at nine." The plan reassures not by sentiment, but by structure.

The most damaging reassurance loops often confuse reassurance with resolution. A person may ask, "Are we okay?" when what they actually need is repair. They may ask, "Do you love me?" when what they need is a changed behaviour. They may ask, "Are you annoyed?" when what they need is a clear conversation about recurring silence. Reassurance can soothe the moment, but it cannot replace a necessary agreement. This is why "one sentence, one hug, one plan" matters. Sometimes the plan is the most reassuring element because it moves the issue out of panic and into time.

A limit also prevents reassurance from becoming a hidden test of devotion. The test says: if you really loved me, you would keep answering without frustration. The limit says: I am asking you to care for me in a way that still leaves you intact. That difference is ethically important. Love should stretch people at times, but it should not require them to become endlessly available to another person's alarm. Care without limits curdles. Limits without care harden. Secure reassurance needs both warmth and shape.

The language of the request should make the boundary explicit. "Could you reassure me once, and then I will try not to ask again tonight?" "Can I have one hug, and then I will give us both a bit of space?" "Can you tell me whether we are okay, and if we are, I will take that as the answer for now?" "Could we make one plan for when we revisit this, so I do not keep circling?" These sentences contain a promise as well as a request. The speaker is not merely asking to be soothed; they are committing to participate in their own settling.

The person giving reassurance may also need language for the limit. "I care about you, and I can reassure you once more, but I do not want us to get stuck in repeating." "I have answered honestly. I am still here." "I can give you a hug, and then I need us to pause." Such sentences can sound firm without sounding cold. They matter because reassurance loops often continue partly because nobody names the loop until irritation has already entered. Early firmness is usually kinder than late exasperation.

There is a delicate difference between believing reassurance and practising with reassurance. Belief may not arrive immediately. Practice can begin sooner. A person can say inwardly, "I do not fully feel settled, but I have received a clear answer." They can notice the urge to ask again without obeying it. They can put the phone down, change rooms, make tea, step outside, or write the sentence they were given. The point is not to become invulnerable. It is to let reassurance become an object that can be carried, rather than a sound that must be repeated until it vanishes.

The lamp motif returns here. A lamp is useful because it lights a limited space. It does not become the sun. Reassurance with a limit works the same way. It lights the next stretch of floor: tonight, this conversation, this pause, this return time. When reassurance is expected to illuminate the entire future, it fails and is blamed for failing. A bounded request respects what reassurance can actually do.

The forward test is not whether fear disappears after one kind sentence. It may not. The test is whether the sentence can be allowed to matter before another is demanded. When the urge comes to ask again, the question becomes sharp: is more reassurance needed, or is the reassurance already given being asked to fight a fear that now belongs partly to self-soothing, time, and the evidence of future behaviour? Secure love is not built by refusing comfort. It is built by giving comfort a shape strong enough to hold.

Chapter 5
Handling Delays and Uncertainty

Why can waiting for a reply feel more difficult than hearing a disappointing answer? A disappointing answer may hurt, but it has edges. It can be named, argued with, grieved, or carried. Waiting has no such shape. The phone lies on the table, quiet and bright-faced, while the mind begins filling the empty space with possibilities. Perhaps they are busy. Perhaps they are upset. Perhaps they have seen the message and chosen not to respond. The kettle clicks. The room keeps going. The body does not.

The hardest part of delay is not always the delay itself; it is the private theatre that grows inside it. A person may check the screen, put it down, pick it up again, open another app, close it, reread the last exchange, inspect the punctuation, remember a tone from earlier, and feel the silence becoming heavier with every minute. Nothing new has happened, yet the story has advanced. Absence starts behaving like evidence.

This is the peculiar cruelty of uncertainty: it asks the nervous system to tolerate what the mind cannot yet organise. A clear no may bruise, but ambiguity breeds. It breeds guesses, comparisons, imaginary conversations, protective anger, and the urge to take action before the feeling becomes unbearable. The easiest action is often escalation. Send another message. Make it sharper. Withdraw visibly. Decide not to care. By the time the reply arrives, the person waiting may already have fought a whole relationship in their head.

The central tension is that love requires responsiveness, but real lives contain delay. Work, fatigue, family, illness, concentration, travel, sleep, overwhelm, poor timing, and ordinary human inconsistency all interrupt availability. A person can be loved and still not answered quickly. A bond can be intact and still pass through hours of practical silence. Yet it is equally true that chronic vagueness corrodes trust. The task is not to pretend uncertainty feels fine, nor to make another person prove devotion on command. The task is to give waiting a structure that does not become punishment.

Delay matters because the body often treats the unknown as unfinished business. Without a time, a reason, or a point of return, the mind tries to create one. This is where anxious guessing becomes relationally expensive. A slow reply becomes "they are pulling away". A busy day becomes "I am not important". A hesitant "I do not know" becomes "the answer must be terrible". The visible behaviours that follow are rarely neutral: repeated checking, colder messages, sudden tests, over-explaining, or a performance of indifference. The person is not merely waiting; they are attempting to seize control of meaning.

The longer cost is subtler. If every delay becomes a crisis, the other person may begin to experience contact as surveillance. If every uncertainty must be resolved immediately, conversations lose the room they need to become honest. If every "I do not know" is treated as abandonment in disguise, people learn to offer premature answers simply to stop the pressure. That may create short-term relief, but it weakens the relationship's tolerance for truth. Some answers need time. Some feelings are not yet organised. Some clarity cannot be forced without being falsified.

A more secure approach begins by asking for timing without demanding attention. A message such as "When you get a moment, can you let me know when we can talk?" does not deny the ache of waiting. It simply turns the ache into a request with edges. While waiting, the work shifts inward without becoming lonely exile: the unsettled person keeps contact with themselves rather than converting discomfort into accusation. If the answer that comes back is uncertain, the next movement is not to wrestle certainty from the other person, but to ask what would make the next step measurable.

The motif here is the unanswered phone, but the deeper subject is orientation. A person can survive delay more steadily when they know whether there will be a call after dinner, a message before bed, a conversation tomorrow, or a pause until the other person has had time to think. Orientation does not remove all anxiety. It gives anxiety somewhere smaller to stand. "I can be unsettled and still be safe" is not a denial of feeling; it is a refusal to let feeling govern the next move without evidence.

The unresolved friction is plain. If a person asks too quickly, they may turn waiting into pursuit; if they waits too long without naming the need, they may turn waiting into resentment. If they demands certainty, they may receive compliance instead of truth; if they accepts uncertainty without structure, they may abandon themselves inside the fog. The next test begins where the phone remains silent and the hand reaches for it again: is another message needed, or is a clearer agreement about time, self-holding, and the next measurable step the more honest request?

When replies are slow

Why can ten silent minutes after a message feel longer than an honest difficult conversation? The message has gone. The phone is face-up on the table, innocent and brutal, showing nothing new. A person tries to return to work, to the washing-up, to the book open beside them, but attention keeps bending towards the screen. The first minute is ordinary. The fifth begins to thicken. By the tenth, the mind has started writing its own reply on the other person's behalf.

The reply, in the imagination, is rarely neutral. It is not usually, "I am in a meeting," or "I am driving," or "I saw this and want to answer properly later." More often, the silence becomes character evidence: they are avoiding me, they are annoyed, they do not care enough, I have asked too much, something has shifted. The body responds to the story before any fact has arrived. The hand reaches. The thumb hovers. Another message begins to form. The phone becomes a courtroom.

Slow replies are difficult because they combine two human sensitivities: the need for connection and the discomfort of not knowing. A delayed message is not merely a gap in information; it is a gap in felt access. When someone matters, their availability carries emotional weight. A quick reply can feel like a thread held between two people. A delayed reply can feel as though the thread has gone slack, even if nothing has actually broken. The problem is not that the feeling is foolish. The problem is that the feeling often arrives faster than evidence.

John Bowlby's attachment work in London across the mid-twentieth century, including his 1951 World Health Organization report, helps explain why access matters so deeply. Human beings are not built to treat important bonds as abstract commitments stored safely in the mind. They look for signs: a returned call, a softened voice, a familiar greeting, a hand reaching back, a message that says, in effect, "I am still here." Digital life has changed the signal but not the underlying need. A reply now carries more than information. It can carry reassurance, priority, warmth, or the absence of all three.

Yet the danger lies in assigning meaning too quickly. A slow reply may mean distance, but it may also mean work, sleep, family demands, poor signal, driving, emotional processing, a dead battery, or the simple wish to answer with care rather than speed. The anxious mind dislikes this range of possibilities. It wants one explanation, preferably one it can act upon. If it chooses the most painful explanation, it may send a second message not to communicate but to manage panic. "Did you see this?" becomes "Are you ignoring me?" becomes "Never mind." What began as waiting becomes escalation.

The more secure move is to request timing without demanding attention. "When you get a moment, can you let me know when we can talk?" is a small sentence with important architecture. It does not insist on immediate emotional service. It does not pretend the need is absent. It asks for orientation. The question is not, "Will you soothe me now?" but "Can you tell me where to place this need in time?" That distinction changes the pressure in the exchange. The other person is not being summoned; they are being asked to mark a point of return.

Mary Ainsworth's Strange Situation research in Baltimore in the late 1960s and early 1970s remains useful here because it made patterns of separation and reunion observable. The adult version is more complex, but the pattern still matters: distress is not only about being apart, but about whether return feels reliable. In messaging, reliability is not the same as speed. A person who replies instantly for days and then disappears unpredictably may create more insecurity than a person who replies slowly but consistently names when they are available. Trust grows around patterns the body can learn.

This is why timing requests should be concrete. "Can we talk later?" may be better than silence, but it still leaves a wide field for anxious guessing. "Can we talk after dinner?" is clearer. "I am busy until late afternoon, but I can call at seven" is clearer still. A slow reply becomes less threatening when it is paired with a visible return. Even a brief acknowledgement can steady the room: "I saw this. I cannot answer properly now, but I will tonight." Such sentences do not require constant access. They provide orientation, and orientation is often what the distressed person is actually seeking.

For the person waiting, a clean follow-up has a different feel from an accusatory one. "When you have a moment, can you let me know when we can talk?" gives the other person room to be occupied without being presumed guilty. "I am feeling a bit unsettled and would appreciate a time to reconnect" names the emotion without making it evidence of neglect. "No rush to reply fully; I would just like to know when you are free" protects the request from becoming pursuit. These messages do not erase longing. They refuse to weaponise it.

The opposite style can be heard in the hidden charge. "Guess you are too busy for me" is not a timing request. "Nice to know where I stand" is not a timing request. "Forget it, clearly this matters more to me than to you" is not a timing request. Such messages are understandable when the body is frightened, but they place the other person in a defensive posture before any explanation has been offered. They also tend to produce the very atmosphere they fear: distance, irritation, guardedness, a reply given under pressure rather than one offered with presence.

A slow reply is not always innocent, and that truth must be kept in view. There are relationships where delay is used carelessly or deliberately: messages ignored as punishment, difficult topics left hanging, promises to call quietly abandoned, "busy" used as a permanent hiding place. In those cases, the issue is not merely the anxious person's interpretation. It is a pattern of unreliability. Clean language should not be used to excuse chronic ambiguity. If someone repeatedly refuses to provide timing, repeatedly disappears after tender exchanges, or repeatedly returns only when pressed, the pattern deserves to be taken seriously.

The reconciliation lies in separating a delayed reply from a recurring absence. One slow response during a heavy day is a moment. A repeated refusal to acknowledge important messages is a pattern. One missed call can be human. A long sequence of broken return times becomes information. The difference should be measured through visible behaviour: does the person come back when they said they would, apologise when they miss the mark, give context without contempt, and show care in other ways? Or do they leave the other person guessing and then criticise them for feeling unsure? Timing is not only about minutes. It is about reliability.

For the person who tends to panic while waiting, the first follow-up should have one job. Not three. Not reassurance, protest, punishment, and scheduling all at once. One job. If the need is timing, ask for timing. If the need is reassurance, ask for one reassurance. If the need is a later conversation, ask for a time. "Can you let me know when we can talk?" is clean because it does not drag the whole emotional history into the message. Once the timing is known, the deeper conversation has a place to happen. Without timing, everything risks leaking into the next text.

There is also dignity in not adding commentary after the clean ask. Many messages begin well and then damage themselves. "When you get a moment, can you let me know when we can talk? I just feel like you never really make time and I am tired of feeling stupid for caring." The first sentence creates a bridge. The second sets fire to it. This does not mean the pain is false. It means the pain belongs in the conversation, not in the anxious afterthought that follows the request. A timing text should be a marker, not a trial.

The quiet skill is to tolerate the space after the message has been sent. This is where secure language becomes more than phrasing. The clean text may still leave the body unsettled. The phone may still feel magnetic. The mind may still produce stories. But the next act matters. Picking up the phone repeatedly, checking whether the message has been read, composing and deleting follow-ups, inspecting online status, or rehearsing accusations in advance all keep the nervous system fastened to the gap. The reply is slow, but anxiety makes the waiting active in the most punishing way.

A different kind of action is possible. The person can send one clear timing request and then turn towards something that does not punish the other person for being unavailable: a task with a beginning and end, a walk round the block, a shower, food, a written note that says, "I have asked for a time; I do not need to ask again yet." This is not indifference. It is containment. The body may still be unsettled, but the relationship is not being made to absorb every wave of that unrest in real time.

The person receiving the message has responsibilities too. "I am busy" is sometimes true, but often incomplete. A caring response gives enough information to reduce unnecessary guessing. "I am tied up until six, but I can call after that." "I saw your message and want to answer properly later." "I do not have capacity for this by text; can we talk tomorrow morning?" "I am not ignoring you; I am with family and will reply tonight." None of these sentences requires dramatic emotional labour. They simply prevent silence from becoming an empty room the other person must furnish with fear.

The danger, for both people, is treating speed as the only measure of care. Speed is seductive because it is visible. It can be counted, compared, and turned into evidence. But care has more than one tempo. Sometimes care is a quick "thinking of you." Sometimes care is waiting to respond until the answer can be thoughtful. Sometimes care is saying, "I cannot talk now, and I do not want to leave you hanging." A relationship built only on speed may become fragile, because life will inevitably interrupt speed. A relationship built on reliable return has a stronger base.

The scripts that serve slow-reply moments often share a calm structure: acknowledgement, request, release. "I know you may be busy. When you get a moment, can you let me know when we can talk?" "I am feeling unsure after earlier. No need to answer fully now, but could you send a time for later?" "I do not want to spiral or keep messaging. Please let me know when you are available." The release matters because it signals that the other person is not being grabbed through the phone. The request remains clear. The pressure lowers.

Still, a person should notice whether they are asking for timing or secretly asking for immediate reassurance. There is no shame in wanting reassurance, but hidden motives make messages unstable. "Just tell me when we can talk" may become painful if the real desired answer is "I love you, do not worry, nothing is wrong." When the need is reassurance, it is cleaner to say so: "I am feeling anxious. Could you send one reassuring line when you can, and we can talk later?" The more honest the ask, the less likely it is to mutate into resentment.

The phone on the table will always have a peculiar power because it makes absence visible. It shows the message, the time, the lack of answer. It tempts the mind to treat silence as speech. But silence is not always speech. Sometimes it is simply a gap awaiting context. The secure move is neither to deny the ache nor to obey every interpretation it produces. It is to ask for a point of return, then let that request stand long enough to mean something.

The forward test comes when the screen stays quiet and the story begins to write itself. Is the next message seeking useful timing, or trying to force relief? Is the delay a moment, or part of a pattern? Can the need be placed in a sentence that gives the other person room to answer without being accused before they arrive? Slow replies will always press on the tender place where love meets uncertainty. The question is whether the pause becomes a bridge with a return time, or a courtroom built in the glow of a silent phone.

What to do while waiting

Why can one unanswered message create more urgency than a real disagreement that lasts an hour? A disagreement has sound, shape, and another person in the room. Waiting has almost nothing: a sent message, a silent phone, a body that keeps checking for a change. The mind begins to supply what the screen withholds. Five minutes become a signal. Twenty minutes become a theory. An hour becomes a verdict, unless something interrupts the private courtroom before it reaches sentencing.

The temptation is action. Anxiety rarely sits still by choice. It wants to do something with the charge in the body: send another text, reread the last reply, inspect the wording, open the chat, close it, make the phone light up, draft a colder message, decide not to care, imagine the apology that should arrive. Some of these actions look harmless. They may even feel responsible. Yet many of them keep the nervous system fastened to the absence. The phone becomes a small altar of uncertainty.

A waiting plan is not a performance of indifference. It is a way to remain connected to oneself while refusing to punish the other person for not being available at once. That distinction matters. Some people try to wait by becoming hard: they tell themselves they do not care, withdraw affection in advance, or turn silence into a weapon they can return later. Others try to wait by dissolving into the gap: they abandon the rest of the day, letting one unanswered message determine their posture, appetite, concentration, and tone. Neither is freedom. One attacks the bond; the other abandons the self.

John Bowlby's attachment work in London across the mid-twentieth century, including his 1951 World Health Organization report, placed emotional availability at the centre of human security. Yet adult availability is not constant presence. A loved person may be unreachable for ordinary reasons: work, sleep, travel, illness, a conversation, a low battery, a mind that needs time before answering well. The body may still read the delay as risk, because attachment does not operate like a calendar. A waiting plan recognises this without letting the alarm become the author of the next move.

The first task is to separate the facts from the story. The fact may be plain: a message has not yet been answered. The story may be elaborate: they are pulling away, they regret the relationship, they are punishing me, I was too much, the warmth is gone. The story may be possible, but possibility is not proof. The private sentence "I do not yet know what this silence means" is powerful because it leaves reality unfinished. It keeps the mind from sealing the gap with fear. It does not soothe by lying. It soothes by refusing to invent.

A useful waiting plan gives the body something to do that does not escalate the relationship. The action should be concrete, limited, and non-punitive: make tea, wash the cup, take a short walk, finish a defined task, shower, eat something ordinary, stand by a window and name what is present, write the message not to send but to understand. The value is not in distraction for its own sake. The value is in giving the nervous system a different object of contact. The hand holds a mug instead of the phone. The room returns.

James Gross's process model of emotion regulation, developed at Stanford University in the late 1990s, is useful here because it treats emotion as something shaped by attention, interpretation, and response. Waiting intensifies when attention narrows to one point and stays there. The unanswered message becomes the entire field. A waiting plan widens the field enough for choice to re-enter. It does not deny the feeling. It changes the sequence: notice the alarm, name the uncertainty, choose the next non-punitive action, return to the phone only at an agreed point rather than every time anxiety spikes.

The phrase "I can be unsettled and still be safe" matters because it separates sensation from emergency. It is not a promise that everything is fine. It is a reminder that feeling unsettled is not itself proof of danger. A tight chest, restless hands, or a sinking stomach may signal distress; they do not automatically supply accurate information about another person's intentions. The sentence gives the body a handrail. It says, in effect, this feeling is real, but it does not get to govern every behaviour.

There are other private lines that can hold the same function. "I have asked clearly; I do not need to ask again yet." "A delay is not a diagnosis." "I can wait without becoming cold." "I do not have to turn uncertainty into evidence." "If there is a problem, I will meet it when it is real." The best self-statements are not sugary. They are sturdy. They do not try to make the person feel delighted about waiting; they help the person remain recognisable to themselves while waiting. The tone should be sober enough to believe.

The danger is that a waiting plan can become another form of control if it is used to suppress need entirely. Some people mistake maturity for not minding. They tell themselves to be calm when the truer sentence is, "I am hurt and I need a time to reconnect." They perform serenity while resentment gathers below the surface. That is not secure waiting. Secure waiting is not silence at any cost. It begins after a clean request has been made, or while one is being prepared. It holds the space between asking and receiving without filling it with accusation.

The credible limitation is important. Waiting patiently is not the right answer to chronic unreliability. If someone regularly leaves meaningful messages unanswered, avoids agreed conversations, disappears after conflict, or criticises the other person for needing basic responsiveness, the issue is no longer the discomfort of a single pause. A waiting plan can prevent escalation in the moment, but it cannot transform a sustained pattern of ambiguity into care. There are silences that need self-soothing, and there are silences that need to be named as part of the relationship's structure. The difference is visible in repetition.

That distinction protects self-respect. One delayed reply during a full day can be met with steadiness. A repeated pattern of vanishing requires a clearer boundary or a different conversation. The question is behavioural: does the other person return, explain, repair, and keep future agreements, or do they leave the waiting person to absorb uncertainty again and again? A waiting plan should never become a private prison in which one person learns to endure what another refuses to make accountable. It is a bridge, not a cage.

The plan also needs a time boundary. Endless waiting makes the mind feral. A person may decide, privately, "I will not check for the next half-hour," or "I will return to the phone after I finish this task," or "If I have not heard by evening, I will send one clear timing request." The exact interval matters less than the principle: the phone is no longer allowed to set the rhythm by constant interruption. The person waiting chooses a point of return. That choice restores agency without creating pressure.

A particularly damaging habit is rehearsing the accusation before the answer arrives. The mind drafts speeches: "You clearly did not care enough to reply," "I knew this would happen," "I am done asking." These rehearsals feel like preparation, but they often prime the body for conflict before facts appear. By the time the other person replies with something ordinary, the waiting person may already be angry from the imagined exchange. A waiting plan interrupts the rehearsal. It says, "I will not argue with a person who is not yet here."

There is wisdom in writing during the wait, but only if writing is used to sort rather than inflame. A useful note might contain three lines: what happened, what I am feeling, what I will ask if needed. "I sent a message and have not heard back. I feel anxious and embarrassed. If I still feel unsettled later, I will ask when we can talk." That is different from building a long indictment. The written page can either become a mirror or a weapon. The purpose is to return to clarity, not to gather ammunition.

Waiting also tests whether care for oneself is being confused with punishment of the other person. Putting the phone down is self-care when it protects attention and steadiness. It becomes punishment when it is done with the hidden aim of making the other person worry. Taking a walk is grounding when it helps the body move through agitation. It becomes protest when every step is fuelled by the fantasy of being chased. The visible action may look the same; the inner contract changes its meaning. Secure waiting does not scheme. It steadies.

Mary Ainsworth's Strange Situation research in Baltimore in the late 1960s and early 1970s showed how separation and reunion reveal patterns of protest, avoidance, and settling. Adult relationships contain more language and choice, but the old structure still appears in miniature. A delay separates. The reply reunites. The question is what happens in the space between. Does protest take over? Does avoidance freeze the need? Or can the person remain available to reconnection without surrendering their dignity to the gap?

A waiting plan should preserve warmth, not merely prevent damage. That may sound subtle, but it is decisive. The aim is not to become emotionally blank until the other person returns. The aim is to remain capable of receiving them without having turned the delay into a private betrayal. A person might say inwardly, "I am allowed to want the reply, and I am allowed to live until it comes." The sentence is modest, but it resists two extremes: clinging to the phone and pretending the phone means nothing.

The person who is waiting may also need to decide what kind of follow-up belongs at the next point. If the issue is simple timing, the follow-up can be simple: "When you get a moment, can you let me know when we can talk?" If the issue is emotional reassurance, the request can name that: "I am feeling unsettled; could you send one reassuring line when you can?" If the issue is a repeated pattern, the message may need to be firmer: "I do not want to keep guessing after difficult conversations. Can we agree on a return time when we pause?" The waiting plan does not erase communication. It makes communication less reactive.

There is also the matter of bodily grounding. The body that checks the phone every few moments is usually seeking a signal. If the signal is not available externally, it can be useful to create internal signals of present safety: feet on the floor, shoulders lowered, jaw unclenched, breath lengthened, eyes deliberately moved from the screen to the room. These actions are small, but their smallness is part of their usefulness. They return the person from imagined future harm to the present surface of the chair, the weight of the mug, the sound of ordinary life continuing. The room returns again.

The quiet motif is the phone on the table. It will not lose its power entirely. Love makes certain silences matter. But the phone need not become the only object in the room. Around it are tasks, textures, doors, windows, water, paper, breath, other relationships, other parts of the self. Anxiety narrows the world to one bright rectangle. A waiting plan widens it just enough for the person to remember that they are not only the one awaiting a reply.

The unresolved test is what happens after the clean message has been sent and no answer has yet arrived. Will the waiting person keep faith with the request, or will they undermine it with protest? Will they stay connected to themselves, or make the other person's delay the sole measure of their worth? Will the next action keep the bridge open, or punish the silence for being silent? The line "I can be unsettled and still be safe" does not end the uncertainty. It asks whether the self can remain present inside it.

If the answer is uncertain

Why can the words "I don't know" feel more threatening than a clear no? A no has a shape. It may hurt, but it gives the mind something to meet. "I don't know" opens the floor. The person hearing it may feel as though they have been left standing in a half-lit corridor, no door closed, no door open, listening for movement on the other side. The conversation pauses, but the body does not. It keeps searching for a verdict.

The uncertain answer often arrives quietly. A partner looks down, rubs a thumb along the side of a glass, and says, "I don't know what I feel yet." Or, "I don't know if I can talk about this tonight." Or, more painfully, "I don't know what I want." The sentence may be honest. It may even be careful. Yet to an anxious ear, uncertainty can sound like danger taking its time. The mind rushes to complete what the other person has not said: they are leaving, they are losing interest, they are hiding the truth, they are softening the blow. The corridor gets longer.

The central difficulty is that uncertainty asks for patience at the exact moment fear wants control. A person who hears "I don't know" may try to force the answer into existence. They ask the question again, in a different tone. They offer interpretations for the other person to accept or deny. They argue against possible outcomes before any outcome has been named. This is understandable; ambiguity is uncomfortable, and intimate ambiguity can feel almost physically unsafe. But forced certainty is rarely genuine certainty. It is often compliance, appeasement, or escape.

A more secure response treats uncertainty as incomplete information rather than immediate rejection. That distinction changes the next sentence. "What do you mean you don't know?" can easily become an accusation. "How can you not know?" adds shame to the fog. "So that means you don't care" turns uncertainty into a verdict before the facts have arrived. A cleaner response asks for the next measurable step: "What would help you get clearer, and when can we revisit this?" The question does not pretend the uncertainty is painless. It simply refuses to convert pain into pressure.

John Bowlby's attachment work in London across the mid-twentieth century remains relevant here because attachment fear is not only fear of loss; it is fear of unavailability. The uncertain person may still be present in the room, yet emotionally unreachable in the specific way the other person wants. That gap can feel like abandonment, especially when the subject is the relationship itself. But adult intimacy cannot demand instant access to every inner answer. People sometimes need time to locate the truth beneath their first defensive reaction, their guilt, their fatigue, or their wish not to hurt someone they love.

Uncertainty has different forms, and each form needs to be heard accurately. "I don't know because I am overwhelmed" is not the same as "I don't know because my feelings have changed." "I don't know how to explain it" is not the same as "I don't know whether I want this." "I don't know tonight" is not the same as "I refuse to think about it." When all uncertainty is treated as one threat, the conversation loses precision. The anxious mind wants certainty at any cost; the secure mind asks what kind of uncertainty is actually present.

The next measurable step gives uncertainty a container. Time to think is a container. A return date is a container. A smaller question is a container. Support for getting clearer is a container. "Would it help to sleep on it and talk tomorrow evening?" "Do you need quiet time, or would talking it through help?" "Can we narrow the question to what you know right now?" "If you are unsure about the larger decision, can you tell me what you are sure of?" These sentences do not solve the uncertainty. They keep it from spreading everywhere.

The phrase "what would help you get clearer?" is powerful because it makes the uncertain person active. It does not let them disappear into vagueness. It asks them to participate in the process of clarification. They may need time alone, a calmer setting, a walk, a written note, a practical detail, a pause in the argument, or a chance to speak without being corrected after each sentence. The answer matters because it turns fog into behaviour. Instead of staring at uncertainty as a blank wall, both people can identify a next action.

A follow-up time is equally important. Without it, "I don't know" can become an indefinite waiting room. The person who asked is left to carry the anxiety alone, while the uncertain person may feel relieved simply because the pressure has stopped. A return point prevents that quiet abandonment. "Can we revisit this after dinner?" "Can we speak on Sunday afternoon?" "Can you take tonight and tell me tomorrow what you know?" These are not demands for instant resolution. They are agreements that the question will not be buried.

The handrail returns here. A person may not be able to hold certainty, but they can hold a next step. The next step should be visible enough to keep both people oriented. "I'll think about it" is vague. "I'll think about it tonight and tell you tomorrow whether I need more time or whether I have an answer" is clearer. "We'll talk later" drifts. "Let's talk after work for twenty minutes" gives the anxiety less room to invent. Precision does not remove discomfort; it reduces the unnecessary suffering caused by formlessness.

There is a credible limitation. Some people use uncertainty as a shelter from accountability. "I don't know" can be honest, but it can also become a way to avoid choosing, avoid disappointing, avoid admitting a truth, or keep another person available while offering very little in return. Chronic uncertainty is not neutrality. If someone repeatedly cannot say what they want, cannot define the relationship, cannot decide whether they will return to a conversation, or cannot offer any next step, their uncertainty begins to function as a decision with consequences. Refusing to choose still shapes the other person's life.

The reconciliation is to honour genuine uncertainty without romanticising endless ambiguity. A person is allowed to need time. They are not entitled to keep someone else suspended without structure. One evening of not knowing deserves patience. A repeated pattern of "I don't know" without reflection, movement, or accountability deserves clearer boundaries. The difference is visible in behaviour: does the uncertain person use the time to become more honest, more specific, more responsible? Or does uncertainty become a room where difficult conversations go to disappear?

The person hearing uncertainty must also resist the urge to become the other person's interpreter. Under pressure, they may begin offering answers: "Maybe you just need space." "Maybe you are scared." "Maybe you do love me but you are overwhelmed." Sometimes such guesses are compassionate; often they are attempts to steer the answer towards something survivable. But interpretation can become another form of pressure. A better move is to ask what the other person can genuinely name. "What part is unclear?" "What do you know for certain?" "What feels true, even if the whole answer is not there yet?"

This is where partial clarity becomes valuable. Not knowing everything is not the same as knowing nothing. A partner might say, "I know I care about you, but I do not know how to handle this conflict." Or, "I know I need space tonight, but I do not want to end the conversation forever." Or, "I know I am upset, but I do not yet know what I need from you." Such statements reduce the threat without pretending the issue is settled. They give the other person something real to hold while the larger answer forms.

There is also a place for asking what support would help, but support must not become persuasion. "Would it help if I listened without responding for a few minutes?" is different from "Let me explain why you should not feel unsure." "Do you need time alone, or would it help to talk it through?" is different from cornering someone into clarity before they have found it. Support creates conditions for truth. Persuasion tries to control the truth that emerges. The distinction is subtle, but the body usually knows the difference.

For the person who feels anxious, uncertain answers can awaken a desperate wish to secure the future immediately. The temptation is to ask large questions at the wrong scale: "Do you still love me?" "Are we going to make it?" "Should I be worried?" These may be real questions, but they may not be the most useful questions in the moment. A more workable scale might be, "Can you tell me whether this uncertainty is about tonight or about us more broadly?" or "Can you reassure me that you are willing to keep talking while you think?" The smaller question may carry more truth than the dramatic one.

Uncertainty after conflict needs particular care. One person may say, "I don't know what I need," because their nervous system is still flooded. If the other person demands immediate clarity, the answer may come from defence rather than reflection. A structured pause can help, but only if it includes return. "Let's pause for an hour, and when we come back, each of us can say one thing we know and one thing we are still unsure about." This keeps the conversation collaborative without pretending that all truth is available on command.

The same principle applies to relational decisions. If someone is unsure about a commitment, a move, a recurring pattern, a repair process, or the future of the relationship, the uncertainty may require more than one conversation. But it still needs form. "I need a month to decide" may be honest, but it should not be the whole sentence. What happens during that month? What will be discussed? What behaviour will change or pause? What contact remains? What would count as progress? Without such questions, time does not necessarily clarify; it merely passes.

There is dignity in saying, "I can give you time, but I cannot live indefinitely inside maybe." This sentence is not a threat. It is a boundary around ambiguity. It respects the other person's process while naming the cost of suspension. Some people fear that setting such a boundary will push the uncertain person away. Perhaps it will. But a relationship that can only continue while one person silences their need for clarity is already asking for too much. Patience must have a spine.

The uncertain person, too, may need language that protects honesty without creating panic. "I do not have the full answer yet, but I am not trying to avoid you." "I need time to think, and I can talk again tomorrow." "I know this is hard to hear; I want to be careful rather than quick." "I cannot give certainty tonight, but I can give you a return time." These sentences do not eliminate the ache for the listener. They show respect for that ache. They make uncertainty less lonely.

The waiting person can use grounding lines that keep fear from finishing the sentence too soon. "Uncertain is not the same as over." "I can ask for a next step without forcing an answer." "A delayed truth is better than a false certainty." "I do not have to solve the whole future tonight." These lines should not be used to deny genuine warning signs. They are meant to hold the body steady long enough to gather reality rather than manufacture it.

The ethical centre of uncertain answers is truth with responsibility. Truth says, "I do not know yet." Responsibility says, "I will not leave you alone with that indefinitely." Truth says, "I need time." Responsibility says, "Here is when I will return, and here is what I will do with the time." Truth without responsibility becomes carelessness. Responsibility without truth becomes appeasement. Secure communication needs the difficult combination: honest uncertainty held inside a clear next step.

The forward test arrives when "I don't know" enters the room. Will the uncertainty be treated as a verdict, a threat, an excuse, or an unfinished place where both people still have work to do? The next sentence decides the shape of the corridor. It can become a place of panic, pressure, and forced answers, or it can become a passage with a handrail: what would help you get clearer, and when can we revisit this?

Chapter 6
Boundaries Around Contact and Space

Why can the sentence "I need space" sound, to one person, like breathing room and, to the other, like the beginning of abandonment? The words are short. They may even be reasonable. A person stands in the hallway after a strained conversation, keys still in hand, shoulders tight, needing quiet before they can speak kindly. The other person hears the request and feels the floor drop. Space, in that moment, does not sound like regulation. It sounds like leaving.

The opposite sentence can be just as charged. "I need you to answer me" may mean, "I am frightened and trying to find the thread between us." But to the person receiving it, the words may feel like a locked room with no air. One reaches because distance hurts; the other steps back because closeness has begun to feel like pressure. Neither response is automatically cruel. Both can become damaging when they arrive without shape, reassurance, or respect for the other person's limits.

Contact and space are often treated as rival needs, as though one person is loving and the other is withholding, one person is needy and the other is cold. That framing is too crude for real intimacy. The need for contact protects the bond from drift, neglect, and unspoken fear. The need for space protects the bond from overwhelm, resentment, and words spoken while flooded. A relationship that honours only contact becomes breathless. A relationship that honours only space becomes lonely. The hard work sits between them.

The central tension is that boundaries can either threaten connection or preserve it, depending on how they are framed and kept. "Leave me alone" may contain a legitimate need for quiet, but it gives the other person nothing to hold. "I need thirty minutes to decompress, then I want to reconnect" changes the meaning of space. It attaches a return. It tells the anxious body that absence is not exile. It tells the overwhelmed body that closeness can wait without disappearing. The boundary becomes a bridge rather than a locked door.

The stakes are practical as well as emotional. Contact expectations quietly govern daily life: when messages are answered, whether bedtime calls are assumed, how long silence can stretch after conflict, what counts as checking in, and what kind of availability is realistic during demanding days. When these expectations remain unspoken, people create private rules and then suffer when the other person breaks rules they never agreed to. One person feels tested; the other feels trapped. The phone becomes an examiner. The pause becomes evidence.

Clear boundaries reduce that secret testing. They move the relationship from moral accusation into practical agreement. "Weekdays are heavy for me; can we do a quick call at nine?" is different from "You never make time for me." "I cannot text through the workday, but I can send a message at lunch" is different from going silent and hoping the other person adapts without pain. The point is not to turn love into a timetable. It is to give care a rhythm that human lives can actually sustain.

Boundaries also become necessary when reassurance requests, however understandable, begin to overwhelm the person receiving them. Love cannot remain generous if every anxious wave must be answered immediately and repeatedly. Yet refusing the pattern does not have to mean rejecting the person. "I care, and I cannot do repeated reassurance texts - can we talk at seven?" holds two truths in the same sentence. It says yes to the bond and no to the loop. That distinction is one of the marks of adult intimacy.

There will be moments when boundaries are not received gracefully. Someone may argue, plead, guilt-trip, reinterpret, or keep negotiating after the answer has already been given. The pressure may be subtle: one more question, one more exception, one more attempt to make the boundary sound unkind. At that point, the work shifts from explanation to consistency. A boundary that must be endlessly defended begins to lose its protective function. Calm repetition is not harshness. It is the boundary remaining itself.

The path ahead moves through space that reassures rather than alarms, contact expectations that are concrete rather than moralised, limits that protect care from becoming depletion, and responses for the moments when a boundary is pushed past the point of honest discussion. The unresolved question is not whether closeness or space matters more. The sharper question is whether two people can build a pattern in which contact does not become possession, and space does not become disappearance.

Asking for space safely

Why can thirty minutes alone sound like a threat when it is meant as protection? A person stands in the doorway after a difficult exchange, hand still on the handle, feeling words crowd the back of the throat. They know that if they stay, the next sentence may come out too sharp. They also know that if they leave abruptly, the other person may hear a louder message than the one intended. The room has gone brittle. Space is needed. The risk is what space might be made to mean.

"I need space" is one of the most easily misunderstood sentences in intimate life. It may mean, "I am overwhelmed and trying not to hurt us." It may mean, "I need quiet so I can think clearly." It may mean, "My body is flooded, and I cannot stay kind if this continues." But to the person already afraid of disconnection, it may land as, "I am leaving you," "You are too much," or "Your needs have driven me away." A boundary spoken without reassurance can become a blank wall. A boundary spoken with care can become a door left visibly unlocked.

The aim is not to avoid space, because space is sometimes the most responsible thing a person can ask for. Staying in the room while resentment, panic, or exhaustion takes over is not devotion. It may be a form of damage dressed as loyalty. The adult question is not whether space is allowed, but whether it can be requested in a way that protects the bond from the meaning anxiety will rush to attach. "I need thirty minutes to decompress, then I want to reconnect" changes the emotional architecture of the moment. It gives the body room and the relationship a return.

John Bowlby's attachment work in London across the mid-twentieth century, including his 1951 World Health Organization report, placed reliable access at the centre of emotional security. The adult relevance is plain: separation is less frightening when return is credible. A partner may not fear space itself as much as they fear space without a map. The visible behaviours matter. Does the person leaving say where they are going? Do they say when they will return? Do they keep that return? Do they still signal care while setting the boundary? Space becomes safer when it is attached to orientation.

A safe request for space has three elements: reassurance, purpose, and return. Reassurance tells the other person that the relationship is not being cancelled in the moment. Purpose tells them what the space is for. Return tells them when contact will resume. "I care about us. I need half an hour to calm down, and I will come back at seven." "I am not walking away from the relationship. I need a quiet break so I can speak more carefully." "I want to continue this, but not while I am this activated." These sentences do not remove all discomfort. They reduce unnecessary fear.

Purpose matters because vague space is easily filled with old stories. "I need to get away from this" sounds different from "I need to settle my body so I do not become unkind." The first sentence may be true, but it leaves the other person with too many possible meanings. The second gives the space a protective function. It says the pause is being taken for the sake of the conversation, not as a punishment for having it. The difference is not cosmetic. It changes whether the person left behind experiences the pause as abandonment, rejection, discipline, or care.

A return time matters even more. "Later" may feel casual to the person requesting space, but to the person waiting it can feel like fog. "After dinner," "in thirty minutes," "tomorrow morning before work," or "once I have walked round the block" gives the pause a boundary. The exact time need not be perfect, but it must be sincere. A return time that is repeatedly missed becomes another wound. If the person asking for space needs more time, the safer move is to update rather than vanish: "I need longer than I thought. I still want to talk tonight. Can we make it nine?"

Mary Ainsworth's Strange Situation research in Baltimore in the late 1960s and early 1970s showed how much meaning gathers around separation and reunion. The adult lesson is not that every pause is a crisis, but that the quality of return matters. A pause that ends in reliable re-engagement teaches the relationship something different from a pause that dissolves into silence. Returning does not always mean resolving everything. It may mean saying, "I am calmer now, and I am ready to listen," or, "I still need sleep, but I did not want to leave this hanging." The point is not theatrical reunion. It is kept faith.

For the person requesting space, the temptation may be to over-explain. When someone looks hurt or frightened, it can feel necessary to justify the boundary until they accept it. Yet excessive explanation often invites negotiation at the very moment the person needs to disengage. A safe space request should be clear enough to hold, not so detailed that it becomes a debate. "I am too overwhelmed to keep talking well. I will come back in thirty minutes" is stronger than a long defence of every reason space is justified. The boundary needs a handle, not an essay.

Tone carries great weight here. The words "I need space" can be spoken like a slammed door or a steady hand on the table. A sharp tone may turn a reasonable pause into a relational threat. A cold tone may make reassurance sound false. A pleading tone may invite the other person to argue the boundary down. Adult tone is neither cruel nor apologetic. It says, in effect, this is necessary, and I am not using it to injure you. Calm firmness protects the pause from becoming another stage of the conflict.

There is a credible limitation. Space can be misused. Some people call it a boundary when it is actually avoidance, stonewalling, punishment, or control. They leave whenever accountability approaches, refuse to set a return time, disappear after hard questions, or use silence to make the other person anxious enough to drop the issue. That is not safe space. It is withdrawal with better vocabulary. A true boundary around space protects the possibility of later contact. It does not erase the obligation to return, repair, or answer for the matter at hand.

The reconciliation lies in accountability. A person has the right to pause a conversation that has become overwhelming. They do not have the right to make the other person live indefinitely inside uncertainty. "I need space" must be paired with "and I will return" if the relationship is to remain held. The return may not produce instant agreement, but it should produce contact. The issue may still be hard. The person may still need more time. But the pause cannot become a corridor with no end.

The person receiving the space request also has work to do. A safe request can still hurt. The body may protest. The mind may race. The urge to follow, argue, demand reassurance, or force the conversation open may be strong. Yet if the other person has named care, purpose, and return, the most secure response is not to pursue the pause until it breaks. "Okay. I feel unsettled, but I will wait for you to come back" is a deeply adult sentence. It acknowledges the ache without making it the other person's emergency. It allows space to function.

This does not mean accepting every pause without question. If the return time is missed again and again, if the same issue disappears after every break, if "space" always protects one person from consequence, then the pattern needs to be named. "I can respect a pause, but I need us to keep the return time" is a fair boundary. "I do not want to continue conversations where space means we never come back" is not neediness; it is structural clarity. Safe space requires trust from the person waiting, and trust requires evidence.

There is an art to choosing the length of the pause. Too short, and the body may not actually settle. Too long, and the other person may be left alone with avoidable uncertainty. A useful pause is long enough to lower intensity and short enough to preserve connection. The exact length will depend on the people and the moment, but the underlying principle remains: space should serve re-engagement. It should not become a private country one person enters whenever closeness becomes inconvenient.

The scripts that work best are plain. "I need twenty minutes to cool down, then I want to come back." "I am getting overwhelmed. I care about you, and I need a pause before I say something badly." "I cannot keep texting about this right now. I will call after work." "I need to be alone for a bit, but I am not leaving the conversation." "I want to reconnect, and I need to settle first." Plainness is important because the moment is already emotionally loaded. Decorative language can sound evasive. A clean sentence gives the anxious mind less to distort.

Safe space also includes small signals of continued connection when appropriate. A hand briefly on the shoulder before leaving the room. A text that says, "Still coming back at eight." A cup of tea placed nearby after a pause. These gestures are not substitutes for the return conversation, but they can reduce the sense that space means emotional exile. The visible behaviour confirms the stated intention: I am taking room, not withdrawing care.

For some people, asking for space safely will require resisting shame. They may have learned that needing quiet makes them cold, avoidant, selfish, or defective. So they stay too long, speak too sharply, and then apologise for words that a pause might have prevented. Space, properly held, is not a rejection of intimacy. It is one of intimacy's maintenance tools. A person who can say, "I need to stop before I become unkind" is not abandoning the relationship. They are protecting the conditions under which tenderness can return.

For others, the challenge will be resisting the fantasy that space must feel comfortable to be safe. It may not. A well-framed pause can still ache. The person waiting may still feel exposed. The person leaving may still feel guilty. Secure communication does not remove all discomfort from boundaries. It makes the discomfort less confusing and less dangerous. The relationship knows what is happening, why it is happening, and when contact will resume. That knowledge matters.

The quiet motif is the door. A door slammed in anger teaches fear. A door locked without explanation teaches helplessness. A door closed with a clear return time teaches something else: separateness can exist without abandonment. Behind that lesson is a mature form of love. It does not demand that two people remain fused in every difficult moment. It also does not permit distance to become disappearance.

The forward test comes when the body says, "I cannot stay in this conversation," and the relationship is still listening. Will the request for space arrive as a threat, a vanishing act, an apology so weak it cannot hold, or a clear boundary with reassurance and return? The difference may live inside one sentence: "I need thirty minutes to decompress, then I want to reconnect." Space becomes safe when it has a purpose, a promise, and a way back through the door.

Setting contact expectations

Why can a missed 9 p.m. call feel less like a scheduling problem and more like a verdict on love? The agreement may never have been spoken, yet the body behaves as though it has been broken. One person assumed there would be a call after work. The other assumed silence meant a full day and no offence. By the time the phone stays quiet, both are living inside different contracts. The calendar becomes a witness.

Unspoken expectations are powerful because they often feel obvious to the person holding them. A morning message may mean steadiness. A goodnight text may mean care. A midday check-in may mean being remembered, not monitored. To another person, the same rhythm may feel excessive, interruptive, or impossible during a demanding day. Neither person is necessarily wrong. The trouble begins when private meanings are treated as public agreements. The disappointed person feels neglected; the overwhelmed person feels accused; the contact pattern becomes a moral trial.

Setting contact expectations moves the conversation out of accusation and into design. "Weekdays are heavy for me; can we do a quick call at 9?" is a different sentence from "You never make time for me." The first names a real constraint, proposes a practical rhythm, and leaves room for negotiation. The second may contain pain, but it makes the other person defend their character before the pattern can be discussed. Secure contact is not built by guessing who should have known what. It is built by making the invisible agreement visible enough to keep.

John Bowlby's attachment work in London across the mid-twentieth century, including his 1951 World Health Organization report, helps explain why contact carries so much emotional charge. Human beings seek signs that important bonds remain accessible. In adult relationships, those signs are often ordinary: a reply before sleep, a call after a long day, a message when plans change, a sentence that says, "I am busy, not gone." The need for access is not childish. But access becomes healthier when it is patterned rather than constantly improvised under stress.

A rhythm is not a cage. It is a form of orientation. A couple might agree that workdays involve fewer texts but one evening call. They might agree that no one is expected to respond during meetings, driving, sleep, or family time. They might agree that after conflict, a pause must include a return time. These agreements are not romantic in the decorative sense, but they are deeply protective. They reduce the number of moments in which silence has to be interpreted from scratch. The phone is no longer asked to carry the entire relationship by mood and timing alone.

Mary Ainsworth's Strange Situation research in Baltimore in the late 1960s and early 1970s made visible the importance of reliable return after separation. Adult contact expectations operate in that same broad territory, though with language, work calendars, temperaments, and phones added. The central question is not whether two people are always available. They will not be. The question is whether absence has a known shape. A delayed reply feels different when the other person has already said, "I cannot text much during clinic hours, but I will call after dinner." Predictability turns some forms of waiting from threat into ordinary time.

The word "realistic" matters. Many contact agreements fail because they are made in the emotional weather of a crisis. After a painful misunderstanding, one person promises to text constantly; the other agrees, not because it is sustainable, but because they want the distress to stop. For a few days, the rhythm may hold. Then ordinary life returns, the promise frays, and the broken agreement hurts more than the original gap. A realistic expectation must account for actual behaviour, actual energy, actual obligations, and the different ways people experience interruption. Love should stretch people, but it should not require a daily performance that life will reliably defeat.

Practical contact language has a distinct tone. It avoids moral verdicts and asks observable questions. "How do your workdays usually run?" "What kind of check-in feels warm but not pressured?" "When you are unavailable, what is a quick way to let me know?" "After an argument, how long is too long for silence?" These questions turn emotional weather into arrangements. The aim is not to make intimacy administrative, but to prevent intimacy from being governed by assumptions no one has named. A shared rhythm can be tender precisely because it is practical.

Private rules cause particular damage because they create tests. One person waits to see whether the other will text first. One withholds a goodnight message to measure pursuit. One deliberately delays a reply to regain power. One says, "No, it is fine," while marking the absence in an inner ledger. Tests are tempting because they promise evidence without the humiliation of asking. But they poison the evidence they collect. If the other person fails, resentment grows. If they succeed, the relief is short-lived because the underlying expectation remains unspoken. The test must be repeated.

A clear expectation is braver than a test. "I like a goodnight message when we are apart; is that something you can do most nights?" risks a real answer. "If you are going offline, could you tell me so I do not keep checking?" names the vulnerable part without making it an accusation. "I do not need long texts during the day, but a small sign of contact helps me feel connected" gives the other person a visible action. These sentences remove the drama of guessing. They also expose whether the relationship can respond to a reasonable request.

There must be space for difference. Some people feel loved through frequent light contact: a photo from the day, a joke, a short voice note, a message between tasks. Others feel most themselves when attention is not constantly divided. They may love deeply and still dislike ongoing digital conversation. A secure agreement does not declare one style morally superior. It asks what rhythm honours both the need for connection and the need for concentration, solitude, or rest. The difference between "You are too needy" and "I cannot text throughout the workday, but I want a reliable check-in" is the difference between shame and structure.

The credible limitation is that contact expectations can be used to control. A request for rhythm becomes unhealthy when it demands constant reporting, monitors movement, punishes harmless delay, or treats normal privacy as betrayal. "Tell me when you are free to talk" is different from "Prove where you are." "Can we check in before bed?" is different from "You must answer whenever I feel anxious." Secure contact respects the other person's separateness. It asks for reliability, not surveillance. The boundary between the two is visible in whether the agreement leaves both people freer and steadier, or smaller and watched.

The reconciliation lies in negotiated specificity. A partner may not agree to be reachable all day, but may agree to send a short message before going quiet for several hours. Another may not want nightly calls, but may offer a longer call on certain evenings and warm texts on others. Someone may need a rule that emotional topics do not unfold by text during work, but can be saved for a voice conversation later. The agreement should be specific enough to reduce guessing and flexible enough to survive real life. Rigid rules break. Vague hopes dissolve.

Good contact expectations also include what happens when the rhythm cannot be kept. This is where many agreements become trustworthy. Life will interrupt. A meeting will run late, a phone will die, a child will need attention, a person will fall asleep, a day will become harder than expected. The repair sentence matters: "I missed our call. I am sorry. I can talk tomorrow at lunch." Or, "I did not realise I would be offline so long. I will warn you next time." A missed expectation does not have to become a wound if it is acknowledged rather than brushed aside. The repair keeps the pattern alive.

The person who needs more contact must be able to say so without shame. "I am calmer when I know roughly when I will hear from you" is not an indictment. "I feel more connected with a small morning message" is not a demand for worship. These statements become secure when paired with openness to the other person's reality. "What feels possible for you?" keeps the request relational. The person who needs less contact must be equally honest. "I care about you, and frequent texts make me feel pulled out of my day" is not rejection. It is information that allows a workable rhythm to be built.

The scripts that serve this territory are plain because contact expectations should not be wrapped in drama. "Weekdays are heavy for me; can we do a quick call at 9?" "I cannot text much at work, but I can send a lunch message." "If you need space after conflict, please give me a return time." "I like hearing from you before bed, even if it is brief." "When plans change, can we both say so directly rather than leaving the other person to guess?" These sentences do not ask anyone to become a different person overnight. They ask the relationship to stop relying on silent contracts.

There is also wisdom in reviewing contact rhythms without treating adjustment as failure. A rhythm that worked during a quiet month may not work during exams, caregiving, travel, illness, a demanding project, or grief. A secure couple does not wait for resentment to expose the mismatch. They notice strain and revise the pattern. "This week is unusually full; can we switch to shorter check-ins and have a longer call on Sunday?" is a relationally intelligent sentence. It keeps care visible while acknowledging capacity. The calendar becomes a tool rather than a witness for the prosecution.

Contact agreements are not meant to remove all longing. Longing is part of attachment. Missing someone is not a defect in the system. The point is to prevent longing from being forced to interpret every gap alone. When expectations are clear, a person may still feel disappointed by a delayed reply, but disappointment has context. When expectations are vague, disappointment recruits fear, fear recruits accusation, and accusation recruits defence. The emotional cost rises because no one defined the rhythm before the body needed it.

The deeper test is whether two people can discuss contact without making it a referendum on worth. More contact does not automatically mean more love. Less contact does not automatically mean less love. The question is what pattern allows both people to feel connected, respected, and uncoerced. That pattern will be imperfect. It will require repair. It will sometimes reveal incompatibilities that cannot be solved by phrasing alone. But without the conversation, incompatibility and misunderstanding look almost identical.

The forward test comes when the old private rule begins to form: if they cared, they would know. That sentence feels powerful because it protects the speaker from asking. It also leaves the relationship trapped in performance and disappointment. The more adult question is less dramatic and more useful: what rhythm of contact can we actually keep, and what meaning will we agree not to attach when ordinary life interrupts it?

Protecting your own limits

Why can one more reassurance text feel kind in the moment and corrosive by the end of the night? A phone lights up on the table after a difficult conversation. The first message asks, "Are you still upset?" The reply is gentle. The next message asks the same fear in different clothing. The third arrives with apology, then worry, then another request for proof. The person answering may still care deeply, yet their body has begun to tighten around the sound of the notification. Care is present. Capacity is not.

This is the painful territory where love and limit meet. Someone is frightened and reaching for contact; someone else is becoming overwhelmed by the form that reaching has taken. The person asking may feel ashamed of needing reassurance at all. The person receiving may feel guilty for wanting the requests to stop. If the limit is spoken harshly, it confirms the fear of being too much. If the limit is never spoken, resentment gathers behind the replies until warmth thins. A boundary delayed too long often arrives wearing irritation.

The central skill is to say yes to the person while saying no to the pattern. "I care, and I cannot do repeated reassurance texts - can we talk at seven?" is not a rejection dressed as maturity. It is a sentence with two loyalties. It remains loyal to the bond by naming care and offering a path back. It remains loyal to the self by refusing a loop that has become dysregulating. The boundary is not against need. It is against a method of seeking reassurance that neither person can sustain without cost.

John Bowlby's attachment work in London across the mid-twentieth century, including his 1951 World Health Organization report, gave enduring weight to the human need for reliable emotional access. Yet reliable access is not the same as unlimited access. A partner, friend, or loved one may be emotionally committed and still unable to answer the same fear repeatedly through the day. The visible behaviour that preserves security is not endless availability; it is a steady return, a clear alternative, and a refusal to treat either person's nervous system as disposable.

A limit becomes harsh when it attacks the person rather than the pattern. "You are exhausting" wounds character. "I cannot keep answering the same question tonight" names behaviour. "You need to stop being so insecure" shames the need. "I want to reassure you once, and then I need us to pause" gives the need a container. The distinction matters because people often remember the tone of a boundary more vividly than its content. A limit that humiliates may succeed at stopping the immediate behaviour, but it teaches the relationship that honesty is dangerous.

Virginia Satir's family therapy work in California during the twentieth century drew attention to communication patterns in which people placate, blame, over-rationalise, or distract when they are under relational strain. Her language belongs to its own therapeutic tradition, but the practical insight remains useful here: people often abandon congruence when pressure rises. The person receiving repeated reassurance requests may placate by answering long after they are depleted, then blame when they can no longer bear it. Congruent speech does neither. It says what is true while keeping the other person's dignity intact.

The cleanest limit usually has three parts: care, boundary, alternative. Care prevents the boundary from sounding like exile. Boundary prevents care from becoming unlimited access. Alternative keeps the conversation from collapsing into a wall. "I love you, and I cannot keep going over this by text. I can talk after dinner." "I hear that you are scared, and I am not able to reassure you again right now. Could you write down what you need and bring it to our call?" "I am with you, and I need a break from this loop. Let us come back at nine." These sentences do not make the other person comfortable. They make the moment clearer.

A boundary without an alternative can sound like abandonment to a frightened person. An alternative without a boundary can become another doorway into the same loop. The two must hold together. "Not now" may be honest, but if it lands after an anxious bid for reassurance, it may leave too much space for catastrophic meaning. "Not by text, but yes by phone at seven" is more precise. "I cannot keep repeating the same answer, but I can give you one sentence and then we pause" is more usable. The boundary becomes a handrail, not a drop.

Protecting one's limits also requires noticing the early signs of depletion before the voice has hardened. The body often knows before the sentence does. The jaw tightens. The reply becomes shorter. The eyes roll before the person can stop them. The hand hovers over the phone with resentment rather than care. These signals matter because they show when reassurance is no longer being freely offered. A reply given through gritted teeth may technically soothe the other person for a moment, but it also seeds the next rupture. Warmth that has been overdrawn does not remain warm.

There is a credible limitation. Some people invoke "my limits" to avoid normal responsiveness. They refuse ordinary reassurance, treat every emotional request as an intrusion, or use boundary language to make distance sound virtuous. That is not the same as protecting capacity. A genuine limit does not erase responsibility to the relationship. It says, "I cannot meet this in this form right now." It does not say, "Your need is inconvenient, therefore it should not exist." The difference is visible in whether the person setting the boundary offers care, timing, repair, or an alternative channel of contact.

The reconciliation lies in pattern and proportion. One tender request after a hard day deserves tenderness if tenderness is available. A repeated cycle of reassurance texts that continues after clear answers have been given may require a firmer edge. A partner who asks, "Are we okay?" once may simply need comfort. A partner who asks it repeatedly, challenges each answer, and escalates when relief fades may be caught in a loop that reassurance alone cannot resolve. The boundary should match the pattern, not punish the need. Proportion is what keeps firmness from becoming cruelty.

It is also important to distinguish reassurance from regulation. Reassurance is a signal of care: "I am here," "I love you," "We are okay for tonight," "I am upset but not leaving." Regulation is the larger process by which a person settles their body and mind enough to continue living inside uncertainty. A loved one can contribute to regulation, but they cannot be made solely responsible for it. When reassurance is repeatedly asked to do the whole job, it starts to fail. Not because love is insufficient, but because the task has been misassigned.

This is why the alternative matters. "Can we talk at seven?" gives the fear a future point. "Could you take a walk and then we check in?" invites self-holding without abandonment. "I can send one reassuring message, and then I need to put my phone away until morning" protects sleep, attention, and goodwill. "Let us write down the concern and discuss it when we are calmer" moves the issue from panic into structure. The alternative should not be a decorative afterthought. It is the bridge that allows the boundary to remain relational.

The person setting the limit may have to tolerate being misunderstood for a while. A frightened person may hear "I cannot do this repeatedly" as "I do not care." That mishearing is painful, but it cannot be solved by abandoning the boundary every time it appears. The response can stay steady: "I know this feels hard. I do care. I am still not going to keep texting about it tonight." Repetition is sometimes necessary, but the repetition should be of the boundary, not of endless reassurance. The tone is calm. The door is not locked. The pattern is still not allowed to continue.

There is a particular discipline in refusing to over-explain. Long explanations may look compassionate, but they often invite debate. The anxious person may argue with each reason: "But I am not asking that much," "But it only takes a second," "But you answered before," "But if you cared, you would want to." A boundary that must win an argument before it can stand is not yet secure. "I have answered, and I am not going to continue this by text" may feel severe to the person who prefers elaborate justification. It is sometimes kinder than a long defence that keeps the loop alive.

The boundary should also avoid contempt. Contempt is the poison that turns a limit into injury. "This is ridiculous," "You are being dramatic," "I cannot deal with your neediness," or "Grow up" may end the exchange, but they damage the ground beneath it. The adult limit does not sneer. It names capacity. "I am at my limit for tonight." "I want to be kind, and I cannot keep repeating this." "I am starting to feel overwhelmed, so I am going to pause." These sentences preserve respect while refusing the pattern.

For the person who struggles to set limits, guilt may be the hardest part. They may believe that love means answering every request as long as the other person is in pain. But love without self-contact becomes performance, then resentment, then withdrawal. The boundary protects future generosity. It prevents a person from giving so much under pressure that they later become cold, avoidant, or quietly angry. A limit set early with warmth can be far more loving than a yes that curdles into punishment.

The person receiving the boundary has dignity too. A well-set limit should not leave them with only shame. It can name what remains available. "I care about you." "I am not leaving." "I can talk later." "I have given the reassurance I can give." "This feeling is real, and this text loop is not helping us." Such sentences help separate the person from the pattern. They say, in effect, *you are not too much; this method is too much for now*. That distinction can change the whole emotional meaning of the boundary.

There are moments when the limit must become firmer because the alternative has already been offered and rejected. "I am not discussing this further tonight." "I will not respond to more reassurance texts before our call." "I have answered, and I am putting my phone away." Firmness is not escalation if it is delivered without attack. It becomes the line that protects both people from continuing a conversation in a form that is actively making things worse. The boundary does not need to become louder to become clearer.

The motif here is the charging cable. Reassurance can connect, but a person cannot remain permanently plugged into another person's alarm without draining. The goal is not to cut the cable in anger, nor to pretend no one needs power. The goal is to charge in ways that do not burn out the socket. One sentence. One hug. One agreed call. One return time. A form of care that can be given without quietly destroying the giver's capacity to keep giving.

The forward test comes when compassion and fatigue arrive together. Will the next sentence collapse into appeasement, harden into rejection, or hold the more difficult middle: I care about you, and I cannot keep doing this pattern? That middle sentence may disappoint the person who wants immediate relief. It may also be the sentence that keeps reassurance from becoming resentment, and closeness from becoming something both people begin to fear.

When boundaries get pushed

Why can the fifth challenge to a boundary feel harder to answer than the first? The first time, the sentence is clear. "I cannot keep texting about this tonight." The second time, there is a reason to explain. The third time, a softer version is attempted. By the fourth, the body is no longer only holding the boundary; it is also holding the pressure of being made to justify it. The phone lights again. The room tightens. The line starts to wobble.

A pushed boundary often arrives disguised as a conversation. "I just want to understand." "So you do not care how I feel?" "It would only take a minute." "You are being cold." "If this mattered to you, you would talk now." Some of these sentences may contain real distress. Some may contain confusion. Some may contain a bid for reassurance that has lost its shape. Yet their effect is the same: the boundary is no longer being heard as information. It is being treated as an obstacle to negotiate, shame, soften, or outlast.

The central difficulty is that a person who keeps explaining may believe they are being kind, while the pattern has already shifted from clarification to erosion. Explanation belongs at the beginning of a boundary, when the other person genuinely does not understand what is being said. Repetition belongs after that. If every challenge receives a new argument, the other person learns that pressure produces more access. The content changes, but the lesson remains: do not accept the line; keep pushing and the line may move. A boundary that must be endlessly defended becomes a debate wearing a name badge.

John Bowlby's attachment work in London across the mid-twentieth century remains useful because it helps illuminate why boundaries around contact can provoke such strong reactions. When a person hears "not now", the attachment system may register threat before reason has interpreted the sentence. A limit can feel like loss. A pause can feel like rejection. A calm exit can feel like abandonment. That emotional reality deserves compassion. It does not, however, give anyone the right to argue another person out of their capacity. Fear explains pressure; it does not justify making pressure the method of connection.

This is where short, repeatable sentences become necessary. "I have answered; I am not discussing this further tonight." "I care about you, and my answer is still no." "I am available tomorrow, not now." "I will not keep repeating this by text." "I am going to step away." These sentences may sound plain, even austere. Their plainness is the point. When a boundary is being pushed, ornate language often becomes fuel. The person pushing can seize on a phrase, dispute a reason, question a motive, or demand a better explanation. A simple sentence gives less to fight and more to respect.

Calm repetition is sometimes mistaken for coldness because it does not perform emotional labour on demand. But consistency is not cruelty. A person can remain warm and still refuse to reopen the same point. "I know this is hard. I am not continuing tonight." That sentence contains care and finality. It does not ridicule the distress. It does not hand over the boundary. It recognises that reassurance, once given, cannot be allowed to become an endless toll paid for the right to leave the conversation.

Mary Ainsworth's Strange Situation research in Baltimore in the late 1960s and early 1970s made patterns of protest and reunion observable in attachment relationships. In adult conflict, protest may appear as repeated questioning, following someone from room to room, sending messages after a pause has been requested, demanding one more answer, or treating every limit as evidence of not being loved. The protest may be an attempt to restore contact, but if it prevents the other person from taking needed space, it damages the conditions for return. Pushed boundaries do not create closeness. They create exhaustion with an audience.

The person setting the boundary must therefore stop trying to make the boundary feel good to the person who dislikes it. This is difficult for those who fear being seen as harsh. They may keep adjusting the sentence, adding reassurance, softening tone, offering more context, or apologising for needing the limit. Some softness may be appropriate at first. But after a boundary has been clearly stated, the aim is no longer to make the other person approve. The aim is to remain consistent without escalating. A boundary is not a contract that requires emotional agreement before it exists.

Guilt-tripping is especially corrosive because it shifts the focus from behaviour to moral identity. "I guess I am just not important." "You are abandoning me." "A real partner would not do this." "You know how hard this is for me." These lines may be spoken from pain, but they ask the boundary-holder to prove love by surrendering the limit. A clean response does not debate the accusation. "I hear that you are upset. I am still not available to talk tonight." "I care about you. I am not changing my answer." The trap is to begin defending one's goodness. Once goodness is on trial, the boundary is already being dragged into court.

There is a difference between being moved by someone's pain and being governed by it. A mature relationship allows pain to be visible. It does not require every visible pain to determine the next action. If someone is distressed by a boundary, that distress may deserve tenderness, acknowledgement, and a future conversation. It does not automatically require immediate access. "I can see this hurts. I will talk tomorrow" honours the feeling without obeying the pressure. The distinction is crucial. Without it, the most dysregulated person in the room sets the terms for everyone.

A pushed boundary also reveals whether the original limit was clear enough. Vague limits invite confusion. "I need some space" may be honest, but it can be too open-ended during conflict. "I am taking thirty minutes and will come back at eight" gives less room for negotiation. "Please stop" is clear in one sense, but "I will not respond to more messages tonight" defines the action that follows. When a boundary is likely to be contested, clarity is kind. It tells the other person exactly where the line is and what will happen if the line is ignored.

Still, even the clearest boundary may be pushed. At that point, the response must move from explanation to consequence, calmly stated and calmly enacted. "If the messages continue, I will mute my phone until morning." "If you follow me from room to room, I will leave the flat for a walk and return at the time I named." "If this becomes insulting, I will end the conversation." A consequence is not a punishment when it is proportionate and protective. It is the behaviour that allows the boundary to remain real. Without action, the boundary becomes a request the other person can decline indefinitely.

The credible limitation is that boundary language can be misused by people who want to avoid accountability. "I have answered" can become a way to shut down legitimate questions. "I am not discussing this" can become stonewalling when important matters are repeatedly dismissed. "Calm exit" can become abandonment if the person exits every time discomfort appears and never returns. A boundary is not automatically healthy because it is firm. Its moral quality depends on whether it protects dignity and future contact, or merely protects one person from being answerable.

The reconciliation lies in timing, return, and proportionality. A calm exit during escalation is different from a permanent refusal to engage. Ending a late-night text loop is different from refusing ever to discuss a painful pattern. Saying "not tonight" while naming tomorrow is different from vanishing. Firmness becomes trustworthy when it is paired with eventual accountability. The person setting the boundary can say, "I am not discussing this further tonight. I will talk tomorrow at seven." That sentence protects the present limit without burying the issue.

There is also a responsibility to avoid escalation in the language of enforcement. A pushed boundary may provoke anger, especially if the pressure feels manipulative or relentless. The temptation is to sharpen the sentence: "How many times do I have to tell you?" "Stop being ridiculous." "You are proving my point." These lines may feel satisfying, but they feed the conflict. The stronger move is often less dramatic: "I have answered." "I am ending this conversation now." "We can speak tomorrow." The voice stays lower than the pressure around it. The sentence does not chase the argument.

For the person whose boundary is being pushed, the body may experience repetition as threat. Heart rate rises. The jaw sets. Thoughts become absolute. This is why repeatable scripts are useful; they prevent improvisation at the exact moment improvisation is most likely to turn punitive. A practised sentence acts like a doorstop. It holds the line open long enough to exit without slamming. "I am not available for this tonight." "I will not debate my boundary." "I am stepping away now." The sentence is not meant to win. It is meant to end the cycle.

For the person hearing the boundary, the work is to notice the impulse to convert discomfort into negotiation. Wanting another answer does not mean another answer is owed. Feeling hurt by a limit does not mean the limit is wrong. Needing reassurance does not mean reassurance must arrive in the exact form and timing desired. A healthier response might be, "I do not like this, but I hear you." Or, "I feel anxious, and I will wait until tomorrow." Such sentences preserve self-respect because they do not require the other person to collapse their boundary in order to prove care.

Short scripts are particularly important in digital contact. Texting invites endless continuation because there is no natural end to the room. A person can keep sending one more thought, one more objection, one more emotional consequence. The boundary must therefore name the medium as well as the issue. "I am not continuing this by text." "I will read messages tomorrow." "I am putting my phone away now." "I will not respond again tonight." These are not hostile sentences. They create an ending where the platform does not provide one.

A calm exit is not the same as disappearing. Disappearing leaves the other person in uncertainty. A calm exit marks departure and, where appropriate, return. "I am going to sleep now. We can speak after work tomorrow." "I am leaving this conversation because it is becoming circular. I will check in in the morning." "I am taking space. I will not respond for the rest of the evening." The clarity may disappoint, but it reduces the confusion that fuels further pursuit. The person knows the line, the action, and the next point of contact.

There are circumstances where the safest boundary is not a script but distance, support, or a more serious reassessment of the relationship. If pushing boundaries includes intimidation, threats, relentless surveillance, humiliation, or refusal to accept physical space, the issue is no longer ordinary conflict management. Secure language should not be used to make unsafe dynamics sound manageable. A short sentence can end a conversation; it cannot make someone else respect personhood if they are determined not to. The pattern itself must be taken seriously.

In ordinary but strained relationships, however, the practice of calm repetition can change the texture of conflict. The person who sets the limit learns that they can disappoint someone without becoming cruel. The person who hears the limit learns that a no can be survived without forcing it open. The relationship learns that pressure is not the path to closeness. Over time, this matters. Boundaries stop appearing only as crises and begin to function as part of the architecture of trust.

The motif is the door again, but now the door has a latch. A boundary without a latch swings open under pressure. A boundary slammed shut in anger teaches fear. A boundary calmly closed, with a clear time for return when return is appropriate, teaches a different lesson: access to one another is real, and so are limits. Love does not require every door to remain open at every hour. It requires people to know which doors can be knocked on, which must stay closed for now, and which conversations will be resumed when the house is quieter.

The forward test comes when the boundary has already been spoken and the next challenge arrives. Will the answer become longer, sharper, more apologetic, more defensive, or simply steadier? The sentence may be brief: "I have answered; I am not discussing this further tonight." Beneath that brevity is a serious relational claim. A limit does not become unloving because someone dislikes it. A boundary becomes secure when it can remain calm under pressure without disappearing, retaliating, or turning the person on the other side into the enemy.

Chapter 7
De-escalation in the Moment

Why can a conversation about one sentence become a quarrel about the whole relationship before either person has noticed the turn? The scene is ordinary enough: two people in a kitchen, a plate left on the side, a tired voice, a question answered too sharply. One says, "You did not need to say it like that." The other says, "I was just answering you." A small defence enters. Then another. The air changes. The plate is no longer the point.

The argument begins to write itself. Each person hears not only the words being spoken, but the injury those words seem to confirm. One hears dismissal. The other hears accusation. One raises the volume to be understood; the other grows colder to stay in control. The faster the exchange moves, the less either person is responding to the present sentence. They are responding to threat, memory, tone, posture, implication, and the unbearable feeling of being misread by someone whose opinion matters.

Escalation is rarely a single dramatic act. It is usually a sequence of small permissions granted too quickly: a sharper phrase, a wider accusation, a refusal to pause, a need to correct every detail, a face that says contempt before the mouth says anything at all. By the time both people recognise the pattern, the conversation may already have become a machine. It feeds on speed. It feeds on certainty. It feeds on the belief that the next sentence must win ground or prevent loss.

The central tension is that intimate conflict often requires care most urgently at the exact moment care is least available. A person may still love, still want repair, still intend no harm, and yet be too activated to speak in a way the relationship can safely use. De-escalation is not the same as dropping the issue. It is the decision to stop feeding the fire before the real issue is burned beyond recognition. The point is not to become calm enough to be impressive. The point is to become steady enough to remain truthful without becoming destructive.

This matters because many couples confuse intensity with seriousness. If the voice is raised, the issue must be important. If someone keeps pushing, they must care more. If the conversation continues late into the night, perhaps that proves commitment. But some forms of intensity do not deepen truth; they deform it. A flooded person may exaggerate, accuse, collapse, deny, or threaten meanings they do not truly wish to live by in the morning. A conversation can be emotionally sincere and still be structurally unsafe.

The future cost of escalation is measured in what people begin to expect from each other. One learns that honesty will become punishment, so they soften the truth until it is no longer clear. Another learns that pausing will be called avoidance, so they stay and become cruel. One expects to be attacked; the other expects to be abandoned. The next conflict then begins before the first word is spoken. The room remembers. So do bodies.

A different pattern begins with interruption, not dismissal: "I want to get this right; I am getting activated, can we slow down?" From there, the work becomes more delicate. Feelings can be acknowledged without surrendering to unfair conclusions. A person can say, "I hear you felt ignored; I did not intend that," and keep both truths alive. When the pace is too fast for either truth to survive, a pause needs structure rather than disappearance: time, purpose, and a promised return.

The quiet motif here is the match. A struck match can light a candle or burn a room, depending on what surrounds it and how quickly it is handled. Conflict is not the enemy of intimacy; unmanaged heat is. A difficult sentence, held with care, can illuminate something that needed to be seen. The same sentence, thrown into defensiveness and fear, can leave both people coughing in the smoke and arguing about who started the fire.

The unresolved question is whether the next rising moment can be treated as a signal rather than a command. When the voice tightens, when the answer comes too fast, when the body wants to prove, correct, pursue, or flee, will the conversation obey the spiral or name it? De-escalation begins at the thin, difficult edge where someone still has enough presence to say: the issue matters, and we are about to handle it in a way that makes it harder to heal.

Stop the spiralling script

Why can ninety seconds of rising intensity do more damage than the issue that started the argument? Two people are standing in the kitchen, both still technically speaking about the same small event. One tone sounded sharp. One reply came too fast. One sentence began with "You always," and another arrived before the first had finished landing. The cupboard door is open. A mug sits near the sink. Nothing in the room has changed, except the air. The match is lit.

At first, both people may believe they are clarifying. One explains. The other corrects. One says, "That is not what I meant," and the other hears, "Your feelings are wrong." The pace increases because each person is trying to prevent misrepresentation. Then the conversation stops being a conversation and becomes a struggle for immediate emotional survival. The body moves ahead of the mind. The voice tightens. The face hardens. The next sentence is chosen less for accuracy than for defence.

The spiralling script has a recognisable rhythm. It begins with an injury, often small but symbolically loaded. It moves into interpretation: you do not care, you are blaming me, you are making me the problem, you are leaving again. Then come the protective moves: accusation, withdrawal, sarcasm, correction, pleading, repetition, coldness. Each move is experienced by the person making it as necessary. Each is experienced by the other as further evidence. The match touches paper. The issue is no longer simply what happened. It is what the reaction now seems to prove.

John Gottman and Robert Levenson's long observational work with couples, associated with the University of Washington in Seattle across the late twentieth century, drew attention to the visible behaviours that make conflict deteriorate: criticism, defensiveness, contempt, stonewalling, and failed repair attempts. Whatever one thinks of any single model of couple research, the practical observation is hard to dismiss. Conflict is shaped not only by what people feel, but by what they do next. A raised eyebrow, a faster interruption, a refusal to answer, a dismissive laugh, a repeated accusation: these are not decorations around the argument. They become the argument.

Stopping the spiral does not mean dismissing the issue. This distinction is essential. Many people resist de-escalation because they have experienced it as silencing: "Calm down," "You are overreacting," "Can we not do this?" Such phrases may lower visible noise while increasing injury. They communicate that the feeling is inconvenient, not that the relationship needs steadier conditions. A true interrupting phrase protects the issue from the intensity around it. "I want to get this right; I am getting activated, can we slow down?" says the matter still matters. It also says the current speed is becoming unsafe for truth.

That sentence works because it takes responsibility for state without assigning total blame. "I am getting activated" is not the same as "You are making me angry." It locates the rising intensity inside the speaker's body, where the speaker has some responsibility, while still naming a shared need to slow the exchange. "I want to get this right" matters just as much. Without it, "Can we slow down?" may sound like avoidance.

With it, the phrase becomes a commitment: the speaker is not leaving the issue; they are trying not to damage it.

The word "activated" is useful because it is less accusatory than "furious" and more honest than "fine." It signals that the nervous system is entering a state in which good language becomes harder to reach. The body may show this before the mind admits it: heat in the face, tightness in the chest, pressure behind the eyes, clenched hands, a rising urge to interrupt, the sudden certainty that the other person must understand now or the relationship is in danger. These signs are not moral failures. They are warnings. The match is still small enough to cup in the hand.

James Gross's process model of emotion regulation, developed at Stanford University in the late 1990s, offers a helpful way to understand this moment. Emotion unfolds through attention, interpretation, bodily response, and action; changing the action can alter the path that follows. In relational conflict, a person may not be able to stop the first surge of heat, but they can change what the surge is allowed to do. A spiralling script thrives on automatic continuation. An interrupting phrase introduces a break in the sequence. It does not solve the conflict. It changes the next available move.

The most effective interruption names three things: intention, state, and process. Intention sounds like, "I want to understand this," or "I do not want to hurt us." State sounds like, "I am getting flooded," "I am starting to feel defensive," or "I am too wound up to hear well." Process sounds like, "Can we slow down?" "Can we take one point at a time?" "Can we lower our voices?" "Can we pause before we keep going?" The sentence is not grand. It is functional. It catches the conversation before it becomes a fire that both people then blame on the original spark.

The phrase must avoid hidden superiority. "You are spiralling" may be accurate in some sense, but it often lands as diagnosis and dismissal. "This is getting heated" is usually safer because it describes the shared field. "I am noticing I want to defend myself rather than listen" is stronger still because it returns agency to the speaker. A person cannot de-escalate well while standing above the other person as the sane observer of their chaos. Secure interruption is not a performance of control. It is participation in slowing the system both people are inside.

Two nervous systems feeding each other can create a speed neither person would choose alone. One person's raised voice may trigger the other's shutdown; the shutdown may trigger the first person's pursuit; the pursuit may trigger more withdrawal; the withdrawal may confirm abandonment fear. This is not an excuse for harmful behaviour. It is a description of sequence. Once the sequence is visible, the question changes from "Who started it?" to "What would stop feeding it?" The answer may be a slower pace, a softer tone, one topic at a time, a pause, or a sentence that names the pattern without turning it into a character attack.

Mary Ainsworth's Strange Situation research in Baltimore in the late 1960s and early 1970s made separation and reunion observable, showing how distress can shape seeking, protest, avoidance, and settling. Adult conflict contains a related pattern: people often protest or withdraw not only because of the content, but because connection itself feels threatened. When someone says, "You never listen," the surface issue may be listening; the deeper fear may be that one's inner world does not matter. When someone replies, "I cannot say anything right," the surface defence may hide the fear of being permanently cast as the villain. A spiralling script keeps both fears alive by speaking from them rather than about them.

Stopping the spiral therefore requires language that honours urgency without obeying it. "This matters, and I am getting too heated to handle it well." "I want to stay with you, and I need us to slow the pace." "I am starting to hear this as an attack, and I do not want to respond defensively." "I can feel myself getting sharp; I am going to lower my voice and try again." These phrases do not ask anyone to pretend the conflict is mild. They ask the conflict to move at a speed where dignity can survive.

There is a credible limitation: some people use de-escalation language to avoid accountability. "I am activated" can become a way to shut down every difficult conversation. "Can we pause?" can become a pattern of disappearance. "This is too heated" can be used to silence justified anger, especially when the other person has been ignored until their pain becomes visible. The phrase itself is not virtuous. Its integrity depends on return. A de-escalation move is trustworthy when it protects the conversation for later contact, not when it buries the issue under the appearance of maturity.

The reconciliation lies in pairing interruption with commitment. "I need to slow down, and I want to come back to the point." "I cannot hear well while we are both this intense; I am not dropping it." "Let us pause the pace, not the issue." These sentences are more honest than a vague plea for calm. They acknowledge the fear that slowing down means losing momentum, being dismissed, or watching the issue disappear. For many people, that fear is not imaginary. They have known relationships where every pause became a graveyard for hard truths. A secure interruption must make clear that slowing is not erasure.

The person who hears the interruption also has a choice. They may experience it as rejection and push harder: "Of course, now you want to slow down." They may treat it as proof of guilt: "You just do not want to answer." Or they may test whether the phrase contains a real promise: "Okay, but I need to know we are coming back to this." That response keeps the boundary and the issue alive together. It is reasonable to ask for reassurance that the topic will not vanish. It is not helpful to force the conversation to continue at a damaging speed simply because fear distrusts the pause.

The shortest scripts are often strongest when both people are flooded. "Pause. Same team." "One point at a time." "Lower voices." "I am listening, but I am getting overwhelmed." "I want to understand, not win." Such phrases may look too simple on the page, but under pressure simplicity is a virtue. A mind in threat mode cannot easily retrieve elegant language. It needs handrail sentences. The purpose is not literary beauty. The purpose is to keep the next sentence from becoming a weapon.

The match motif returns because escalation depends on fuel. Some fuel is verbal: "always," "never," "typical," "you people," "of course you would." Some is tonal: contempt, mockery, pleading, coldness. Some is procedural: interrupting, following, texting repeatedly, refusing a pause, dragging in a catalogue of past injuries. Stopping the spiral means removing fuel before debating the flame. "Let us stay with this one point" removes the fuel of the catalogue. "I am not going to use 'always'; I am going to name tonight" removes the fuel of global accusation. "I need a minute before I answer" removes the fuel of reflex.

There is a particular courage in naming one's own defensive move before the other person names it. "I am about to argue every detail because I feel ashamed." "I am tempted to go cold, and I do not want to punish you." "I can feel myself trying to win rather than connect." These sentences are disarming because they reveal the machinery of escalation as it starts to move. They do not make the speaker helpless. They make the speaker accountable. The conversation is given a chance to become conscious before it becomes automatic.

The body must often be involved in slowing down. Words spoken at high speed from across a room may not calm anything. Sitting down, putting the phone aside, lowering volume, taking a sip of water, facing slightly sideways rather than squared off, allowing a few seconds between sentences: these visible behaviours support the script. "Can we slow down?" means little if delivered while pacing aggressively or typing three more messages. The phrase and the behaviour must belong to the same intention. Otherwise the body will believe the behaviour.

The person who wants to stop the spiral may have to accept that the other person will not immediately join. This is frustrating. One person may lower their tone while the other stays heated. One may ask for pace while the other insists on finishing the argument. Secure de-escalation does not require controlling the other person's response. It begins with withdrawing one's own fuel. "I am not going to keep raising my voice." "I want to answer, but I will not do it while we are interrupting." "I am going to pause for a minute so I do not make this worse." These lines protect the speaker's part of the pattern even before the whole pattern changes.

Not every conflict should be de-escalated into softness. Some truths need firmness. Some boundaries need to be unmistakable. Some harms should not be smoothed over for the sake of a calmer room. The distinction is between intensity that serves clarity and intensity that destroys it. A firm sentence can be calm. A raised voice can sometimes mark the seriousness of pain, but if it begins to frighten, dominate, or prevent listening, it has crossed from expression into damage. De-escalation does not require diminishing truth. It requires choosing a form in which truth can still be received.

The forward test comes at the moment the conversation begins to accelerate. The next line may promise relief: correct them, prove it, defend yourself, send the sharper message, make them feel the size of it. Or the next line may interrupt the old script: "I want to get this right; I am getting activated, can we slow down?" The issue remains. The fire is not denied. But someone has noticed the match before it reaches the curtains, and that noticing may be the first act of care the conversation can still use.

Validate without conceding

Why can six words - "I hear that hurt you" - lower the heat of a conflict more than a perfect defence of what really happened? A person says, "You ignored me all evening," and the body of the listener prepares for trial. They remember answering questions, making dinner, asking about the day, sitting in the same room. The accusation feels unfair. The next sentence rises quickly: "That is not true." It may be accurate. It may also be the spark that keeps the fire alive.

The trouble is that the injured person may not be making a clean factual claim, even though the sentence sounds like one. "You ignored me" may mean, "I felt alone beside you." "You do not care" may mean, "I could not find evidence of care when I needed it." "You always dismiss me" may mean, "This moment has touched an old place where I expect not to matter." The conclusion may be exaggerated, but the feeling underneath may be real. If the response attacks only the conclusion, the feeling goes unheard. The match finds paper.

Validation is the art of acknowledging the felt experience without surrendering the whole interpretation. It does not require false agreement. It does not require confession to motives one did not have. It does not require accepting a distorted account of reality in order to seem kind. The sentence "I hear you felt ignored; I did not intend that" holds two truths in the same hand. One truth belongs to the other person's experience. The other belongs to one's own intention. Neither has to erase the other.

Carl Rogers, working in the United States in the mid-twentieth century and publishing *Client-Centered Therapy* in 1951, helped give modern psychology a durable language for empathic understanding. Rogers was not writing a script manual for couples at a kitchen table, but the practical insight travels: people are more able to examine their own reactions when they first feel accurately heard. Empathy is not agreement. It is an disciplined effort to understand the meaning of another person's experience from inside their frame of reference. In conflict, that effort can interrupt the reflexive fight over who owns reality.

The reflex is powerful because unfair interpretations feel like threats to identity. "You ignored me" can land as, "You are selfish." "You only care when it suits you" can land as, "Your love is fraudulent." "You wanted to embarrass me" can land as, "You are cruel." Once a person feels morally accused, they often defend the self rather than respond to the pain. The visible behaviours follow quickly: rapid correction, raised voice, narrowed eyes, interruption, counter-examples, a catalogue of one's good intentions. The defence may contain facts. It may still miss the relational moment.

Validation shifts the first response from correction to contact. "I can see that felt lonely." "That landed as rejection for you." "I understand why that would sting." "You felt exposed when I went quiet." These sentences do not say, "Your conclusion is entirely accurate." They say, "Your emotional experience has registered with me." The difference is precise. It allows the other person's nervous system to stop shouting long enough for the facts to become discussable. Without that pause, facts often arrive as weapons, not information.

Marsha Linehan's work on dialectical behaviour therapy, first systematised in her 1993 treatment manual in the United States, made validation a central clinical skill while also insisting on change. The dialectic matters here. One can validate the sense a feeling makes without endorsing the behaviour that followed it. One can say, "I understand you panicked when I did not reply," while also saying, "It was not okay to send twenty angry messages." One can say, "I see why my silence frightened you," without saying, "My silence meant I was abandoning you." Validation and boundary are not enemies. They often need each other.

The most useful validation separates three layers: emotion, interpretation, and behaviour. Emotion is the felt state: hurt, fear, shame, loneliness, anger. Interpretation is the meaning attached to it: you ignored me, you do not care, you wanted to hurt me. Behaviour is what happened next: raised voice, withdrawal, repeated texts, accusation, refusal to speak. Conflict becomes less confusing when these layers are not treated as one object. "I hear you felt ignored" validates emotion. "I did not intend to ignore you" addresses interpretation. "I want us to talk about it without name-calling" addresses behaviour. Each layer receives the sentence it deserves.

This is why "I hear you felt ignored; I did not intend that" works better than "I did not ignore you." The second sentence may be factually relevant, but it starts with denial. The first begins with acknowledgement and then clarifies intention. It gives the other person evidence that their pain has not been brushed aside, while refusing to accept a motive that is untrue. The phrase is not soft in the weak sense. It is structurally strong. It keeps the conversation from collapsing into either appeasement or defence.

Appeasement is the shadow side of validation. Some people, desperate to end conflict, validate by conceding too much. "Yes, I am terrible." "I always mess everything up." "You are right, I do not know how to love you." Such statements may appear accountable, but they often move the focus away from the hurt person's experience and towards the speaker's shame. They also distort reality. A concession made to stop distress is not the same as repair. It may soothe the moment while teaching both people that emotional intensity can rewrite the facts.

The opposite error is precision without tenderness. A person may respond, "Technically, I did not ignore you; I responded to three separate points and was merely tired." The sentence may be defensible. It is also relationally useless if the other person is still standing in the pain of feeling alone. Accuracy matters, but timing matters too. A fact delivered before acknowledgement can sound like erasure. A fact delivered after acknowledgement can become part of repair. The order changes the meaning.

Validation also protects against the exhausting debate over who is "right" about an emotional event. Emotional reality and factual reality are not identical, but neither is disposable. If one person says, "I felt embarrassed when you corrected me in front of your friends," the other can validate the embarrassment without agreeing that humiliation was intended. "I hear that you felt put on the spot. I was trying to clarify something, but I can see the impact was painful." This sentence does not surrender intent. It acknowledges impact. The conversation can now move beyond courtroom logic.

John Gottman and Robert Levenson's observational work with couples in Seattle across the late twentieth century gave sustained attention to repair attempts, defensiveness, contempt, and the small moves by which conflict either escalates or softens. One practical lesson is that the response to a bid for emotional recognition matters enormously. When someone says, "That hurt," a reflexive defence may protect the speaker's pride but leave the relationship more brittle. A validating response does not require self-betrayal. It requires recognising that impact can be real even when intention was different.

The credible limitation is that validation can be demanded as agreement. A person may say, "Validate me," when what they mean is, "Admit my conclusion is true." They may treat any clarification as invalidation. They may insist that if they feel ignored, then the other person must accept that they were ignored in every meaningful sense. This is not emotional honesty; it is emotional absolutism. Feelings deserve respect. They do not automatically possess full authority over facts, motives, or moral judgement. The phrase "my feelings are valid" should not become a royal seal placed on every interpretation.

The reconciliation lies in disciplined language. "I accept that you felt ignored" is different from "I agree I ignored you." "I can see how it landed that way" is different from "That was what I meant to do." "Your hurt makes sense to me" is different from "Your whole reading of my character is accurate." These distinctions are not evasions. They are the grammar of fairness. They allow care without false confession and self-respect without coldness.

The person offering validation must listen for the vulnerable meaning beneath the harsher sentence. "You never think about me" may conceal, "I wanted to feel considered." "You made me look stupid" may conceal, "I felt exposed and unprotected." "You do not care about my time" may conceal, "I feel unimportant when plans change without warning." The validating sentence should meet the vulnerable meaning, not merely the hostile surface. "You wanted to feel considered, and that did not happen tonight" will usually reach further than "That is not fair; I do think about you."

There is also a place for validating without solving. Many people move too quickly from acknowledgement to explanation, reassurance, or repair plan. The other person says, "I felt dismissed," and the response becomes, "I am sorry, but I was tired, and next time I will..." The haste may be sincere, yet it can skip the moment of recognition. Sometimes the needed sentence is shorter: "That felt dismissive to you." Silence after such a sentence is not failure. It allows the acknowledgement to land. The cup can stay on the table for a breath before anyone reaches for the next tool.

Tone determines whether validation sounds real. "I hear you felt ignored" can be generous, flat, resentful, patronising, or weaponised. If spoken like a line from a training manual, it may inflame rather than soothe. Adult validation requires the voice to carry the same message as the words: I am not admitting a falsehood, and I am not treating your hurt as a nuisance. The body participates. Eye contact, softened pace, an unclenched jaw, and a pause before correction may communicate as much as the sentence itself.

For the person receiving validation, there is responsibility too. If someone says, "I hear that hurt you," it matters not to reply immediately, "But do you agree you were wrong?" That may be the next part of the conversation, but if every validation is rejected until it becomes full concession, the bridge collapses. Receiving validation means allowing acknowledgement to count, even if the facts still need discussion. It does not require giving up the issue. It requires not moving the goalpost the moment care appears.

The scripts are strongest when they keep emotion and conclusion separate. "I hear you felt ignored; I did not intend to ignore you." "I can see that my delay scared you; I was not trying to punish you." "I understand that my tone landed as criticism; I was frustrated, and I want to say it better." "It makes sense that you felt lonely when I went quiet; I was overwhelmed, not withdrawing from the relationship." "I hear the impact, and I want to be careful with the meaning we attach to it." These sentences are not evasive. They are exact.

Sometimes validation must be paired with a boundary around unfair claims. "I will listen to how hurt you felt, and I will not accept being called cruel." "I want to understand the impact, but I do not agree that I did it to humiliate you." "Your fear matters to me; the accusation that I never care is not something I can accept as true." This is adult speech at its most difficult. It refuses the false choice between submitting to the other person's interpretation and dismissing their pain. It keeps the match away from the curtains.

The deeper purpose of validation is not to be nice. It is to make reality shareable. In conflict, each person can become trapped inside a private courtroom, prosecuting the other with evidence gathered from tone, memory, and fear. Validation opens a window in that courtroom. It says, "I can see where you are standing, even if I do not agree with every conclusion you reached from there." That sentence, in various forms, makes it possible for two people to compare realities instead of trying to destroy one another's.

The forward test comes when an unfair interpretation arrives wrapped around a real feeling. The old reflex will be to correct the unfairness first, perhaps because the accusation feels intolerable. The more secure move is harder: touch the feeling without swallowing the conclusion. "I hear you felt ignored; I did not intend that." The sentence is small, but the discipline beneath it is large. It asks whether love can remain truthful when hurt is inaccurate, and tender when accuracy alone would be easier.

Take a structured pause

Why can twenty minutes away from a conflict save a conversation, while twenty minutes of unexplained silence can injure it? Two people are standing in the same room, still arguing about the original issue, though the original issue has begun to vanish beneath tone, speed, and defence. One person says, "I cannot do this," and walks out. The door closes. The person left behind hears not a pause, but abandonment. The person who left hears not abandonment, but survival. The match is no longer small.

The pause itself is not the problem. The absence of structure is the problem. A pause without timing, purpose, or return becomes an empty space into which each person pours their worst interpretation. The one who needs distance may think, "I am stopping this before I say something damaging." The one who is left may think, "They have withdrawn love until I behave differently." Both may be sincere. Both may be frightened. Without a shared frame, the break becomes another argument conducted in separate rooms.

A structured pause protects the conversation from two opposite dangers: escalation and disappearance. Escalation says, "Stay until this is resolved, no matter how much damage we do." Disappearance says, "Leave the heat, and let the issue dissolve into avoidance." A secure pause refuses both. It says, "This matters too much to keep handling it badly, and it matters too much to abandon." The sentence "Twenty minutes, then we come back and take turns speaking" is powerful because it gives the pause a job. It is not an escape hatch. It is a temporary scaffolding.

John Gottman and Robert Levenson's observational work on couple conflict, associated with the University of Washington in Seattle across the late twentieth century, gave particular attention to physiological arousal during arguments and the way heightened states can narrow people's capacity to listen, repair, and think flexibly. The practical lesson is not that emotion should be suppressed. It is that some levels of activation make good conversation unlikely. When a person is flooded, the issue may remain important, but the conditions for addressing it have deteriorated. The fire needs less fuel before the room can be entered again.

A structured pause begins with naming the reason without blaming the other person for the entire state of the room. "I am getting too activated to listen well." "I want to answer carefully, and I cannot do that while we are interrupting each other." "I am starting to shut down, and I do not want to disappear." These sentences differ from "You are impossible" or "This is pointless." The former names capacity; the latter condemns the relationship. A pause called through contempt is not de-escalation. It is an exit wound.

Timing gives the pause its walls. "Later" is too vague when fear is already in the room. "Tomorrow" may be appropriate for exhaustion, but not if it is used to avoid every hard moment. "Twenty minutes" works in many ordinary conflicts because it is long enough to reduce intensity and short enough to keep the thread visible. The exact length is less important than the agreement: both people know when the break begins, when it ends, and what will happen if more time is needed. If the pause must be extended, the extension should be named, not smuggled in through silence.

Purpose gives the pause its dignity. The break is not for rehearsing arguments, recruiting allies, scrolling furiously, composing a colder text, or building a prosecution. It is for returning to a state in which speech can be less damaging. One person may walk, breathe, drink water, write the one point they need to make, or sit quietly until the body stops demanding immediate victory. The other may do the same. A pause used to inflame the case is not a pause. It is a private continuation of the fight.

What each person will do during the break matters because unstructured time can become fantasy time. The anxious person may imagine abandonment. The avoidant person may enjoy relief and never want to return. The angry person may rehearse the devastating line. The ashamed person may collapse into self-attack. A clear agreement interrupts these tendencies: "During the break, let us each write down the one thing we want understood." Or, "Let us not text during the break." Or, "Let us cool down separately and come back to take turns." The pause becomes active, but not aggressive.

Mary Ainsworth's Strange Situation research in Baltimore in the late 1960s and early 1970s made visible the emotional significance of separation and reunion. Adult conflict is not infancy replayed in simple form, but the lesson of return remains relevant. A pause that includes reunion teaches something different from a withdrawal that leaves the other person uncertain. The moment of coming back matters. It says, through behaviour rather than theory, that distance can serve the relationship rather than threaten it. A kept return time is a small act of trust made visible.

A structured pause also reduces stonewalling by making silence accountable. Stonewalling often looks calm from the outside, but inside it may be overwhelm, shutdown, punishment, or a refusal to engage. The person on the receiving end cannot always tell the difference. "I cannot speak right now, and I will come back in twenty minutes" is different from staring, leaving, or going mute without explanation. The words do not require eloquence. They require enough contact to prevent the other person from having to interpret absence alone.

The credible limitation is that pauses can be misused by people who want permanent escape from accountability. Some people call for a break whenever the conversation becomes inconvenient, then fail to return. Others take pauses that stretch into days while the issue quietly dies. Some use calm language to control the terms of every conflict, allowing their own discomfort to decide when the other person may speak. This is not structure. It is avoidance with a polished surface. A legitimate pause must protect the future conversation, not bury it.

The reconciliation lies in the return plan. A pause becomes trustworthy when it includes a specific time, a specific purpose, and a specific method for resuming. "Twenty minutes, then we come back and take turns speaking" contains all three. The timing prevents indefinite uncertainty. The purpose is regulation, not escape. The method prevents the same chaotic pattern from restarting immediately. If both people return only to interrupt and accuse again, the pause was incomplete. If they return with one point each and a slower rhythm, the pause has served its purpose.

There is an art to asking for a pause before the conversation has become unbearable. Many people wait until they are already near the edge, then leave abruptly because they have no language left. Earlier is kinder. "I can feel this getting too heated. I want to pause before we make it worse." "I am still here, and I need a short break so I do not shut down." "I want to keep talking, but not at this pace." These sentences are not dramatic. They are preventative. They treat escalation as something to notice, not something to obey.

For the person who fears abandonment, a structured pause may still feel painful. The body may protest even when the words are clear. That does not mean the pause is wrong. It means the return must be credible enough to survive the discomfort. The person taking space can help by saying, "I am not leaving the relationship; I am pausing the conversation." The person waiting can help by saying, "I do not like pausing, but I will respect the twenty minutes." Both sentences preserve the bridge. Neither asks the other to pretend the bridge is effortless.

For the person who tends to withdraw, a structured pause may feel uncomfortably accountable. It is easier to disappear into silence than to name a return. Yet naming a return is precisely what turns withdrawal into adult space. "I need time" becomes meaningful when it is attached to "and I will come back." Without that second half, the person left behind may experience the pause as emotional exile. With it, the pause becomes a boundary with a door.

The return should not begin with a fresh prosecution. If the first words after the pause are "As I was saying, you always do this," the body learns that the break only delayed the attack. A better return begins by re-establishing process. "I am ready to take turns." "The one thing I want understood is..." "Can I say my part, then I will listen?" "I want to start with impact rather than blame." The structure keeps the conversation from sliding back into the old groove. The match has been set down; it should not be struck again immediately.

Taking turns is not childish. It is containment. Under pressure, people interrupt not because they lack intelligence, but because they fear losing the chance to be understood. A turn structure reassures both people that being heard does not depend on fighting for the floor. One speaks. The other reflects what they heard before responding. Then the roles switch. This may feel slow to people accustomed to rapid defence, but slowness is sometimes the price of accuracy. A conversation that moves too fast often mistakes momentum for truth.

The language of the pause should be short because conflict is a poor environment for complicated instructions. "I am flooded. Twenty minutes, then we return." "I need to cool down. I will come back at eight." "Let us pause and each write one point." "I do not want to say this badly. I am taking ten minutes." "We are getting heated. Let us stop and restart." These are handrail sentences. They are designed to hold weight when the mind is not at its finest.

There is also a need to define what not to do during the pause. Do not keep arguing through the door. Do not send a string of texts. Do not post, hint, punish, or recruit spectators. Do not use the break to sharpen contempt. Do not drink in order to return bolder or numb. The point is not moral purity. The point is to stop feeding the system that made the pause necessary. If the break becomes another arena, it cannot do its work.

The structured pause carries a moral claim about love: remaining in a conversation is not always more loving than leaving it briefly. Sometimes staying is a refusal to regulate. Sometimes leaving is an act of care. But leaving becomes care only when the other person is not left to wonder whether the bond has been suspended with the conversation. The return time is the difference between a protective exit and a wound.

The motif is the match again. A structured pause does not deny that there is fire in the room. It removes both people from the immediate flame long enough to decide what actually needs tending. The issue may still be serious. The hurt may still be real. The apology may still be owed. The decision may still be difficult. But after a structured pause, the conversation has a better chance of handling those truths without adding unnecessary burns.

The forward test comes at the instant one person knows they cannot continue well. Will they vanish, endure until they explode, or call a pause with enough structure for trust to remain intact? "Twenty minutes, then we come back and take turns speaking" sounds simple because it has to be simple. Beneath it is a serious promise: I will not let intensity force me to harm us, and I will not use space to escape what still needs to be said.

Chapter 8
Repair Statements After Conflict

Why can the sentence after the argument matter almost as much as the argument itself? The room is quieter now. No one is interrupting. The plate has been moved, the phone turned face-down, the sharpest words already said and impossible to unsay. One person stands near the doorway, replaying the moment their voice changed. The other sits on the sofa, not crying now, but not softened either. The conflict has ended in sound. It has not ended in the body.

This is the strange afterlife of a rupture. The visible fight may be over, yet both people continue living with what it seemed to reveal. One may be thinking, "I frightened them." The other may be thinking, "They can speak to me like that when they are angry." One may want to explain the pressure they were under; the other may want to know whether the impact has actually been understood. The silence after conflict is not empty. It is full of unfinished meanings.

Repair begins where performance fails. A vague "sorry" may be polite, but it often leaves the wound unlocated. A dramatic apology may look remorseful, yet quietly asks the injured person to comfort the one who caused harm. A long explanation may contain useful context, but if it arrives before ownership, it can sound like an argument wearing softer clothes. The relationship does not need a speech first. It needs a clean line of responsibility.

The central tension is that repair must hold two truths without letting either erase the other. The behaviour must be named clearly, and the underlying need must not remain buried beneath shame. "I raised my voice; that was frightening and unfair. I am sorry" does not collapse into self-hatred, and it does not hide behind intention. It names what happened, acknowledges its effect, and leaves room for change. Later, a person may also say, "Under that, I needed reassurance that we were OK." The need explains the pressure; it does not excuse the harm.

This matters because relationships are not made safe by never rupturing. They are made safer by what happens after rupture. If conflict is followed by denial, minimising, sulking, or a rushed return to normal, the body learns that pain has no proper place to land. If conflict is followed by self-attack, the injured person may learn that honesty creates collapse. But if conflict is followed by specific ownership, the relationship receives a different message: harm can be named without destroying the bond, and accountability can exist without humiliation.

The future cost of poor repair is cumulative. A single raised voice may hurt; a pattern of unowned raised voices teaches vigilance. One sharp text may sting; repeated apologies with no behavioural change teach disbelief. One defensive explanation may be understandable; a habit of explaining before acknowledging impact teaches the other person not to bring hurt forward. Trust is not rebuilt through intensity of remorse. It is rebuilt through visible evidence: a changed sentence, a different pause, a smaller next step kept over time.

A repair statement has to move from ownership to need to action, but not as a tidy formula recited without feeling. The point is to make the invisible sequence of the conflict visible enough to alter. What did I do? What did it cost you? What need was I trying to meet badly? What will I try differently next time? These questions return dignity to both people. The harmed person is not asked to forget impact. The person who caused harm is not reduced to their worst sentence. The relationship is invited to become more truthful than the conflict allowed.

The repair must also be believable. Grand promises often fail because they are designed to relieve guilt rather than guide behaviour. "I will never do that again" may sound comforting, but it can be too large to trust. "Next time I feel panicky, I will ask for a ten-minute call instead of sending five texts" is smaller and stronger. It gives the relationship something observable. The apology steps out of mood and into practice. The words become a hinge, not decoration.

The unresolved question after conflict is not simply "Who was wrong?" It is sharper and more useful: can this rupture become information without becoming a life sentence? Someone must be able to say, "This is the part I did," without disappearing into shame. Someone must be able to say, "This is what I needed," without turning need into blame. Someone must be able to propose a next step small enough to keep. The first repair begins at the place where regret could become another performance, or finally become responsibility.

Own your part clearly

Why can a short apology repair more than ten minutes of explanation? The argument is over, at least in the ordinary sense. No one is speaking over anyone now. A chair has been pushed back from the table, a glass of water sits half-finished, and the sentence that did the damage is still hanging in the room. One person wants to explain the pressure they were under. The other is waiting to know whether the impact has been seen. The hinge is small.

The first instinct after conflict is often self-protection. A person wants to say, "I did not mean it like that," or "You have to understand how stressed I was," or "I only raised my voice because I felt cornered." Some of those statements may contain truth. Intention, context, and pressure are not irrelevant. Yet when they arrive before ownership, they ask the hurt person to step over the injury in order to understand the one who caused it. The apology becomes a detour. The wound remains unnamed.

Clear ownership begins with behaviour. Not personality. Not global shame. Not a foggy "sorry if things got heated." Behaviour. "I raised my voice." "I interrupted you." "I sent repeated messages after you asked for space." "I walked out without saying when I would return." A relationship cannot repair what remains vague. The more specific the behaviour, the less the apology depends on emotional theatre. The sentence points to the exact place where responsibility belongs.

The distinction matters because vague regret often sounds safe while doing very little. "I am sorry for everything" may appear generous, but it leaves the other person holding the work of definition. What, precisely, is being acknowledged? The tone? The threat? The silence? The dismissive phrase? The failure to return? The apology becomes a mist through which the injured person must walk alone. Specific ownership says, "I know where the harm occurred." That knowledge steadies the room.

The next element is impact. An apology that names behaviour but not impact can sound like a legal admission without human comprehension. "I raised my voice" is a start. "I raised my voice; that was frightening and unfair" goes further. It shows that the speaker understands why the behaviour mattered. Impact is not always identical to intention. A person may not have intended to frighten, belittle, pressure, confuse, or abandon. But if their behaviour had that effect, repair requires contact with the effect. The other person needs to know that the harm has registered.

Erving Goffman, in *Relations in Public*, published in 1971, wrote about remedial exchanges and the social labour by which people repair disruptions in ordinary interaction. His work was not a manual for intimate apologies, yet the insight travels well: repair is not merely a feeling inside the offender; it is an act performed in the shared world. A person has to show that they understand the breach. In a close relationship, that showing is often painfully concrete. A lowered voice. A stopped explanation. A sentence that does not wriggle away.

Self-attack is not ownership. This is one of the most common confusions. "I am awful," "I ruin everything," "You should not have to deal with me," or "I am the worst partner" may sound remorseful, but it often shifts the emotional burden onto the injured person. Now they must choose between staying hurt and comforting the person who hurt them. Self-attack collapses accountability into shame. Clear ownership stays upright: "I raised my voice. That was frightening and unfair. I am sorry." The speaker does not become the wound. They name the wound and stand responsible beside it.

Aaron Lazare, a psychiatrist and former chancellor of the University of Massachusetts Medical School, examined apology in his 2004 book *On Apology*. One of his enduring contributions was to treat apology not as a social nicety but as a structured act that can restore dignity when it includes acknowledgement, responsibility, and an offer of repair. In intimate life, dignity is often the missing element. The hurt person does not merely want regret. They want the truth of their experience recognised without having to prosecute it. A clean apology gives that recognition before the defence brief is opened.

Defensiveness often enters through the word "but." "I am sorry I shouted, but you were not listening." "I am sorry I kept texting, but you know silence scares me." "I am sorry I walked away, but you were pushing me." The material after "but" may be important later, but inside the apology it usually cancels the ownership. The listener hears the sentence reassigning the centre of gravity: the behaviour was unfortunate, yet understandable, perhaps inevitable, perhaps partly your fault. A better sequence separates ownership from context. "I am sorry I shouted. That was not okay. I want to talk later about how unheard I felt, but that does not excuse my volume."

This separation is not merely polite. It protects accuracy. Conflict often contains more than one truth. One person may have raised their voice and also felt persistently dismissed. One may have sent too many messages and also received too little clarity. One may have gone silent and also felt overwhelmed by relentless questioning. Repair fails when these truths are collapsed into a contest. Owning one part clearly does not mean owning the whole conflict. It means refusing to use the complexity of the whole conflict to evade the part that belongs to the speaker.

The apology should also include intent to change, but the intent must be believable. "I will never do that again" often sounds comforting in the moment and hollow later. Human beings under stress may repeat patterns they sincerely dislike. A stronger statement is more behavioural: "Next time I feel that activated, I will ask for a pause before my voice gets loud." "If I need reassurance, I will ask once instead of sending repeated texts." "If I need space, I will name a return time rather than disappearing." These commitments give the relationship something observable. Trust requires visible behaviour, not grand remorse.

There is a credible limitation here. Not every conflict requires a formal apology, and not every hurt feeling means someone has done wrong. A person can feel disappointed because a boundary was held. They can feel rejected when a reasonable request for space was made. They can feel upset by truthful feedback. Clear ownership should not become automatic self-blame. The question is whether one's behaviour crossed a line of respect, honesty, care, proportion, or consent. If it did, ownership is necessary. If it did not, the repair may require validation rather than apology.

The reconciliation lies in precision. "I am sorry you were upset" is often too evasive when harm was done, because it apologises for the other person's feeling rather than the speaker's behaviour. Yet "I am sorry I hurt you" may be too broad if the hurt came from a necessary boundary spoken respectfully. A precise repair might say, "I am sorry for the contempt in my tone," or, "I am not sorry I asked for space, but I am sorry I left without giving you a return time." Precision prevents both over-apology and under-apology. It keeps repair honest.

Owning one's part also means resisting the urge to demand immediate forgiveness. An apology is offered; it is not inserted like a coin to release absolution. "I said sorry, why are you still upset?" reveals that the apology was being used to hurry the other person out of pain. Repair may begin with the offender's clarity, but it is completed, if it is completed, in the injured person's body over time. The person apologising can ask, "Is there anything about the impact I have not understood?" They cannot require the answer to be convenient.

Timing matters. An apology delivered too early may be a way to stop the discomfort before the impact is heard. An apology delivered too late may feel like something extracted by exhaustion. The cleanest timing is often after enough regulation has returned for the sentence to be accurate and owned. The apology should not be used as a sedative for conflict. It should be used as a repair tool. That means the speaker must be capable of staying present while the other person says, "Yes, that did frighten me," or "I am still hurt," without turning the apology into another defensive exchange.

The body participates in apology. A rushed apology can feel like evasion. A collapsed apology can feel like a plea for rescue. A cold apology can feel like compliance. A steady apology requires pace, eye contact where appropriate, and enough stillness to let the words land. "I raised my voice; that was frightening and unfair. I am sorry." The sentence needs space after it. The silence is not a failure. It is where the impact has room to be acknowledged rather than buried under follow-up explanation.

A clean apology may also name the relational value that was violated. "I want our conversations to feel safe, and I did not protect that when I shouted." "I care about your need for space, and I ignored it when I kept messaging." "I want to be honest with you, and I hid what I was feeling until it came out sharply." This kind of statement is useful when it does not become grandstanding. It connects the behaviour to the shared standard. The apology is not merely, "I regret feeling bad." It is, "I see the gap between what I value and what I did."

There is a particular courage in apologising without asking the other person to applaud the growth. "I am working on this" may be true, but if it arrives too soon, it can sound like a request for credit. "I know I have been better lately" may also be true, but it can dilute the present ownership. Repair asks for humility at close range. The speaker may have made progress. They may have handled other moments well. This moment still deserves clean attention. The injured person should not have to grade a trend before receiving acknowledgement of the specific harm.

The apology should not smuggle in a demand that the other person own their part at the same time. "I am sorry I raised my voice, but you need to admit you provoked me" breaks the repair. There may indeed be another conversation about provocation, misunderstanding, timing, pursuit, withdrawal, or repeated patterns. But the ownership sentence must be able to stand alone. "I am sorry for my volume. I want to talk about the pattern between us, and I can do that after I have owned my part." This order matters because it prevents accountability from becoming a bargaining chip.

In secure repair, the person apologising remains neither superior nor small. They do not lecture the other person on the mature way to receive an apology. They do not grovel until the other person has to rescue them. They do not turn the apology into a performance of sensitivity. They remain adult: specific, affected, responsible, and oriented towards change.

The dignity of this posture is easy to underestimate. It says, "I can face what I did without making you carry my shame."

There are moments when the injured person may not respond generously. They may be too hurt, too guarded, too accustomed to empty apologies, or too activated themselves. The apology still matters. It plants a marker of reality. It may not repair everything immediately, but it refuses denial. A person can say, "I understand you may not be ready to respond. I wanted to name my part clearly." That sentence releases the apology from the demand for instant repair. It allows ownership to be an ethical act, not merely a strategy for restoring comfort.

The quiet motif is the hinge. After conflict, a relationship can swing towards denial, shame, argument, or repair. The hinge is rarely a dramatic speech. It is the exact sentence that bears the weight of responsibility without breaking into self-attack or defence. "I raised my voice." "I dismissed your concern." "I kept pushing after you asked me to stop." "I left without saying when I would return." These are hinge sentences. They let the door move.

The forward test comes when regret rises and the old escape routes appear: explain, collapse, blame the pressure, apologise vaguely, demand forgiveness, or pretend it was not so bad. The more secure move is narrower and braver. Name the behaviour. Name the impact. Name the intent to change in a form that can be seen. The sentence may be short, but it must be strong enough to hold reality: "I raised my voice; that was frightening and unfair. I am sorry."

Ask for what you needed

Why can an apology still leave the argument strangely unfinished? The behaviour has been named. The raised voice, the repeated texts, the abrupt exit, the cold silence: each has been placed on the table with enough honesty to be seen. Yet something remains under the table, alive and unspoken. The person who apologised may have taken responsibility for the damage and still not revealed what they were reaching for before the damage began. The hinge has moved, but the door has not fully opened.

After conflict, it is tempting to believe that ownership is the whole repair. "I interrupted you." "I was sharp." "I pushed after you asked me to stop." These statements matter. They protect the injured person from being asked to pretend harm did not happen. But repair is incomplete if the distorted need remains hidden, because the relationship then knows only the symptom, not the signal. It knows that someone shouted. It does not yet know what fear, longing, embarrassment, or loneliness came through the voice before the voice became too loud. The need waits.

The sentence "Under that, I needed reassurance that we were OK" changes the repair because it does not excuse the behaviour; it explains the emotional pressure beneath it. That distinction is crucial. Explanation without ownership becomes evasion. Ownership without need can become a sterile confession. Together, they allow the relationship to learn. The person is not saying, "I raised my voice because you failed me." They are saying, "I raised my voice, and I am responsible for that. Beneath it was a need I did not ask for well." The repair becomes not only moral, but instructive.

John Bowlby's attachment work in London across the mid-twentieth century, including his 1951 World Health Organization report, helps make sense of why conflict so often disguises need. When an attachment bond feels uncertain, human beings may reach for contact through behaviours that do not look like contact at all. Protest can masquerade as anger. Fear can speak as accusation. Shame can hide inside withdrawal. The visible behaviour may be sharp, but the underlying movement is often towards safety, closeness, recognition, or reassurance. Naming the need after the rupture helps separate the reach from the wound it caused.

This separation protects both people. The injured person does not have to accept the behaviour as justified. The person who acted badly does not have to pretend the need was shameful simply because the strategy was harmful. "I needed reassurance" is not the same as "I was entitled to frighten you." "I wanted to feel chosen" is not the same as "I was allowed to punish you for disappointing me." "I needed a pause" is not the same as "It was fine that I disappeared." The need can be dignified while the behaviour remains accountable. That is the adult balance.

Marshall Rosenberg's *Nonviolent Communication*, first published in 1999 in the United States, popularised a distinction that remains useful when handled without formula: observations, feelings, needs, and requests are not the same thing. The practical value lies in refusing to confuse blame with information. "You ignored me" may be the accusation. "I felt alone" may be the feeling. "I needed reassurance that I still mattered" may be the need. "Next time, could you tell me when you need quiet rather than going silent?" may be the request. When these layers are collapsed, conflict thickens. When they are separated, repair gains a map.

The need should be named without making it the other person's indictment. This is where many repairs falter. "I needed you to stop being so dismissive" still contains the charge. "I needed to know my feelings mattered to you" moves closer to the centre. "I needed you to prove I was important" may be honest in its intensity, but it risks turning reassurance into a trial. "I needed a clear sign that we were still connected" gives the other person something more human to understand. The sentence should move from accusation to longing, from verdict to request.

Need-language is not automatically clean. It can be used to dress up control. "I need you to answer every time I text" may be phrased as need, but it is really a strategy demanding compliance. "I need you never to take space during conflict" turns anxiety into a rule that may suffocate the other person. A truer version might be, "I need reassurance that space has a return time." Or, "I need to know you are pausing, not leaving." The difference is not academic. A need can be met in more than one way. A controlling strategy usually insists on only one.

After conflict, the underlying need is often embarrassingly simple. "I needed comfort." "I needed to feel heard." "I needed to know you still liked me." "I needed time before answering." "I needed help making sense of what had happened." These sentences may feel too plain for the size of the argument that grew around them. But that is precisely why they matter. Much relational damage begins when a simple need becomes intolerable to state directly. The need hides, gathers pressure, and emerges as an accusation with teeth.

The person naming the need must do so after, not instead of, accountability. Order matters. "I am sorry I kept pushing after you asked for space. Under that, I was frightened and needed reassurance that we were still okay" will land differently from "I only kept pushing because I needed reassurance." The word "only" is often where repair dies. It shrinks the harm beneath the explanation. A cleaner repair allows the behaviour and the need to stand side by side, neither cancelling the other. "That was not okay. And I want to understand what I was trying to get badly."

There is a quiet severity in asking for what was needed without reopening the prosecution. The speaker must resist turning the repair into a second trial: "I needed reassurance, which you never give me unless I drag it out of you." That may contain a real grievance, but it has shifted from repair into indictment. A more workable sentence might be, "I realise I needed reassurance, and I did not ask for it cleanly. I would like us to talk later about how we handle reassurance after conflict." The larger pattern may still need attention. It does not have to ambush the repair.

Mary Ainsworth's Strange Situation research in Baltimore in the late 1960s and early 1970s remains relevant because it showed how much meaning gathers around reunion after stress. In adult relationships, repair is a form of reunion. It answers not only "What happened?" but "Can we come back into contact after what happened?" Naming the need helps that return become meaningful. If the only message after conflict is "I behaved badly," the relationship may gain accountability but not understanding. If the message becomes "I behaved badly because I was trying to protect a tender need in a poor way," the relationship gains material for change.

The credible limitation is that some conflicts are not primarily about unmet needs being poorly expressed. Some involve disrespect, dishonesty, coercion, contempt, repeated boundary violations, or patterns that cannot be softened by explaining the need beneath them. A person may say, "I needed reassurance," but if the behaviour included intimidation, surveillance, or punishment, the need does not become a shield. Naming need is not a moral solvent. It clarifies motive; it does not erase impact. The more serious the harm, the more carefully need must be separated from entitlement.

The reconciliation lies in proportion. A distorted need may explain why someone became sharp during a tender exchange; it does not excuse cruelty. It may explain why repeated texting began; it does not justify harassment or refusal to respect a boundary. It may explain why someone withdrew; it does not justify disappearing for days without accountability. In ordinary conflict, need-language opens repair. In harmful patterns, it must be paired with firmer responsibility and, where necessary, external support or serious relational reassessment. The sentence "I needed reassurance" should deepen accountability, not dilute it.

The person hearing the underlying need also has work to do. It can be tempting to respond, "Well, you should have just said that," especially if the conflict caused real hurt. The statement may be true, but it can close the door too quickly. A more useful response is, "I understand that was the need. I still need us to address how it came out." This keeps both truths alive. The need is received. The behaviour remains accountable. Repair does not require choosing between compassion and boundaries.

Asking for what was needed also changes the future script. If the need is reassurance, the next conflict can contain a cleaner request: "I am feeling panicky and need to hear we are okay." If the need is space, the next conflict can contain a safer boundary: "I need twenty minutes, and I will come back." If the need is understanding, the next conflict can contain a smaller ask: "Could you reflect back what you heard before responding?" The repaired sentence becomes a rehearsal for the next difficult moment. That is why naming need after conflict is not indulgent; it is practical.

The language should be specific enough to guide behaviour. "I needed love" may be true but too broad to help. "I needed a kind sentence after we disagreed" is more usable. "I needed respect" may be legitimate but vague. "I needed you not to interrupt while I finished the hard part" gives the next conversation a visible shape. "I needed safety" can mean many things. "I needed your voice lower and a return time before you left" turns safety into practice. Abstractions become reparative only when they can be translated into behaviour.

The person naming the need should avoid making the other person responsible for having guessed it. "I needed reassurance, and you should have known" is understandable when the need feels obvious internally, but it pulls the repair back into blame. "I needed reassurance, and I see that I asked for it by criticising you instead" is more mature. It acknowledges that the other person may have been responding to the strategy rather than the need. This distinction can soften defensiveness because it admits the confusion the speaker helped create.

There is a particular kind of grief in recognising that a conflict might have been smaller if the need had been spoken earlier. The repeated texts might have been one sentence. The sharp tone might have been a request for a pause. The accusation might have been a bid for comfort. This grief should not become self-attack. It can become information. "I see now that I was trying to ask for closeness by complaining about your distance" is a brave sentence. It allows the relationship to understand the route by which need became harm.

A good repair statement may therefore sound like this: "I am sorry I accused you of not caring. Under that, I felt scared by the distance between us and needed reassurance that we were okay. Next time I want to ask for that directly." Or: "I am sorry I went cold after you said no to talking. Under that, I felt rejected and needed a return time. I should have asked for one instead of shutting down." Or: "I am sorry I kept arguing after you said you were overwhelmed. Under that, I needed to feel understood, but I pushed too hard." Each version honours the wound and names the hidden need without making the need a weapon.

The quiet motif is the hinge again. Ownership opens the door to responsibility; need opens the door to understanding. Without the first, the second becomes excuse. Without the second, the first may leave the pattern intact. The hinge needs both plates fixed firmly: what I did, and what I was trying to ask for badly. Only then can the door swing towards a different future rather than back into the same room.

The forward test comes after the apology, when shame wants to end the conversation quickly and fear wants to start the blame again. Can the underlying need be spoken without turning it into a defence? Can the person say, "Under that, I needed reassurance that we were OK," and let the sentence remain both tender and accountable? Repair becomes deeper when the relationship learns not only where the harm occurred, but what unmet need was distorted on its way into the room.

Rebuild trust with next steps

Why does "I promise I will change" often feel less reassuring than one plain agreement about what will happen next time? The conflict has been named. The apology has been spoken. The underlying need has emerged from beneath the sharper behaviour. For a moment, the room may seem softer. Then a quieter question arrives: what will be different when the same fear returns, the same tone appears, the same silence stretches, the same old pressure finds the same old doorway? The hinge has opened. Now the door needs somewhere to lead.

Repair without a next step can leave both people stranded inside sincerity. One person may feel genuine remorse, even tenderness. The other may believe the apology, yet still feel their body bracing for the next repetition. This is not cynicism. It is memory doing its work. If a pattern has happened before, words alone cannot carry the weight of trust for long. Trust listens politely to remorse, then watches behaviour. It waits to see whether the next difficult moment contains any evidence that the repair has entered the body.

Grand promises are emotionally seductive because they sound total. "I will never send those messages again." "I will always pause before I raise my voice." "I will be different from now on." Such statements often come from an honest wish to end the pain, but they ask the relationship to believe in a transformed future before any new behaviour has been practised. They can also create a trap. The next imperfect moment then feels like proof that the apology was false, when the real problem may be that the promise was too vast to guide action. The repair needs a handle.

A next step turns remorse into behaviour. "Next time I feel panicky, I will ask for a ten-minute call instead of sending five texts." That sentence has strength because it is modest, visible, and testable. It identifies the trigger, names the old strategy, and proposes a different action. It does not claim that panic will never return. It does not pretend the person has become permanently serene. It says: when the familiar pressure rises, here is the move I will practise instead. Believability begins there.

John Gottman and Robert Levenson's observational work with couples in Seattle across the late twentieth century gave close attention to repair attempts, escalation, withdrawal, and the behaviours by which partners either return to each other or deepen rupture. The practical lesson is valuable here: repair is not only a feeling state after conflict, but a sequence of observable moves. A softened tone, a pause taken earlier, a return time honoured, one message sent instead of several, a boundary named without contempt - these are the small acts through which trust becomes visible again.

The next step should fit the actual injury. If the harm was a raised voice, the step might be, "When I feel myself getting loud, I will ask for a pause before continuing." If the harm was repeated messaging, it might be, "I will send one clear request for timing, then step away from my phone." If the harm was disappearing, it might be, "If I need space, I will give a return time before I leave the conversation." If the harm was contempt, it might be, "If I feel myself becoming mocking, I will stop and restart the sentence plainly." The change must meet the wound where it occurred.

Specificity protects the agreement from becoming sentimental fog. "I will communicate better" sounds worthy, but it is difficult to recognise in practice. "I will tell you when I am overwhelmed instead of going silent" is clearer. "I will be more thoughtful" may soothe briefly, but it does not guide the next tense evening. "If plans change, I will message you as soon as I know" gives the relationship something concrete. Abstractions can inspire repair; behaviours rebuild it. The difference is the difference between a wish and a practice.

A believable next step also respects the limits of human change. People do not usually become secure by deciding never to be activated again. They become more trustworthy by catching the pattern earlier, repairing faster, and choosing one different behaviour at a time. This is humbler than the fantasy of total transformation, but it is more durable. A person who says, "I may still get anxious, but I will not make my anxiety the whole conversation," is often more credible than someone who says, "I will never be anxious again." The smaller sentence knows the terrain.

There is a credible limitation. Some harms require more than a small agreement. Repeated dishonesty, intimidation, chronic contempt, coercive control, or sustained emotional unavailability cannot be repaired by a neat behavioural tweak. A next step may still matter, but it cannot be used to minimise the scale of the problem. "I will speak more softly next time" is inadequate if the wider pattern involves fear. "I will text less" is inadequate if the wider pattern involves surveillance or punishment. In serious patterns, trust may require wider accountability, sustained change, outside support, or a clearer decision about whether the relationship is safe enough to continue.

The reconciliation lies in proportion. Ordinary ruptures need concrete next steps. Serious ruptures need concrete next steps inside a larger structure of accountability. The principle remains the same: repair must become visible. The difference is the scale of visibility required. For a small rupture, one changed sentence may be meaningful. For a repeated pattern, the next step may need a review point, a clearer boundary, and evidence over time. Trust does not demand perfection, but it does ask for a pattern that can be seen.

A next step should belong primarily to the person making it. "Next time, you should reassure me sooner so I do not spiral" may contain a real desire, but it shifts the repair away from personal accountability. A stronger version is, "Next time I feel the spiral starting, I will ask directly for reassurance once, and I will tell you I am going to take a walk after that." This does not mean the other person has no part in the pattern. It means the speaker begins with the part they can actually change. Repair becomes cleaner when each person owns their own next move rather than designing the other person's personality.

Some agreements will need to be shared. If one person says, "I will ask for a ten-minute call instead of sending five texts," the other may need to answer honestly: "I can usually do that in the evening, but not during work." That response does not reject the repair; it makes it realistic. The final agreement might become, "If I feel panicky during the day, I will send one message asking when we can talk. If it is evening and you have capacity, I will ask for a ten-minute call." The repair becomes less dramatic and more usable. Real life has been admitted.

Follow-up is the part many couples neglect. A next step made in the warm aftermath of apology may feel complete, but it needs to be checked in the world where the pattern usually appears. "Let us see how this goes this week and talk on Sunday" gives the agreement a return point. "If I miss it, I will name that rather than pretend it did not happen" gives the repair resilience. Without follow-up, the next step risks becoming another good intention swallowed by habit. The hinge needs oil, not applause.

Checking later should not become a trial. The purpose is not to gather evidence for punishment, but to measure whether the new behaviour is becoming available. "How did we do with the pause this week?" is different from "See, you failed again." "It helped when you gave me a return time" is different from silent scoring. "I noticed I still wanted to send extra texts, but I stopped after one" is a useful piece of data. Repair grows through observation. It shrinks under surveillance.

Trust is rebuilt partly through the injured person's freedom not to be instantly reassured by the agreement. A person may hear the next step and still feel guarded. That guardedness should not be treated as punishment. It may simply be the body waiting for evidence. "I understand you may need to see it more than hear it" is a mature repair sentence. It acknowledges that the agreement is the beginning of credibility, not its completion. The person repairing does not demand immediate restoration of confidence as a reward for having spoken well.

The person receiving the next step may also need to avoid turning vigilance into permanent prosecution. If the agreement is being practised sincerely, every imperfect attempt should not be used as proof of hopelessness. Growth often appears awkwardly before it appears elegantly. Someone may catch their tone halfway through a sentence rather than before it begins. Someone may ask for a pause after one sharp reply rather than none. Someone may send two texts instead of five. These are not full repair, but they may be movement. Trust does not have to be naive to notice direction.

The most useful next steps often include a replacement behaviour, not merely a prohibition. "I will not get defensive" is too vague; defensiveness needs a substitute. "When I feel defensive, I will say, 'I want to answer, but I need to reflect back what I heard first.'" "I will not shut down" is incomplete; shutdown needs a safer exit. "When I go blank, I will say, 'I am overwhelmed and still here; I need ten minutes.'" "I will not chase" becomes stronger as, "I will ask for a time to reconnect, then put my phone down until that time." A habit is easier to change when the body knows what to do instead.

There is a place for mutual agreements, but they should remain small enough to keep. "When either of us gets activated, we will pause for twenty minutes and return" is useful if both people intend to honour the return. "We will never argue late at night again" may be unrealistic unless paired with a practical alternative. "We will be kinder" is too soft to carry pressure. "We will avoid emotional texting after ten and schedule a call if something feels urgent" is clearer. The agreement should be strong enough to guide the next difficult moment and flexible enough not to collapse under ordinary life.

A repair agreement also needs language for failure. Not because failure is the goal, but because shame often makes a slip worse. If a person promises a new step and then misses it, the old instinct may be to hide, minimise, or defend. A better repair includes a recovery sentence: "I missed the pause and raised my voice again. I am naming it now, and I want to reset." Or, "I sent extra texts after saying I would not. I am going to stop now and wait for our call." Recovery is part of trust. The relationship learns not only whether people can avoid mistakes, but whether they can catch themselves without being forced.

The next step should be framed as practice, not as proof of moral worth. A person who ties every slip to identity will either collapse into shame or deny the slip. Practice allows attention without humiliation. "I am practising asking directly instead of protesting." "I am practising giving a return time when I need space." "I am practising one reassurance request rather than repeated checking." The language of practice is sober. It does not excuse harm. It makes change something the body can rehearse.

Aaron Lazare's work on apology, particularly his 2004 book *On Apology*, treated repair as a process that may involve acknowledgement, responsibility, remorse, and reparation. In intimate life, reparation is often not a grand gesture but a changed micro-behaviour in the exact place where harm used to repeat. The person who used to disappear now sends a return time. The person who used to accuse now names fear. The person who used to flood the phone now asks for one call. Reparation becomes ordinary enough to be trusted.

There is a temptation after conflict to seek a clean emotional ending: apology given, need named, hug exchanged, pain resolved. Some repairs do end softly. Many do not. Some end with an agreement that feels slightly awkward because both people know it will have to be tested later. This is not failure. It is realism. A relationship that can leave a repair with one concrete next step may be stronger than one that insists on immediate emotional closure and then repeats the old pattern unchanged.

The quiet motif is the hinge. Ownership opened it. Need gave it meaning. The next step determines whether it swings differently next time. Without a behavioural agreement, the door may simply return to its old frame. With one small practised change, the next conflict has a different route available. Not a perfect route. A better one. A route that can be recognised under pressure.

The forward test comes when the apology begins to fade and ordinary life returns. What will the relationship be able to observe? A promise, however heartfelt, cannot be watched unless it becomes behaviour. The stronger repair asks for a future small enough to enter: next time I feel panicky, I will ask for a ten-minute call instead of sending five texts. The sentence does not claim to heal everything. It places trust where trust can actually grow - in the next visible choice.

Chapter 9
Texting and Digital Reassurance

Why can a message of fewer than ten words change the whole temperature of a relationship? The screen lights up in a quiet room. "Fine." Nothing more. No voice, no face, no hand reaching across the table, no softness to correct the sharp edge the mind has already supplied. The person reading it stares at the small word until it grows teeth. Perhaps it means fine. Perhaps it means hurt. Perhaps it means the conversation has already become a fight, though only one person knows it yet.

Text is efficient until it is asked to carry tenderness. It can arrange a train time, confirm a meal, send a joke, keep affection alive across distance, and offer a small signal of care during a crowded day. But it is a thin medium for thick feeling. It strips away tone and leaves punctuation to do dangerous work. A full stop becomes coldness. An ellipsis becomes threat. A delayed reply becomes evidence. A short answer becomes a psychological crime scene. The phone is not neutral when the body is afraid.

The trouble is not that texting is shallow. It is that texting is powerful in precisely the places where it is most ambiguous. A message arrives quickly and reassures. A message fails to arrive and unsettles. A phrase lands warmly one day and sharply the next because the reader brings fatigue, memory, longing, and fear to the glass. The same screen that keeps people close can make them vigilant. The same thread that carries affection can carry protest, punishment, and private tests that neither person has formally agreed to take.

The central tension is that digital contact invites instant expression while intimate truth often needs better conditions. A frightened person can send the sharp sentence before the steadier one has had time to form. A hurt person can type "never mind" and watch the other person scramble. A person who wants reassurance can ask for it indirectly through baiting, silence, double-texting, or a message designed to sting. The screen gives the feeling a door. It does not guarantee that the feeling should walk through it.

The stakes are larger than etiquette. Digital habits train emotional expectations. If reassurance arrives only after panic texts, panic learns to text. If silence by phone is used to punish, silence stops being rest and becomes threat. If every tender subject is pushed through a medium that cannot carry tone well, both people may begin to associate contact with misreading. The relationship becomes less a place of connection than a sequence of notifications, interpretations, corrections, and apologies. A thread can fray.

There is another cost: text can create the illusion of having communicated when only fragments have been exchanged. A person may feel they have explained their hurt because they sent several long messages. The other may feel attacked because those messages arrived without voice, pacing, or the possibility of real-time repair. One person writes to be understood; the other reads under pressure. The medium turns feeling into evidence and response time into character. What should have become a conversation becomes a file.

A better digital script has to do more with restraint than cleverness. Short, specific messages reduce the space where fear invents meaning. A useful text can name the feeling, make one request, and give timing without accusation: "I am feeling a bit anxious - can you send a quick 'thinking of you' when you can?" A healthier pause can say, "I am going to take a break from my phone so I do not spiral." A tender topic can be moved out of text without drama: "This feels tender; can we talk for ten minutes later?" These are not perfect sentences. They are safer doors.

The movement now turns towards digital language that lands without unnecessary shrapnel: messages that say what they mean, protest patterns that can be interrupted before they become proof of insecurity, and the judgement to recognise when the phone is too narrow for the conversation being forced through it. The question is not whether texting belongs in love. It does. The sharper question is what kind of love the text is training: one built on signals, clarity, and return, or one built on testing, guessing, and the long stare at a silent screen.

The unresolved friction sits in the hand before sending. The body wants relief. The thumb wants action. The screen offers speed, and speed can feel like power when uncertainty hurts. But the next message will either lower the cost of being close or raise it. Before the word leaves the phone, the real test is already present: is this text asking for connection, or is it making the other person pay for the fear of not having it?

Write messages that land well

On 3 December 1992, Neil Papworth sent the words "Merry Christmas" from a computer to a mobile phone on the Vodafone network in the United Kingdom. The first SMS was not a love note, not an apology, not a trembling request for reassurance. It was a seasonal greeting, brief enough to fit the technology that carried it. Yet the form it helped introduce would later carry everything human beings find hardest to say plainly: desire, irritation, longing, fear, delay, repair. A tiny message can hold too much.

That is the trouble with texting. It is wonderfully useful for practical life and dangerously thin for emotional life. A message has no breath in it. No softened mouth. No hand reaching across the table. It arrives as marks on glass, and the reader supplies the missing weather from memory, mood, and fear. "Fine" can mean fine, or wounded, or furious, or finished. The word is small. The room it opens is not.

A text lands well when it reduces the number of meanings the other person has to invent. This does not mean writing long explanations. In anxious moments, length can become another kind of pressure: a flood of feeling delivered into a medium too narrow to hold it. The best reassurance texts are often short because they have a single job. They name the state, make one request, and give the other person room to respond. "I am feeling a bit anxious - can you send a quick 'thinking of you' when you can?" carries more security than three paragraphs about feeling ignored. It tells the truth and gives it a handle.

The first discipline is to remove sarcasm from tender messages. Sarcasm feels protective because it says the painful thing while pretending not to care. "Nice to know I matter" may be trying to say, "I felt hurt when I did not hear from you." But the form punishes the person before inviting them close. The recipient now has to respond to the sting, not only the need. A clean text gives up the small pleasure of the blade. "I felt a bit unimportant when I did not hear back. Can you tell me when we can reconnect?" is less dramatic and far more courageous.

Ellipses can do similar damage. Three dots may look harmless on the screen, but in a tense exchange they often function as a threat left unfinished. "Okay..." does not communicate a need. It creates suspense. It asks the other person to guess whether the speaker is sad, angry, disappointed, testing, or preparing a later case. The same is true of "sure." or "fine." when used as emotional punctuation rather than communication. These words may briefly protect pride, but they increase the cost of understanding. The screen becomes a fogged window.

A message that lands well is specific about timing. Much digital anxiety begins when emotional need and schedule are tangled together. "Can we talk?" may be sincere, but it gives no clue whether the request means now, later, urgently, briefly, or for the rest of the evening. "This feels tender; can we talk for ten minutes after dinner?" gives the relationship a shape. "I do not need a full reply now, but could you tell me when you are free?" lowers pressure while still asking for orientation. Timing turns a vague emotional summons into a practical invitation.

WhatsApp, founded in 2009 in California by Jan Koum and Brian Acton, helped normalise the quick, continuous thread as a central form of personal contact. The technology made it easier to send affection in the middle of a day, but it also made it easier to send agitation before it had been translated. A person can now move from alarm to message in seconds. That speed is convenient when the message is simple. It is dangerous when the message is loaded. The thumb often moves faster than the self.

The second discipline is to separate the text that seeks connection from the text that seeks relief through impact. A connection text says, "I miss you - can we have a quick call later?" A relief-through-impact text says, "Do not worry, I will stop bothering you." The first invites. The second wounds and waits to be repaired. The person sending it may feel briefly powerful because the pain has been made visible. But the visibility comes at a price: the other person is pulled into reassurance through guilt, not generosity. The thread frays.

Need and timing can often be held in one sentence. "I am feeling unsettled after earlier - could you send one reassuring line when you have a moment?" "I want to talk about this, but I do not want to do it badly by text. Are you free tonight?" "I am reading your short reply as distance, and I know I might be wrong. Are you busy or upset?" These messages are not emotionally sterile. They are emotionally edited. They let feeling enter the thread without making feeling the only author.

Short does not mean abrupt. A message can be brief and still warm. "Thinking of you. No rush to reply." "I am tender after earlier, but I want us to be okay." "I need a little reassurance when you have space." The warmth matters because digital communication easily tilts towards efficiency, and efficiency can sound cold when closeness is at stake. A few human words can change the whole landing. Not ornamental words. Accurate ones.

There is a credible limitation. Some people use careful texting to avoid fuller conversation. They send tidy messages that sound mature while refusing voice, eye contact, or real repair. A well-written text is not a substitute for presence when the subject is complex, painful, or recurring. It can open the door, mark a pause, ask for timing, or offer a small reassurance. It cannot carry everything. A person who keeps trying to resolve attachment injuries by text may end up polishing sentences inside a medium that cannot provide enough relational information.

The reconciliation is to let text do what text can do well. Text is good for signals, timing, brief reassurance, clean requests, and transitions into fuller conversation. It is poor for interpreting tone, resolving layered conflict, proving motives, or processing the whole emotional history of a pattern. The skill is not to abandon texting, but to stop asking it to become a room when it is only a thread. "This is bigger than text. Can we speak for ten minutes later?" is often the most secure digital sentence available.

A message that lands well also avoids hidden tests. "I guess you are too busy" is a test. "Do you even want to talk to me?" may be a test, especially if the only acceptable answer is immediate reassurance. "Never mind" after asking for closeness is usually a test. The cleaner alternative states the request directly: "I would like to talk. If now is not good, please send me a time." This allows the other person to answer the actual need rather than perform loyalty under pressure.

The sender should also notice when they are trying to make the other person feel the force of their anxiety. Long emotional texts can sometimes be attempts at intimacy, but they can also become a way of transferring urgency. The message arrives, and the recipient must now carry the whole storm at once. A better text may hold the door open without pushing the storm through it: "I have a lot of feelings about this, and I do not want to unload by text. Can we talk later?" That sentence is restrained, but not avoidant. It respects the weight of the issue.

There is an art to the unsent text. Not every true sentence deserves to be sent in its first form. The first draft may be for the body, not the relationship. It may say, "You made me feel pathetic." It may say, "I hate that I care this much." It may say, "Please come back and fix this feeling." Such lines can be written privately to reveal what is underneath. Then the sent version can become cleaner: "I am feeling exposed and would like reassurance when you can." The private text finds the heat. The sent text carries the light.

The person receiving a clear text has responsibility too. A well-written message should not be punished with vagueness when a small answer is possible. "I hear you. I am busy now but can call at eight" is a generous reply. "Thinking of you too - I will message properly later" can steady a tender moment. "I am tired, not distant" can prevent unnecessary guessing. Secure digital contact is not created by one perfect sender. It is created by a rhythm in which clarity is met with enough responsiveness to make clarity worth practising.

The quiet motif is the thread. A text thread can stitch connection through a difficult day, or it can tighten into a knot. The difference often lies in whether the message is carrying a request or a punishment, a time or a test, a feeling or a verdict. "I am anxious" is not the same as "You are making me anxious." "Can you send a quick line when you can?" is not the same as "Why can you not do one basic thing?" These distinctions may look small on the screen. In the body, they are enormous.

The forward test comes before pressing send. Does the message reduce guessing, or does it create more? Does it ask for one clear thing, or does it smuggle in accusation, punishment, and proof? Does it respect timing, or demand immediate regulation? The best text is not the cleverest or the most emotionally complete. It is the one that can be received without decoding a threat. It keeps the thread open without pulling so hard that it snaps.

Avoiding protest texting

Why can a message sent to reduce panic become the very thing that makes the relationship feel less safe? The first text is a question. The second is a correction to the question. The third is a small accusation wearing the clothes of concern. The fourth says, "Forget it." The phone is still in the hand, warm from use, and the body is no calmer than it was before. Something has been done. Nothing has been settled. The thread tightens.

Protest texting is contact-seeking under pressure. It is not usually born from indifference; indifference rarely works this hard. It grows from the ache of waiting, the fear of being dismissed, the humiliation of needing a reply, the hope that one more message might finally make the other person understand. Yet the form of the message often fights the need beneath it. A person wants reassurance and sends a trap. They want closeness and send a sting. They want a return and create a reason for the other person to brace before coming back.

The pattern is old, even when the technology is new. John Bowlby's attachment work in London across the mid-twentieth century gave language to protest as a response to threatened separation. In childhood, protest may look like crying, searching, clinging, calling. In adult digital life, it may look like double-texting, monitoring replies, baiting questions, sudden coldness, or an abrupt "never mind" designed to provoke pursuit. The medium has changed. The nervous system still wants to know whether the important person is reachable.

Double-texting is not always protest. Sometimes it is a practical correction, an added detail, a joke sent after a thought, a harmless continuation of a warm exchange. The difference lies in the emotional contract underneath it. Protest double-texting says, "I cannot bear the gap, so I will press on it." It often escalates in tone: "Did you see this?" becomes "Are you ignoring me?" then "Fine, clearly this is not important to you." The visible behaviour is repeated contact. The hidden demand is immediate relief. The cost is that the other person begins to experience the thread as pressure rather than connection.

Baiting questions carry a similar charge. "Do you even care?" "Are you done with me?" "Should I just stop trying?" These questions sound as though they are seeking information, but often they are seeking proof through emotional force. They make the other person disprove an accusation before comfort can begin. The answer may soothe for a moment, but the method trains both people badly. One learns that panic must become dramatic to receive attention. The other learns that reassurance arrives through cross-examination. The thread tightens again.

Silent treatment by phone is protest in the opposite direction. Instead of sending too much, the person sends absence with intention. They stop replying not because they need grounded space, but because they want the other person to feel the gap. They read the message and leave it unanswered as punishment. They become visible online while withholding response. They use silence to make the other person pursue, worry, or apologise without being told what hurt. This may feel like dignity in the moment. It is often control with a quiet face.

The common feature in all protest texting is indirectness. The real sentence is rarely sent. "I am scared your silence means distance." "I wanted warmth and did not know how to ask." "I feel embarrassed that I care this much." "I need a time when we can reconnect." Instead, the phone carries a performance of the need: sharpness, withdrawal, bait, repetition, coolness.

The protest gives the body a burst of agency, but it does not give the relationship a clean request. It makes the other person respond to smoke rather than fire.

Mary Ainsworth's Strange Situation research in Baltimore in the late 1960s and early 1970s showed how strongly separation and reunion can organise behaviour. The adult application must be careful, but one point remains useful: the way a person seeks reunion matters. Seeking contact through protest may bring the other person closer physically or digitally, but it can make the reunion less secure. A reply extracted by guilt is not the same as a reply offered freely. A reassurance given under threat does not settle as deeply. The bond is contacted, but also strained.

A replacement text must do what the protest text was trying to do, only without punishment. "I am going to take a break from my phone so I do not spiral" is a strong sentence because it names the inner state without assigning blame. It does not say, "You made me spiral." It does not say, "I hope you notice my absence." It marks a self-protective pause. The person is not disappearing to punish; they are stepping away to prevent escalation. The thread is not cut. It is loosened.

The best replacement texts are honest, brief, and non-punitive. "I am feeling anxious and tempted to send too much, so I am going to pause and wait for your reply." "I want to talk, but I do not want to do it by spiralling through messages." "I am hurt, and I would rather speak later than send something sharp now." "I am reading the silence as distance, and I know I may be wrong. Please let me know when you can talk." These messages do not pretend the feeling is tidy. They simply refuse to make the feeling injure the channel of contact.

There is a crucial difference between taking space and staging distance. Taking space says what is happening and, where appropriate, when contact may resume. Staging distance withholds information in order to produce anxiety. "I am putting my phone away until after dinner, then I will check back" is space. Going cold after sending "whatever" is protest. "I need time before I can answer kindly" is space. Reading messages while refusing to respond in order to make a point is punishment. The same outward pause can carry very different ethics.

Protest texting often becomes harder to stop because it sometimes works. The other person may reply faster after the second message. They may reassure more intensely after the baiting question. They may chase after the cold withdrawal. The immediate relief teaches the anxious body that escalation is effective. But the long-term lesson is corrosive. The partner may become less relaxed, less spontaneous, less willing to engage tenderly by text. They may answer to prevent consequences rather than to connect. Security purchased through pressure is rarely secure for long.

There is a credible limitation. Not every repeated message is anxious protest, and not every delayed reply deserves infinite patience. If someone routinely disappears after conflict, refuses to set return times, ignores agreed contact rhythms, or uses ambiguity as a way to avoid accountability, a firmer text may be necessary. "I do not want to keep guessing after difficult conversations. Please tell me when we can talk" is not protest; it is a boundary around ambiguity. The difference is visible in the aim. Protest tries to provoke relief. Clarity seeks information, timing, or accountability.

The reconciliation lies in measuring the pattern rather than judging a single impulse. One extra message during a stressful day may simply be human. A repeated habit of escalating through the phone deserves attention. One period of silence to cool down may be healthy. A pattern of using silence to punish is harmful. The question is not, "Did I send more than one message?" The better question is, "Was I trying to communicate, or trying to make the other person feel my distress?" That question cuts close, which is why it is useful.

The screen intensifies protest because it makes small signals visible and easy to overread. Delivered. Read. Typing. Online. Last seen. These markers appear to offer information, but they rarely offer enough context to be emotionally reliable. A person may be online and unable to reply. They may type, delete, and rethink. They may read quickly and plan to answer properly later. The anxious mind turns fragments into certainty. Protest texting then responds not to reality, but to a story built from fragments. The thread becomes evidence before it becomes conversation.

A non-punitive text should usually avoid three moves: verdict, bait, and withdrawal-as-threat. Verdict says, "Clearly I do not matter." Bait says, "Do you even care?" Withdrawal-as-threat says, "Fine, I will stop bothering you." The cleaner versions are less theatrical and more exact: "I am feeling unimportant and would like reassurance when you can." "I am scared I misread the silence; are you busy or upset?" "I am going to stop texting for a bit because I do not want to make this worse." These lines preserve dignity. They give the other person a way towards the speaker rather than a maze of penalties.

The body will often protest the cleaner text. It may feel too mild. Too exposed. Too easy for the other person to ignore. A sharp message can feel safer because it gives the sender armour. A clean message leaves the need visible without a weapon in front of it. That vulnerability is exactly why it has more chance of landing. "I miss you and feel anxious" can be answered. "Nice of you to remember I exist" must first be survived. The former invites repair. The latter invites defence.

Timing matters. A replacement text is most useful before the protest has gathered speed. After the fifth message, the nervous system may be too activated to write cleanly. Earlier is kinder. "I am noticing I want to send another message, so I am going to pause" catches the pattern while it is still small. "I want to say this well, and I do not think texting more right now will help" turns self-awareness into protection. The message becomes a small gate before the field, not a fence built after damage has already spread.

There is also a private component to avoiding protest texting. The unsent message can be used as a diagnostic tool. Write the protest line privately: "You obviously do not care." Then translate it. What is the feeling? Fear. What is the need? Reassurance. What is the request? A time to reconnect, one kind sentence, context about the delay. The sent version might become, "I am feeling scared by the silence. Could you let me know when you can talk?" This translation is not censorship. It is stewardship of impact.

The person receiving a non-punitive pause should not punish the effort. If someone says, "I am going to take a break from my phone so I do not spiral," a caring reply, when possible, might be, "I understand. I will message when I can, and I do want to talk." Or, "Thank you for telling me. I am busy until seven, but I will call then." Such responses help make secure behaviour worth repeating. When clean bids are ignored and only protest gets attention, the relationship trains itself towards protest.

Yet the sender cannot make clean behaviour dependent on immediate reward. A replacement text is not a guarantee of instant soothing. It is a decision about who the sender wants to be under strain. The other person may respond well, badly, late, or not at all. That response will provide information. But the sender's side of the thread remains intact: no bait, no punishment, no performance of indifference, no escalation disguised as honesty. This is not passivity. It is discipline with a pulse.

The motif remains the thread. Protest texting yanks it. Silent punishment cuts it and waits for the other person to tie it back together. Clean digital communication holds it with enough tension to stay connected and enough looseness to let both people breathe. "I am going to take a break from my phone so

I do not spiral" is not a retreat from love. It is a refusal to let panic type in love's name.

The forward test comes in the charged second before the next message is sent. Is this text a bridge, a hook, a blade, or a locked door? Does it tell the truth, or perform the wound? Does it ask for connection, or punish the fear of not having it? The phone will always offer speed. Secure love asks for one more beat before the thumb obeys.

When you need a real conversation

Why can a message sent in seconds create a misunderstanding that takes an hour to repair? The phone makes emotional speech feel deceptively available. A person can type while standing in a doorway, waiting for a train, lying awake, washing a cup, or sitting in a meeting with half their attention elsewhere. The subject may be tender, but the medium is thin. Tone is absent. Timing becomes evidence. A pause looks like avoidance. A short reply sounds like contempt. The thread begins to carry weight it was never built to hold.

The first sign is usually a shift in the body. The message has been read twice, then three times. The reply has been drafted and deleted. The sentence that began as "I felt hurt earlier" becomes longer, sharper, more legally precise. The person starts answering objections that have not yet been made. The conversation is no longer happening between two people; it is unfolding between one person and the feared version of the other. The screen glows. The room narrows.

A real conversation is needed when the emotional content has outgrown the channel. Text can carry signals, timing, brief reassurance, small repairs, and ordinary affection. It is poor at carrying layered meaning, especially when fear, shame, desire, disappointment, or apology is involved. A tender issue needs vocal tone, pacing, interruption repair, silence that can be understood in context, and the ability to say, "That landed wrong; let me try again." Text offers none of that easily. It preserves the words and strips away the living conditions that help words become humane.

The crucial move is to shift medium without making the shift dramatic. "This feels tender; can we talk for ten minutes later?" is a clean bridge. It does not announce catastrophe. It does not punish the other person for texting badly. It does not turn a call into a tribunal. It names the nature of the issue, proposes a limited container, and gives the other person a real chance to say when they can show up. The phrase "ten minutes" matters not because every tender issue can be solved quickly, but because scope lowers threat. The call has edges.

A text that asks for a real conversation should usually avoid unloading the whole case first. Many people write, "Can we talk later?" and then immediately send the argument anyway, as though unable to bear the delay. The first sentence opens a door; the following paragraphs crowd through it before the other person has answered. A cleaner version protects the future conversation: "I have feelings about earlier, and I do not want to process them badly by text. Can we talk tonight?" The need is visible. The evidence is saved for a place where repair can breathe.

This restraint is not avoidance. It is respect for complexity. Some subjects require the full human signal: conflict about feeling ignored, uncertainty about closeness, hurt after a boundary, apologies that need to land, repeated patterns of distance, physical affection, sexual boundaries, family pressure, money tension, future plans, the quiet ache of feeling unwanted. These are not always emergencies, but they are rarely best served by rapid paragraphs on a small screen. When a subject has moral weight or relational history, text can make both people sound flatter and harsher than they are.

The request for a call should contain a clear scope, not merely a mood. "Can we talk?" can sound ominous because it has no size. "Can we talk for ten minutes about earlier?" is less frightening. "Could we have a quick call so I can explain what I meant by my message?" is more workable than sending a defensive essay. "I do not think text is helping; can we talk by voice before bed?" names the problem without blaming the person. Scope turns the unknown into a container. The phone stops being a courtroom and becomes a bridge.

There is a difference between moving to voice and demanding immediate access. "Call me now" may be necessary in rare urgent circumstances, but in ordinary relational tension it often carries pressure. "When you have space, can we speak for ten minutes?" respects capacity. "I would rather not continue this by text. Please send me a time that works" is firm without being punishing. The aim is not to seize the other person's attention; it is to find a medium where the subject can be handled with less distortion.

A real conversation does not always mean a long one. In fact, many emotionally charged topics benefit from a limited first contact. A ten-minute call can clarify whether someone is tired or upset. A short walk can establish whether both people are willing to return to the issue. A brief face-to-face exchange can replace a page of anxious interpretation with one softened look. The conversation may not complete the repair. It can stop the digital thread from becoming the injury. Sometimes the first goal is not resolution, but restoring enough human presence to continue later.

The credible limitation is that voice or in-person conversation is not automatically safer. Some people become more intimidating, dismissive, evasive, or overwhelming in real time. Some need written words because live conversation makes them freeze or lose clarity. Some long-distance relationships have no immediate option beyond digital contact. Some neurodivergent people, highly anxious people, or people with conflict histories may communicate more accurately when they can write and revise. A real conversation is not a universal superior form. It is the right form when it increases clarity, safety, and mutual responsibility rather than merely increasing intensity.

The reconciliation is to match the medium to the task. Text can open, pause, signal, schedule, reassure briefly, and preserve a record of agreed next steps. Voice can carry tone, warmth, hesitation, and repair attempts. In-person conversation can add body language, proximity, and embodied reassurance, though it can also intensify pressure if one person feels trapped. Written reflection can help when the issue is complex and both people need time. The question is not which medium is morally best. The question is which medium gives this particular truth the best chance of being understood without unnecessary harm.

When moving out of text, the phrase should be non-punitive. "Since you clearly cannot understand me by text, we need to talk" starts the call with contempt already in the room. "This feels like it is getting tangled by text; can we talk later?" keeps responsibility shared. "I am worried I am reading tone into this. Could we switch to voice?" names the limitation of the medium rather than the failure of the person. This is a subtle but decisive difference. It reduces shame and invites cooperation.

The person receiving the request can also make or break the moment. A dismissive "Just say it here" may force the tender issue back into the narrowest channel. A vague "later" may increase anxiety. A better reply is simple: "Yes, I can talk at eight," or "I cannot tonight, but I can tomorrow morning," or "I agree text is not helping; let us pause and speak later." If a call is not possible, the answer can still provide orientation: "I do not have privacy right now, but I want to hear you properly." Such replies do not solve the issue; they keep it held.

The danger is using the request for a real conversation as a threat. "We need to talk" has become culturally loaded because it often arrives like a summons. It gives no information except dread. In secure language, the request should reduce uncertainty, not inflate it. "Nothing catastrophic; I just want to talk about how earlier landed for me" can be kind if true. "I am not angry, but I do want to clear something up" can prevent unnecessary alarm. "This is tender, not an emergency" may help the other person arrive with less defence. The invitation should match the seriousness without theatrical smoke.

There is also danger in continuing by text after both people know it is not working. The signs are usually clear. Replies become longer and less understood. Each clarification creates another wound. One person starts quoting the other's words back as evidence. The conversation splits into multiple topics. Tone is repeatedly misread. Someone types, "That is not what I meant," more than once. At that point, staying in the thread may feel like persistence, but it is often stubbornness disguised as care. The more loving move may be to stop adding fuel to the written record.

A useful bridging message might sound like, "I think we are both trying, but text is making this sharper. Can we pause and speak later?" Or, "I want to answer properly, and I do not trust myself to do that well by message." Or, "I care about this, so I do not want to keep sending fragments." These sentences preserve dignity because they do not accuse the other person of ruining the exchange. They recognise a shared constraint. The medium is named as part of the problem, not the entire character of the person on the other side.

Scope should also include emotional purpose. "Can we talk for ten minutes so I can explain what I need?" is different from "Can we talk?" "Can we have a quick call just to reassure each other and decide when to discuss the bigger issue?" is different from launching the bigger issue immediately. "Could we speak in person about the pattern rather than texting every time it comes up?" places the conversation in a wider frame. The clearer the purpose, the less the other person has to guess whether the call is for repair, reassurance, planning, apology, decision, or emotional processing.

A real conversation still needs boundaries. Moving to voice does not give either person permission to flood, interrogate, or keep talking past capacity. "Ten minutes" should mean something. If the conversation needs longer, both people can agree to extend it or schedule a fuller discussion. Without this discipline, the person who feared being trapped by the call learns to resist future calls. Scope is not cosmetic. It is how the request remains trustworthy.

The person asking for the call should also be prepared for a delayed yes. "Later" is not necessarily rejection if it comes with a real time. The anxious impulse may insist that the conversation must happen now or the bond is in danger. Sometimes immediacy is necessary; often it is not. The more secure sentence is, "I would like to talk soon. Please tell me when you can give it attention." That phrase makes attention more important than speed. A conversation held by someone half-available may be less reassuring than one held later by someone actually present.

The motif is the bridge. Text can bring two people to the edge of a difficult subject, but it cannot always carry them across. A bridge message does not solve the issue; it changes the conditions under which the issue will be met. "This feels tender; can we talk for ten minutes later?" is a bridge because it holds feeling, timing, and containment in one line. It prevents the thread from becoming the terrain of the whole relationship.

The forward test comes when the message box is open and the subject has become larger than the screen. Will the next text try to force tone, apology, history, reassurance, and repair through a narrow channel, or will it build a bridge towards a fuller form of contact? The distinction is not about being dramatic. It is about being exact. Some truths need a voice, a face, a pause that can be understood, and a chance to try the sentence again before it becomes evidence.

Chapter 10
Working With Different Patterns

Why can one person's attempt to get closer make the other person feel the need to move further away? The scene is familiar: a question asked too urgently, a silence that lasts too long, a face turning towards and another turning inward. One person says, "Can we just talk about this?" The other says, "I need a minute." The first hears avoidance. The second hears pressure. The more one reaches, the more the other retreats. The more one retreats, the more the other reaches.

Neither person may be trying to harm the relationship. That is what makes the pattern so convincing from the inside. The one who pursues often feels they are fighting for connection, not control. The one who withdraws often feels they are protecting the relationship from a conversation that has become too hot to handle. Yet each strategy becomes evidence against the other. Pursuit looks like attack. Withdrawal looks like abandonment. The knot tightens.

The danger is that partners begin to mistake a loop for a character flaw. The anxious one becomes "needy", "dramatic", "too much". The avoidant one becomes "cold", "selfish", "emotionally unavailable". These judgements may contain fragments of pain, but they do not describe the machinery of the moment. A loop is not an excuse. It is a sequence. One action cues the next, and soon both people are responding less to each other than to the threat each behaviour appears to confirm.

The central tension is that different protective strategies can create the very danger they are trying to prevent. The person seeking reassurance may intensify until reassurance becomes harder to offer freely. The person seeking space may withdraw until space begins to resemble disappearance. One nervous system says, "Come closer so I can calm down." The other says, "Give me room so I do not shut down." Both requests can be legitimate. Both can become damaging when they are delivered without regard for the other person's alarm.

This matters because pattern language can restore dignity where blame has narrowed the room. If the problem is only that one person is clingy or the other is distant, the relationship becomes a trial of personalities. If the problem is a pursue-withdraw cycle, then both people can begin to notice their part without becoming the whole villain. The anxious partner can ask for reassurance without turning it into pursuit. The withdrawing partner can ask for space without turning it into vanishing. The door is not yet open, but at least the handle is visible.

The stakes extend beyond single arguments. A repeated loop teaches the body what to expect. One person may begin every difficult conversation already braced for abandonment, so they speak faster, ask harder, and accept less ambiguity. The other may enter already braced for engulfment, so they give shorter answers, delay harder topics, and ration emotional availability. Soon the relationship seems to prove both fears. "I knew you would leave." "I knew you would push." What began as protection becomes prediction.

The work ahead follows the pattern where it actually shows itself: in the reach and recoil of anxious and avoidant loops, in the blankness that can take over when someone shuts down mid-sentence, and in the sharpness that can seize the voice when intensity rises too fast. The point is not to crown one pattern healthier than the other. It is to make each pattern speak in a way the relationship can use: reassurance for the one who fears disconnection, space with a return for the one who fears overwhelm, quick ownership when volume or edge begins to injure the point being made.

There is a quiet mercy in saying, "I will give you space, and I need a time we reconnect." The sentence refuses the old false choice between contact and freedom. It tells one body that space is real and tells the other that return is real too. The same mercy appears in "I am getting overwhelmed and struggling to speak; I am still here," which turns shutdown from rejection into process. It appears again in "I am getting sharp - I am going to lower my voice and start again," which stops intensity from pretending to be truth.

The unresolved question is not which pattern a person has, as though intimacy were a sorting exercise. The sharper question is what happens when that pattern is under pressure. Does reaching become pursuit, or can it become a clean request? Does space become disappearance, or can it come with a bridge back? Does intensity become injury, or can it be named before it burns the room? The next conversation will not ask for a perfect personality. It will ask whether the old protection can learn a new sentence.

Anxious and avoidant loops

Why can the person reaching for closeness become the reason closeness feels unsafe to offer? A message goes unanswered for a while, a voice sounds flat, a conversation pauses at the wrong moment. One partner moves towards the gap with questions, explanations, another text, a sharper bid for reassurance. The other partner feels the air leaving the room and steps back: fewer words, slower replies, a blank face, the promise to talk "later". The first person sees distance and reaches harder. The second feels pursued and retreats further. The knot tightens.

The loop is cruel because each person experiences their own move as protection. The anxious partner is not usually trying to control for the pleasure of control; they are trying to restore contact before the absence becomes unbearable. The avoidant partner is not usually trying to punish with distance; they are trying to preserve enough inner space to avoid overwhelm, shame, or a conversation that seems to have no exit. Each strategy makes sense from the inside. Each becomes frightening from the outside. Pursuit says, "Do not leave me alone in this." Withdrawal says, "Do not trap me inside this." Both are asking for safety in languages that clash.

John Bowlby's attachment work in London across the mid-twentieth century, including his 1951 World Health Organization report, gave language to the importance of reliable emotional access. Mary Ainsworth's Strange Situation research in Baltimore in the late 1960s and early 1970s later made patterns of separation and reunion visible in controlled observation. Adult relationships are more complex than those early studies can capture, but the central insight still travels: when connection feels uncertain, people do not merely think differently; they organise behaviour around regaining or protecting safety. Some move towards. Some move away. Some do both in alternating sequence.

The mistake couples often make is treating these moves as fixed moral identities. The anxious partner becomes "too much". The avoidant partner becomes "cold". These labels may express pain, but they rarely create change. A pattern is more useful than a verdict because a pattern can be interrupted. "When you go quiet, I panic and push; when I push, you shut down; when you shut down, I panic more" is a different kind of sentence from "You never care" or "You are always needy." The first sentence maps the machine. The others feed it.

The pursue-withdraw cycle has a visible architecture. A cue appears: delay, tone, conflict, tiredness, a request, a refusal, a change of plan. The anxious side reads the cue as disconnection and seeks contact quickly. The avoidant side reads the quick seeking as pressure and seeks distance quickly. The anxious side reads distance as confirmation of danger. The avoidant side reads increased pursuit as confirmation of threat. Soon neither person is responding only to the original cue. They are responding to the other person's protection. The relationship becomes a hall of mirrors, each fear reflected back as proof.

Sue Johnson, who developed Emotionally Focused Therapy in Canada in the 1980s, described negative interaction cycles as central to couple distress. The specific language of that therapeutic model is not necessary for ordinary conversation, but one principle is invaluable: the pattern is often the enemy, not either person alone. This does not erase responsibility. It does not mean every behaviour is acceptable because it belongs to a loop. It means that each person must learn to see how their own protective move lands inside the other person's nervous system. The anxious partner must see how pursuit can feel like pressure. The avoidant partner must see how withdrawal can feel like abandonment.

For the anxious side, the work is not to stop needing reassurance. That would be a false and lonely solution. The work is to ask for reassurance in a form that does not corner the other person. "I am feeling the distance and could use one reassuring sentence" is different from "Why are you being like this?" "Can you tell me when we can reconnect?" is different from sending five messages that each carry more injury than the last. "I am scared this means something bad, and I know I may be reading into it" is different from treating fear as fact. The need for connection remains. The protest softens into a request.

For the avoidant side, the work is not to stop needing space. That, too, would be a false solution. Space may be necessary for thinking, settling, or staying respectful. The work is to make space relational rather than disappearing. "I need twenty minutes to settle, and I will come back" is different from leaving the room without a word. "I am overwhelmed and struggling to answer, but I am not rejecting you" is different from a blank stare that the other person must interpret alone. "I cannot do this by text, and I can talk at seven" is different from silence that stretches until anxiety fills it.

The sentence "I will give you space, and I need a time we reconnect" belongs at the centre of this work because it holds both nervous systems in one frame. It tells the avoidant side that space is respected. It tells the anxious side that return matters. It does not demand immediate closeness, and it does not accept indefinite absence. Its moral intelligence lies in refusing the false choice between pursuit and disappearance. It says: your need for space is real; my need for orientation is real; the relationship needs both to be named.

A loop begins to loosen when each person offers the medicine the other can actually use. The anxious partner needs reassurance that does not require begging, testing, or escalation. The avoidant partner needs space that does not require going cold, vague, or unreachable. The anxious partner might say, "I want to push for an answer, and I am trying not to. Could you give me a return time?" The avoidant partner might say, "I want to pull away, and I am trying not to vanish. I need half an hour, then I will come back." These sentences are not glamorous. They are skilled.

There is a credible limitation. Pattern language can be misused to flatten real harm. Not every painful dynamic is simply an anxious-avoidant loop. Sometimes one person repeatedly lies, controls, threatens, humiliates, withholds affection as punishment, or refuses accountability. Sometimes "I am avoidant" becomes a shield for chronic emotional unavailability. Sometimes "I am anxious" becomes a shield for surveillance, coercion, or refusal to respect boundaries. A pattern is not a pardon. It is a map. If the map keeps leading to fear, contempt, or loss of dignity, the issue has moved beyond better phrasing alone.

The reconciliation lies in pairing compassion with behavioural standards. It is compassionate to understand why someone pursues when they feel unsafe. It is also fair to say repeated hostile texts are damaging. It is compassionate to understand why someone withdraws when overwhelmed. It is also fair to say vanishing without return corrodes trust. The pattern explains the pressure; it does not remove the need for changed behaviour. Secure love does not ask people to become patternless. It asks them to become responsible for the way their pattern enters the room.

The most practical scripts therefore name the pattern without accusation. "I think we are in our loop: I am reaching harder, and you are getting quieter." "I do not want to chase you, and I also need not to be left guessing." "I can respect space if I know when we reconnect." "I hear that my questions feel like pressure; I am trying to ask more clearly." "When you go silent, I make it mean rejection; could you tell me if you are overwhelmed rather than upset with me?" These sentences do not solve everything, but they change the level of conversation. Instead of fighting inside the pattern, the couple begins to speak about it.

The anxious partner often fears that reducing pursuit means surrendering the need. It does not. It means giving the need a form the other person is more likely to meet. "Please reassure me once, and then I will take a walk" may feel less powerful than demanding repeated proof, but it preserves dignity. "Can you send a quick message before you go quiet?" may feel less satisfying than demanding constant contact, but it creates a workable rhythm. The anxious side does not heal by pretending distance is painless. It heals, in part, by learning that asking clearly can be more effective than grabbing.

The avoidant partner often fears that offering reassurance means losing autonomy. It need not. A sentence of reassurance can be brief and bounded. "I care about you, and I need space to think." "I am not leaving; I am overwhelmed." "I want to reconnect after dinner." These phrases do not give up the right to a pause. They make the pause less frightening. The avoidant side does not become secure by disappearing efficiently. It becomes more relationally trustworthy by staying intelligible while taking space.

The loop also changes when both people stop arguing about whose need is more legitimate. Contact is legitimate. Space is legitimate. The problem is not either need, but the unregulated strategy attached to it. Pursuit without regard for the other person's capacity becomes pressure. Space without regard for the other person's fear becomes abandonment in practice, even if not in intent. A secure exchange asks, "How can contact have enough air?" and "How can space have enough connection?" These questions are more useful than deciding who is the difficult one.

A common turning point comes when one person names the pattern early. Early is everything. Once the anxious partner has sent several angry messages, or the avoidant partner has gone silent for hours, the pattern has gained momentum. A small early sentence can interrupt it: "I am starting to feel anxious and want to chase. Can we set a time to talk?" Or, "I am starting to shut down and want to disappear. I need a pause with a return." These sentences require self-awareness before the body feels fully ready. That is why they have to be practised before the crisis.

There is no virtue in forcing sameness. An anxious-leaning person may always be more sensitive to signals of distance. An avoidant-leaning person may always need more transition time before emotional conversations. The aim is not to create identical nervous systems. It is to create translations good enough for love. One says, "When you need space, give me a time." The other says, "When you need reassurance, ask without accusing." Each learns the other's alarm language and stops using it as proof of bad character.

The quiet motif is the knot. A knot tightens when both ends are pulled in opposite directions. It loosens when the pressure changes. In anxious and avoidant loops, one end pulls for closeness and the other pulls for space. The answer is not to cut the rope. It is to stop yanking. Reassurance loosens one side. Space-with-connection loosens the other. A return time, a kind sentence, a pause with a bridge: these are small fingers working patiently at the knot.

The forward test comes when the familiar cue appears: the late reply, the quiet face, the urgent question, the need for space. The old pattern will offer its old protections immediately. Chase. Defend. Withdraw. Accuse. Go numb. Get louder. The more secure move is not dramatic. It is a sentence that makes the loop visible before the loop becomes the whole room: "I will give you space, and I need a time we reconnect." Beneath that sentence is the beginning of a different agreement: neither person has to abandon their need, and neither person gets to make their need the only one that matters.

If you shut down

Why can a person who cares deeply suddenly look as though they have left the conversation altogether? The room is still occupied. The body is present. The eyes may be open, the hands resting on the table, the other person's words arriving in sound if not in meaning. Yet inside, language has gone out. A moment ago there were answers, explanations, perhaps even tenderness. Now there is a blank wall where speech should be. The mouth is closed. The mind is elsewhere.

The person watching this happen may read it as refusal. They may see the silence and think, "You do not care enough to answer." They may feel abandoned in the very moment they were asking for contact. They may grow louder, not because they want to dominate, but because the silence feels like a door closing in their face. The person shutting down may be trying, with considerable effort, not to make things worse. The person left speaking may feel punished. Both are frightened by the same stillness.

Shutting down is often mistaken for indifference because it is quiet. But quiet is not always calm. Sometimes it is overload without sound. The body may be flooded, the mind unable to organise words, the chest tight, the face flat because expression itself has become difficult. A person can look composed while internally scrambling for the simplest sentence. They may not be withholding clarity; they may not have access to it yet. The silence has meaning, but not always the meaning the other person assigns.

John Bowlby's attachment work in London across the mid-twentieth century helped show how strongly human beings respond to perceived disconnection. Mary Ainsworth's later observational research in Baltimore made visible different behaviours under separation and reunion: some people protest, some cling, some appear strangely still. Adult shutdown belongs in that wider human field, though it should not be reduced to any single theory. When a conversation becomes too threatening, some nervous systems move towards speech and pursuit; others move towards stillness, numbness, or exit. The pattern is protective before it is relationally effective.

The task is not to force fluency. Forced fluency often produces worse language: defensive fragments, false agreement, harsh withdrawal, or a clipped answer given simply to end the pressure. The task is to communicate process before silence is misread as rejection. "I am getting overwhelmed and struggling to speak; I am still here" is a small sentence with large consequences. It tells the other person that the absence of words is not the absence of care. It gives the silence a label. It keeps the thread visible.

That sentence works because it separates state from intention. "I am struggling to speak" names capacity. "I am still here" names commitment. Without the first, the person may feel pressured to perform eloquence they do not possess in that moment. Without the second, the other person may hear only withdrawal. Together, the words create a bridge between inner overwhelm and relational presence. The speaker is not promising to answer everything immediately. They are promising not to disappear without explanation.

Shutdown often follows a predictable sequence. The conversation quickens. Questions arrive close together. The person feels criticised, cornered, ashamed, or unable to satisfy the demand for clarity. Their thoughts slow or scatter. The body may become heavy, cold, tense, or oddly distant. Words begin to feel dangerous because any answer might be wrong, incomplete, or used as evidence. At that point, silence may seem safer than speech. The difficulty is that silence, unframed, rarely feels safe to the other person.

Stephen Porges's polyvagal theory, introduced in the 1990s, has influenced many clinical discussions about threat, social engagement, and shutdown. The theory is debated in places, but the ordinary observation remains useful: under stress, people can move not only into fight or flight, but into states that look like collapse, numbness, or disconnection. In intimate conflict, this matters because the silent person may not be choosing absence in the way their partner imagines. They may be losing access to social speech. The relational skill is to signal that loss before it becomes another wound.

A shutdown script should be short enough to retrieve under pressure. "I am overwhelmed and need a minute." "I am not ignoring you; I am blank." "I want to answer, but I cannot find words yet." "I am still here, and I need us to slow down." "Please ask me one question at a time." These sentences do not solve the issue. They stop the other person from having to decode silence alone. They also give the person shutting down a way to remain accountable without pretending they are more available than they are.

The phrase "one question at a time" is especially valuable because shutdown often worsens when the conversation becomes crowded. A person may be asked what they meant, why they said it, whether they care, what they will do differently, why they did not answer sooner, and whether the relationship matters. Each question may be legitimate. Together, they can become impossible. Asking for one question does not reject the conversation. It makes participation possible. It converts a flood into a sequence.

There is a credible limitation. Shutdown can become a method of avoidance. Some people go quiet whenever accountability appears, not because they lack all capacity, but because silence protects them from discomfort. Others use blankness to make the other person drop the issue, apologise for bringing it up, or work harder to restore contact. A shutdown script should not become a shield against responsibility. "I am overwhelmed" is trustworthy when paired with a return: "I need ten minutes, then I will answer your question." Without return, shutdown may become stonewalling with softer language.

The reconciliation lies in distinguishing temporary incapacity from chronic disappearance. A temporary shutdown says, "I cannot speak well yet, and I will come back." Chronic disappearance says, "My discomfort ends the conversation whenever I choose." The difference is visible in behaviour. Does the person return when they said they would? Do they make a good-faith effort to answer later? Do they acknowledge the impact of going quiet? Do they learn earlier signals so the pattern can be interrupted sooner? If yes, shutdown is being handled responsibly. If not, the relationship is being asked to accommodate absence without accountability.

The person who shuts down may need to prepare language before conflict, because once blankness arrives, invention becomes difficult. A practised sentence is not artificial; it is compassionate design. "If I go quiet, it usually means I am overwhelmed, not that I do not care." "If I cannot answer, I will try to say, 'I need a pause and I will return.'" "Please do not keep asking faster when I freeze; one question helps me stay." Such sentences are best shared outside the heat of conflict, when both people can understand them without fear doing all the translating.

The other person also has responsibility. If someone says, "I am overwhelmed and struggling to speak," the response should not be to fire more questions at the closed gate. Nor should it be to mock the shutdown as convenient. A steadier response might be, "Okay. I need us to come back to this. How long do you need?" Or, "I can slow down, but I do not want this to disappear." These sentences protect both needs: room for the overwhelmed person and assurance for the person afraid of being abandoned in the middle of pain.

A useful shutdown script often includes a time marker. "I need ten minutes." "I need to write this down and come back after dinner." "I cannot answer tonight, but I will talk tomorrow morning." Time gives silence a boundary. Without it, the other person may wait in a fog of interpretation. With it, the pause becomes structured. The time marker does not have to be perfect, but it must be honoured or updated. If more time is needed, saying so is part of repair: "I need longer than I thought. I have not forgotten. Can we speak at nine?"

Writing can help when speaking is unavailable. Some people can access language on paper before they can say it aloud. "I cannot speak yet, but I can write the one thing I want understood" is a practical bridge. A written sentence can slow the pace, reduce interruptions, and give the blank mind a surface to work on. But writing should not become a way to avoid real-time contact forever if the relationship needs voice, tone, or shared repair. It is a tool, not a hiding place.

Shutdown also asks for honesty about shame. Many people go blank not because they have no thoughts, but because every possible thought feels wrong. They fear being accused, misunderstood, exposed, or inadequate. Shame narrows the field until silence seems like the only non-dangerous option. A sentence such as "I feel ashamed and I am going blank" can be profoundly de-escalating when the relationship is safe enough to hold it. It names the inner event rather than acting it out. It gives the other person a chance to respond to the real material.

The shutdown script must avoid subtle blame. "You are overwhelming me" may sometimes be a fair statement, but it often lands as accusation. "I am getting overwhelmed" keeps the first responsibility inside the speaker. If the other person's behaviour is genuinely contributing, the next sentence can name a specific request: "Please lower your voice," "Please ask one thing at a time," or "Please stop following me while I take a pause." Specific requests are more useful than global blame. They tell the other person what behaviour would help the conversation continue.

There is a difference between engagement and eloquence. A person who shuts down may believe that if they cannot offer a full answer, they have nothing useful to offer. This is false. Tiny signals of engagement can matter: "I heard you say you felt dismissed." "I need a moment." "I do want to answer." "I am not ready, but I am not leaving." Such fragments are relationally valuable because they prevent the other person from falling into the worst interpretation. The sentence may be small. The reassurance is not.

The quiet motif here is the blank page. A blank page can mean nothing has been written yet; it does not mean there is no story. Shutdown is similar. The absence of speech may indicate overwhelm, fear, shame, or the need for more time. But a blank page left on the table without explanation invites others to write on it. "I am still here" places a title at the top. It tells the other person not to mistake the blankness for rejection.

For shutdown to become safer, both people must stop treating immediate verbal fluency as the only proof of care. Some people speak quickly when distressed; others lose speech. Some organise thoughts by talking; others need silence before they can talk honestly. Neither style is inherently more loving.

The question is whether each person's style remains accountable to the bond. The speaker who floods must slow enough for the quieter person to stay. The quieter person must signal enough for the speaker not to feel abandoned.

The forward test comes when the mind goes blank and the other person is waiting. The old move is to disappear behind silence and hope the moment passes. The more secure move is smaller and braver: name the process before it is mistaken for rejection. "I am getting overwhelmed and struggling to speak; I am still here." It may not be eloquent. It may not answer the question yet. But it keeps contact alive at the exact moment silence would otherwise begin to speak for itself.

If you get loud or sharp

Why can one raised sentence pull attention away from the very point it was trying to make? The issue may be real. The hurt may be legitimate. The need may be urgent, even tender. Then the voice hardens, or the words acquire an edge, and suddenly the room is no longer listening to the content alone. It is listening to impact. The other person's face changes. The body across from you braces. The point is still there, but it has been knocked sideways by the way it arrived.

Sharpness often feels clarifying from the inside. It cuts through fog, forces a pause, gives the speaker a brief sense of control. Loudness can feel like evidence of seriousness: if the issue mattered less, the voice would not rise. Yet what feels like emphasis to one person may land as threat to another. What feels like precision may land as contempt. What feels like self-protection may land as attack. The voice becomes a second conversation, and it may contradict the first. The point needs a steadier carrier.

A quick ownership line interrupts that second conversation before it takes over. "I am getting sharp - I am going to lower my voice and start again." The sentence does not deny the issue. It does not collapse into shame. It does not demand reassurance from the person who has just been affected by the tone. It names the behaviour, takes responsibility for it, and returns to the subject in a safer form. The correction is immediate. That immediacy matters.

John Gottman and Robert Levenson's long observational work with couples in Seattle across the late twentieth century gave attention to how quickly conflict can shift through criticism, defensiveness, contempt, withdrawal, and repair attempts. One practical lesson is plain: small moments of repair can change the direction of an argument if they arrive early enough and are received. A softened tone, a reset sentence, a brief acknowledgement of impact - these moves do not erase the problem, but they stop the delivery from becoming a fresh injury layered on top of the original one.

The first task when loudness or sharpness appears is to resist justification. The mind may rush to defend the tone: "I only sounded like that because you were not listening," "I would not have snapped if you had answered properly," "I am not shouting, I am just upset." These lines may contain fragments of context, but they evade the immediate responsibility. They ask the other person to understand the tone before the tone has been owned. A cleaner sentence begins closer to the present fact: "My tone got harsh. I am going to say that again differently."

Owning tone is not the same as surrendering the issue. This distinction protects people who fear that apologising for sharpness will invalidate their concern. A person can say, "My tone was too sharp; the issue still matters." Or, "I do not want to speak to you like that. What I am trying to say is that I felt dismissed." These sentences hold both truths. The delivery caused impact. The content still deserves attention. Without that distinction, people often choose between defensiveness and self-erasure, when the better path is precise correction.

Loudness has social meaning beyond volume. A raised voice can signal danger even when the speaker does not intend danger. For someone who has known intimidation, a louder tone may register in the body before any rational interpretation is possible. For someone who grew up in loud families where raised voices were ordinary but not threatening, this may feel unfair or bewildering. The mismatch does not make either person morally superior. It does mean impact has to be taken seriously. If the other person is bracing, withdrawing, flinching, freezing, or growing smaller, the volume is already part of the exchange.

Sharpness is often less audible but equally damaging. It can live in a clipped phrase, a sarcastic aside, a cold correction, a contemptuous laugh, or a sentence designed to make the other person feel foolish. "Obviously." "You always do this." "That is convenient." "Right, because your needs are the only ones that matter." The words may be brief, but the edge carries rank. It places one person above the other for a moment. Adult repair begins by stepping down from that height: "That came out contemptuous. I am sorry. I want to say it plainly."

There is a credible limitation. Not every firm tone is harmful, and some people use "tone" to avoid content. A person may be told they are too intense when they are simply being direct, too emotional when they are naming a real injury, too loud when the listener would prefer not to hear the truth. This matters. The goal is not to make every difficult sentence soft enough to be ignored. The question is whether the tone preserves dignity on both sides. Firmness can be clean. Contempt cannot. Volume can express urgency. Intimidation cannot.

The reconciliation lies in separating force from harm. A strong sentence may be necessary: "I am not okay with that." "Do not speak to me that way." "I need this to change." Such sentences can be delivered without sneering, shaming, or overpowering. The problem is not strength; the problem is using intensity to dominate the room. A quick ownership line does not ask the speaker to become meek. It asks them to stop making the other person pay for the speaker's activation.

James Gross's process model of emotion regulation, developed at Stanford University in the late 1990s, is useful here because it treats emotion as a sequence that can be shaped at different points. In conflict, the feeling may have already risen before the speaker notices. The voice may already be sharper than intended. But the response is still available. A person can catch the tone mid-sentence, stop, and reset. Regulation does not always happen before impact. Sometimes it happens in the moment immediately after impact, quickly enough to prevent the pattern from hardening.

The reset should be brief. Long self-analysis can pull attention away from the person affected and turn the moment into a discussion of the speaker's inner process. "I am sorry, I am just so triggered because when you said that it reminded me..." may be true, but it may also become another demand for care. A quick reset is cleaner: "I got sharp. I am lowering my voice." Then the speaker returns to the point. The economy of the sentence protects repair from becoming performance.

A good ownership line has three movements: notice, name, restart. Notice: "I can hear myself getting loud." Name: "That is not fair to you." Restart: "Let me try again." The full sentence may be, "I can hear myself getting loud; that is not fair. Let me try again." Or, "I am getting sharp. I am going to slow down and say the actual need." These lines do not need ornament. Under pressure, the simplest words are the ones most likely to survive the heat.

The speaker must avoid making the other person responsible for the reset. "Calm me down," "Stop making me shout," or "If you would just listen, I would not sound like this" gives away responsibility while pretending to explain. Another person's behaviour may influence the level of stress, but each person remains responsible for how their own intensity enters the room. A more accountable sentence is, "I am getting too heated, and I need to pause before I continue." The regulation belongs where it can be practised.

There is a difference between asking for help and outsourcing control. "Please lower your voice too; I am finding it hard to stay steady" is a relational request. "You are making me lose it" is blame. "Can we both slow down?" invites shared regulation. "You need to stop before I snap" threatens. The wording matters because a frightened or defensive room hears responsibility very carefully. Secure speech names the support that would help without making another person accountable for preventing one's harmful behaviour.

Quick ownership becomes especially important for people whose intensity rises before they recognise it. They may not intend to frighten or cut, but intention does not erase impact. A practised phrase gives the body another route. "I am starting to sound harsher than I mean." "I am going to take a breath and restart." "That came out as an attack. The real point is..." "I do not want my tone to bury what I am trying to say." These lines make the speaker less dependent on post-conflict apology because they repair in real time.

For the person on the receiving end, a quick ownership line should be allowed to count if it is sincere and followed by changed delivery. It can be tempting, especially after repeated hurts, to respond, "Yes, you are sharp, as usual." That may be understandable, but it can punish the very moment of self-correction the relationship needs more of. A steadier response might be, "Thank you for noticing. Please say it again more slowly." This does not excuse the sharpness. It reinforces the repair path.

If the tone keeps rising despite repeated ownership attempts, the next move may need to be a structured pause. A reset line is not magic. Sometimes the body is too activated to remain in the conversation without causing further harm. "I tried to restart, and I am still too heated. I need twenty minutes, then I will come back" is more responsible than forcing continued speech. The aim is not to finish the point at any cost. The aim is to protect the conditions under which the point can be heard.

The pattern matters. One sharp moment, quickly owned, is different from a recurring habit of harshness followed by charming apologies. If a person repeatedly raises their voice, makes cutting remarks, then resets only after the other person is already hurt, the reset must deepen into a larger commitment. "I keep catching this too late. I need to work on pausing earlier" is more honest than expecting the same repair line to keep restoring trust. A script is only secure when it is tied to behavioural change.

There is also a private shame that often follows getting loud or sharp. Some people, once they hear themselves, collapse into self-disgust: "I am awful," "I sound just like the people I never wanted to become," "I ruin everything." Shame may look like accountability, but it often pulls repair away from the other person. The injured person now has to comfort the speaker or deny the harm. A better internal line is firmer and less theatrical: "That was my tone. I can own it and change the next sentence." Shame freezes. Responsibility moves.

The quick ownership line should return to the actual point in cleaner form. If the sharp sentence was, "You never listen," the reset might be, "That was too broad. What I mean is, I felt unheard when I was interrupted." If the loud sentence was, "Just leave me alone," the reset might be, "I said that harshly. I need a break, and I will come back in twenty minutes." If the cutting sentence was, "Of course you forgot," the reset might be, "That sounded contemptuous. I am hurt that the plan slipped, and I want to talk about how we handle it next time." The point survives because the weapon is put down.

The motif here is the volume dial. A dial can be turned down without switching the whole system off. Lowering intensity does not mean abandoning truth. It means adjusting the delivery so the truth can travel without damaging the listener. Some people fear that if they turn the dial down, they will not be taken seriously. That fear may come from real histories of being ignored. Still, the answer is not to keep turning the dial until the room shakes. The answer is to make the content clearer, the boundary firmer, and the tone less injurious.

A relationship becomes safer when both people can notice intensity early and name it without humiliation. "You are getting loud" may sound like accusation if delivered sharply. "I want to hear you, and the volume is making it hard" is more useful. The person getting loud can answer, "You are right. I am going to lower it." This exchange is small, but it teaches the relationship that tone can be adjusted without a fight about whether anyone is a bad person. The correction becomes practical rather than moral.

The forward test comes at the instant the voice changes. The old reflex will justify it: they pushed, they ignored, they needed to hear it, the point is important. The more secure move is quicker and stronger: "I am getting sharp - I am going to lower my voice and start again." The issue remains on the table. The speaker remains accountable for how they place it there. And the relationship learns that intensity can be interrupted before it becomes injury.

Chapter 11
Self-Soothing Without Going Solo

Why can telling yourself "I do not care" feel like strength for a moment and loneliness by the end of the night? A person puts the phone down after a difficult exchange and decides, with impressive speed, to become untouchable. No more waiting. No more needing. No more asking for reassurance from someone who might not offer it quickly enough. The room goes quiet. The body is still unsettled, but pride has entered with a coat over its arm, ready to cover the ache.

This kind of independence can look elegant from the outside. It does not send repeated messages. It does not plead. It does not ask whether everything is all right. It may even sound wise: "I am fine on my own." Yet beneath the surface, the need has not disappeared. It has simply lost permission to speak. The person who was longing for warmth now has to manage not only the longing, but the shame of having longed at all. The armour works. It also isolates.

Self-soothing is often misunderstood because it is treated as the opposite of needing other people. That is too crude for real love. A person can steady themselves without pretending they are unaffected. They can breathe, walk, write, make tea, soften their body, and say inwardly, "Needing reassurance does not make me too much," while still wanting contact. The aim is not to become self-sufficient in a way that makes intimacy unnecessary. The aim is to stay with oneself long enough to ask for connection without panic, punishment, or collapse.

The central tension is that comfort has two sources, and neither can replace the other entirely. Self-comfort without relationship can become exile. Relational comfort without self-contact can become dependence that exhausts both people. A secure bond needs the movement between them: the ability to hold one's own feelings for a while, and the courage to ask another person for the kind of support that would actually help. The blanket matters, but so does the hand that may be offered.

This matters because many people confuse dignity with emotional concealment. They believe they are being mature when they minimise the wound, make themselves busy, speak coldly, or rehearse not caring. But denial has a cost. It turns the need for reassurance into resentment. It turns the wish for touch into private accusation. It turns waiting into evidence that one should never have reached in the first place. The person may appear composed, while the relationship quietly loses access to the truth.

There is an opposite danger too. When distress is sent outward too quickly, the other person is asked to guess the right form of comfort under pressure. Should they listen, reassure, touch, solve, apologise, distract, advise, or simply stay close? Without guidance, even a willing partner can miss the mark. One person brings solutions when listening was wanted. Another offers a hug when space was needed. Another says, "It will be fine," when the real request was, "Tell me you are with me while I feel this." Love becomes clumsy when support is left to guesswork.

A more secure movement begins with inward honesty and then outward clarity. The private sentence keeps dignity intact: "I can be upset and still remain kind." "I do not have to punish the wait." "My need is real, and it does not have to run the room." Then the relational request becomes more precise: "Could you listen for five minutes and then tell me you are with me?" That sentence gives support a shape. It asks neither for mind-reading nor rescue. It invites presence with instructions clear enough to be followed.

The path now turns towards comfort that does not deny attachment and support that does not require performance. A person learns to soothe without becoming armoured, and to ask without making the other person guess the task. Listening, touch, practical help, and reassurance are different medicines; the relationship becomes steadier when the right one is named rather than demanded through mood, silence, or tests.

The unresolved question is tender and demanding: when distress rises, will the self become a prison or a place to return to? Will asking for support mean surrendering dignity, or can dignity make the request cleaner? The next moment of waiting, fear, hurt, or longing will offer the old extremes again: need no one, or need someone urgently enough to lose yourself. Somewhere between them is the quieter skill of staying with yourself while still reaching for another hand.

Comfort yourself without denial

Why can the sentence "I do not care" feel like control for five minutes and exile by midnight? The phone is silent. The house has settled into its small evening sounds: water in the pipes, a radiator ticking, a cup cooling on the bedside table. A person decides not to look needy. They will not ask again. They will not wait. They will not be the kind of person who needs reassurance from anyone. The posture is composed. The body is unconvinced.

Denial often arrives dressed as dignity. It says, "I am fine," when the truer sentence is, "I am hurt and trying not to make it worse." It says, "I do not need them," when the ache is precisely about needing and not knowing whether the need will be met. It says, "Whatever," because "I miss you" feels too exposed. For a short while, denial seems to reduce pain by reducing the importance of the bond. But love does not become less important because the mind has issued a command. The blanket is thin.

Self-soothing without denial begins by refusing both extremes: collapse and armour. Collapse says, "I cannot be all right unless the other person responds exactly as I need." Armour says, "I will be all right because I will stop wanting."

Neither is a secure position. One hands the entire nervous system to another person. The other cuts off the very attachment that makes reassurance meaningful. A steadier sentence is humbler and harder: "I am unsettled because this matters, and I can care for myself while it remains unsettled."

John Bowlby's attachment work in London across the mid-twentieth century, including his 1951 World Health Organization report, challenged the idea that human beings can be understood through physical care alone. Emotional bonds are not decorative extras. They are part of how people organise safety, belonging, and distress. That matters here because self-soothing should not be confused with pretending attachment is unnecessary. A person who wants reassurance is not failing independence. They are experiencing one of the ordinary facts of bonded life: the people we love have power to steady us.

The question is what happens when that steadiness is not immediately available. A partner may be busy, tired, uncertain, asleep, overwhelmed, or simply not yet ready to respond. In that gap, the distressed person needs language that does not shame the need and does not turn the need into pressure. "Needing reassurance does not make me too much" is a compact sentence, but it does real work. It separates the existence of the need from the urgency of the strategy. The need may be valid. The next action still has to be chosen.

A useful internal script should be believable, not ornamental. The body in distress rarely trusts grand declarations. "Everything is fine" may be too false. "I am completely safe" may be too large. "I can be unsettled and still remain kind" is more credible. "This feeling is real, but it is not an instruction." "I can want a reply without chasing one." "I do not have to punish the waiting." Such sentences do not erase discomfort. They give discomfort a frame that prevents it from running the room.

Kristin Neff's work on self-compassion, developed through research at the University of Texas at Austin and widely published from the early 2000s onward, offers a useful distinction: compassion towards oneself is not self-pity, indulgence, or avoidance of responsibility. It is a way of meeting distress without adding contempt. In this context, self-compassion does not say, "My anxiety is always right." It says, "My anxiety is painful, and I do not need to insult myself for having it." The visible behaviour changes: the person stops calling themselves pathetic, stops drafting punishing texts, and starts choosing a steadier next step.

The same principle appears in the difference between soothing and suppressing. Suppression pushes the feeling out of sight while the body continues to carry it. Soothing makes contact with the feeling without obeying every demand it makes. A person might notice the tightness in the chest, the impulse to check the phone, the story forming around a delayed reply. Then they might say, "I am afraid of distance right now." That sentence is not dramatic. It is accurate. Accuracy itself can settle the mind because it stops the feeling from needing to shout in disguise.

Denial often creates secondary pain. First there is the original ache: the need for contact, clarity, or reassurance. Then comes the judgement: I should not need this, I am too sensitive, I am weak, I have no self-respect. The judgement does not make the need disappear; it merely makes the person lonelier inside it. A kinder internal script removes the second wound. "This is a tender place for me." "I can feel needy without acting desperately." "Wanting comfort is human." "I am allowed to ask clearly, and I am allowed to wait." The tone is not sentimental. It is sane.

The blanket motif matters because self-soothing is often modest. It is rarely a revelation. It may be a cup of tea, a shower, a walk round the block, a hand placed on the chest, a written note that says what will be asked later, or the deliberate choice to stop reading the last message as if hidden meaning will appear on the seventh pass. These gestures are not cures. They are ways of keeping the body company. The person is not pretending not to care. They are refusing to let care become self-abandonment.

A short waiting script can also protect the other person from being punished for ordinary unavailability. "They may be busy; I do not yet know." "A delay is not a diagnosis." "I have asked for a time; I can let the ask stand." "I can wait without becoming cold." These sentences are not excuses for chronic neglect. They are brakes against premature certainty. When the evidence is incomplete, the mind may try to finish the story with fear. Self-soothing says: not yet. Let reality arrive before sentencing the bond.

There is a credible limitation. Self-soothing can be misused as a private command to tolerate too much. A person may tell themselves to stay calm while a partner repeatedly ignores agreed contact, mocks vulnerability, disappears after conflict, or refuses basic repair. In such cases, soothing should not become a silencing practice. The internal script must remain allied with reality. "I can soothe myself while I wait" is healthy in a moment of ordinary delay. "I must soothe myself so I never ask for accountability" is abandonment wearing a calm face.

The reconciliation lies in pairing self-comfort with discernment. A single delayed reply may call for grounding. A repeated pattern may call for a boundary. A partner's temporary overwhelm may call for patience. Chronic dismissal may call for a more serious conversation about the relationship's structure. Self-soothing is not the same as explaining everything away. It steadies the person enough to see clearly. The calmer question is not, "How do I make this stop hurting at once?" It is, "What is actually happening, and what response protects both my dignity and the bond?"

This distinction gives self-soothing moral force. It is not a technique for becoming easier to neglect. It is a way of staying connected to oneself while deciding what the moment asks for. If the right response is a clean request, self-soothing helps the request come without accusation. If the right response is waiting, it helps the waiting remain warm rather than punitive. If the right response is a boundary, it helps the boundary come without contempt. The inner work serves the outer sentence.

The best internal scripts are often written in the language of permission. "I am allowed to want closeness." "I am allowed to feel disappointed." "I am allowed to need reassurance, and I am also responsible for how I ask." "I can miss someone without making them guilty for being unavailable." Permission softens shame without removing accountability. It gives the person back their own company. That matters because shame isolates before anyone else has actually left.

Another useful kind of script names the difference between feeling and behaviour. "I feel the urge to send another message; I do not have to send it." "I feel rejected; I do not yet know that I have been rejected." "I feel angry; I can wait before choosing words." "I feel exposed; I can be gentle with myself." This language creates a small gap between impulse and action. In that gap, dignity becomes possible. Not perfection. Dignity.

Marsha Linehan's work on dialectical behaviour therapy, formalised in her 1993 treatment manual, placed strong emphasis on holding two truths at once: acceptance and change. That dialectic is useful here. "I accept that I am distressed" can live beside "I will not act from every wave of distress." "I accept that I want reassurance" can live beside "I will ask for it in a way that respects the other person's capacity." This is not contradiction. It is emotional maturity with both feet on the ground.

The body needs attention as well as language. Words alone may not settle a nervous system that is flooded with sensation. The person may need to unclench their jaw, lower their shoulders, feel the floor, step outside, wash their face, or turn away from the screen for a defined period. The point is not to perform wellness. It is to give the body evidence that something other than the feared absence exists. The room has surfaces. The breath has rhythm. The cup is warm. The blanket is real.

Self-soothing without denial also means not weaponising independence after the fact. Some people manage the waiting by deciding the other person no longer gets access to them. When the reply finally comes, they answer coldly or not at all, not because they need space, but because they want the other person to feel the cost of the delay. That is not self-soothing. It is protest with a polished exterior. A steadier response might be, "I felt anxious while waiting, and I took some time to settle. I would still like to reconnect." This preserves truth without turning recovery into revenge.

The person who practises self-comfort may find that their need becomes clearer rather than smaller. After settling, they may realise they do not need a long discussion; they need one reassuring line. Or they may realise the issue is not the delay, but the repeated lack of return time. Or they may realise they are too tired to have the conversation well and should ask for tomorrow. Soothing does not erase need; it refines it. The unsoothed need often arrives as a storm. The soothed need may arrive as one clean sentence.

There is courage in not becoming hard. The culture around self-sufficiency often praises the person who needs least, asks least, waits without visible disturbance, and calls it strength. But love requires a more demanding strength: the ability to remain tender without becoming ruled by tenderness. "Needing reassurance does not make me too much" is not an excuse to demand endless reassurance. It is the refusal to begin from self-contempt. A person who is not ashamed of the need can ask for it more cleanly, and can also hear a limit without collapsing into humiliation.

The blanket returns at the end because comfort is not always dramatic. Sometimes it is the inner warmth that prevents a cold reply. Sometimes it is the sentence that keeps the phone on the table. Sometimes it is the decision not to become a stranger to oneself while waiting for someone else. A secure person is not someone who never aches. A secure person is someone who can keep the ache company without making it the ruler of the house.

The forward test comes in the private moment before any script is spoken aloud. Will self-soothing become denial, a tightened jaw, a vow never to need again? Or will it become honest companionship with the self: I care, I am unsettled, I can stay kind, I can ask clearly, and I do not have to abandon myself while I wait? The answer shapes what happens next, because the way a person speaks inwardly becomes the weather from which the next outward sentence is born.

Ask for support explicitly

Why can a willing partner still offer the wrong comfort? A person sits on the edge of the bed after a hard day, wanting to be understood, not fixed. Their partner, seeing distress, begins to solve: make a plan, list options, suggest a practical next step, point out what can be done tomorrow. The help is sincere. It is also misaligned. The distressed person feels more alone, not because support was absent, but because the support arrived in the wrong language. The blanket was offered when what was needed was a hand.

The reverse happens just as easily. Someone wants practical help because the body is tired and the situation is concrete: dishes, travel, a difficult call, a task that has become too much. Instead, the partner offers emotional reassurance, a hug, or the gentle sentence, "It will be okay." The words may be kind, but kindness without fit can feel strangely useless. The need was not to be told that life would continue. The need was for someone to take the bin out, proofread the message, sit with the child, make the call, or help decide what happens next. Support that misses the target can intensify the loneliness it was meant to relieve.

Explicit support requests prevent this unnecessary miss. They remove the expectation that love should read the room perfectly every time. That expectation sounds romantic until real stress enters, because stress distorts signals. One person becomes quiet and is assumed to want space, when they are actually waiting for comfort. Another becomes tearful and is assumed to want touch, when touch would feel overwhelming. Another complains about the problem and is assumed to want advice, when the deeper request is to be heard without interruption. Guessing is a poor substitute for clarity.

The sentence "Could you listen for five minutes and then tell me you are with me?" is powerful because it names the form of support, the duration, and the emotional landing. It does not ask the other person to become a mind-reader. It does not demand endless availability. It gives them a role they can step into with confidence. Listen first. Stay present. Then offer reassurance. The request has edges, and those edges protect both people from the fog of mismatched care.

John Bowlby's attachment work in London across the mid-twentieth century, including his 1951 World Health Organization report, placed emotional responsiveness at the centre of human security. Responsiveness, however, is not only a matter of being present; it is a matter of responding to the actual need. A person who needs reassurance may not feel soothed by analysis. A person who needs practical help may not feel loved by sympathy alone. A person who needs quiet presence may feel crowded by advice. To be responsive is not merely to show up. It is to notice, or be told, what kind of showing up is needed.

There is no indignity in giving instructions for care. Many people resist explicit requests because they believe the right support should be spontaneous. "If I have to ask, it does not count" is one of the most damaging private rules in intimate life. It turns love into a test and sets both people up to fail. The person needing support waits to be known without speaking. The other person tries, guesses, misses, and then feels criticised for not intuiting the hidden answer. The wound becomes doubled: one person feels unseen, the other feels set up.

A menu of support is not mechanical when it is offered with feeling. It is humane. "I do not need solutions yet; could you just listen?" "Could you hold me for a minute while I calm down?" "Could you help me make a plan?" "Could you remind me that you are on my side?" These are different requests. They ask for different forms of presence. Listening gives witness. Touch gives bodily reassurance. Practical help gives relief from burden. Spoken reassurance gives the attachment system a clear signal. None is superior. The right support depends on the moment.

The request should name the immediate need rather than the whole emotional history. "Could you listen for five minutes?" is easier to meet than "I need you to be more emotionally available." The larger concern may be valid, but it may not be the first doorway. "Could you put your phone down while I say this?" is more actionable than "You never really pay attention." "Could you tell me you understand why I feel shaken?" is clearer than "Make me feel better." Specific support does not reduce the seriousness of the feeling. It gives seriousness a form.

Research and clinical writing on social support often distinguish between emotional, informational, and instrumental support, though ordinary couples need not use those terms at the kitchen table. The distinction is useful because support fails when the category is wrong. Emotional support sounds like listening, validating, reassuring, staying close. Informational support sounds like helping someone think through options or understand a situation. Instrumental support looks like doing, lifting, arranging, calling, driving, cooking, checking, sharing the load. A partner cannot know which kind is wanted simply because distress is visible. Distress is not specific enough.

The person asking for support must also take responsibility for capacity. A clear request is not a command. "Could you listen for five minutes?" allows the other person to answer honestly. "I need you to stop everything and be with me until I feel better" may come from real pain, but it asks too much without checking whether the other person has the space to help. A secure request includes room for a yes, a later, or an alternative. "Do you have capacity to listen for a few minutes?" is sometimes the kindest beginning. It honours the need and the other person's limits at once.

The credible limitation is that explicit requests can be misused by someone who expects care to be delivered exactly to specification, without regard for the other person's humanity. "I told you what to do, so do it" is not vulnerability; it is control. There is a difference between naming what would help and managing another person as though they were an emotional appliance. Support remains relational only when both people remain subjects, not functions. The person asking names the desired form; the person receiving the request retains the right to capacity, timing, and consent.

The reconciliation lies in collaborative clarity. "This is what would help me; what can you offer?" is a more mature posture than either silent hoping or rigid demand. The partner might say, "I can listen, but I do not have energy for problem-solving tonight." Or, "I cannot talk for long, but I can hold you for a minute." Or, "I want to support you, and I need to eat first so I can be present." Such replies are not failures of love. They are the conditions under which love can remain honest. Support that ignores capacity becomes resentment. Support that names capacity can remain generous.

Over-helping is often the shadow side of care. Some people cannot bear to witness distress without doing something immediately. They give advice before the story is finished. They reframe pain too quickly. They suggest solutions not because solutions are requested, but because helplessness makes them uncomfortable. The person receiving this may feel subtly corrected rather than held. An explicit request can protect against this: "I know you will want to solve it, and I love that about you, but I need listening first." That sentence honours the impulse while guiding the form.

Under-helping has a different shape. Some partners freeze because they are afraid of doing the wrong thing. They become quiet, offer a vague "I'm sorry," or wait for the distress to pass on its own. The distressed person experiences this as distance. Explicit requests help here too. "I do not need you to fix it; I just need you to say you are with me." "Could you ask me one gentle question?" "Could you sit beside me while I finish explaining?" These instructions give the hesitant partner a way in. They make support less mysterious.

The most useful requests often combine duration and task. Duration lowers fear of being overwhelmed. Task lowers fear of getting it wrong. "Could you listen for five minutes?" gives a boundary. "Could you help me decide the next step?" gives a role. "Could you hold my hand while I make this call?" gives both. "Could you remind me this moment will pass, but not rush me out of it?" is more delicate, yet still clear. The more tender the need, the more important the edges become. Edges do not make the request colder. They make it safer to meet.

A person can also ask for a sequence of support. "Could you listen first, then help me think?" prevents the common collision between emotional and practical care. "Could we have a hug, then talk about what to do?" recognises that the body may need settling before the mind can plan. "Could you reassure me that you are with me, and then ask what happened?" gives the nervous system a starting place. Sequencing is not fussiness. It is respect for how distress moves through a person.

Tone matters. "I need support" can sound like an accusation if the atmosphere is already tense. "I am having a hard time and could use support" opens the door more gently. "You never know what to do when I am upset" may contain a history of disappointment, but it gives the partner a character flaw rather than a next action. "When I am upset, listening helps me more than advice at first" is cleaner. It turns criticism into instruction. The old complaint may be true. The new sentence is more useful.

The person receiving an explicit request should resist the urge to treat clarity as criticism. If someone says, "I need listening, not advice," they are not necessarily saying the advice is worthless or the adviser is unloving. They are offering a map. A secure response might be, "Thank you for telling me. I can listen." Or, "I can do five minutes now, and more after dinner." Or, "I am not sure I can give the right support, but I want to try." Such responses make explicit asking feel safe enough to repeat.

There will be moments when the requested support cannot be given. The person asked may be exhausted, triggered, working, unwell, or emotionally saturated. A refusal does not have to become abandonment if it offers an alternative. "I cannot listen well right now, but I can after my shower." "I do not have the capacity for a big conversation, but I can sit with you for a minute." "I cannot offer reassurance repeatedly tonight, but I can say once: I am here, and we can talk tomorrow." This is not perfect comfort. It is honest contact.

The person asking for support may need to hear a later without collapsing into shame. That is where self-soothing and explicit support meet. "I can want support and still survive waiting for it." "A later is not always a no." "I asked clearly; now I can let the answer be real." These internal sentences keep the request from becoming a test. If every limit is treated as rejection, the other person will begin to fear being asked. If every request is swallowed before being spoken, the relationship will lose access to need. The middle path is cleaner: ask, hear the answer, negotiate the next available form.

Explicit support requests also reduce resentment because they prevent hidden labour. Without clarity, one partner may keep offering the wrong help and feel unappreciated. The other may keep feeling unmet and secretly angry. Over time, each builds a private case. "I am always trying." "They never understand me." The real problem may be less moral than practical: support was not specified, and the forms did not match. A simple sentence can prevent a long ledger. "When I cry, I usually need comfort before solutions." "When I am overwhelmed, practical help is what reaches me fastest." "When I go quiet, please ask whether I want space or company."

The blanket motif returns here because support should fit the cold. Sometimes the blanket is listening. Sometimes it is a hand. Sometimes it is a plan, a cup of tea, a short call, a lift to an appointment, a sentence of reassurance, or help making the first move. Offering the wrong blanket may still show love, but it may not warm the place that is cold. Asking explicitly is not a failure of intimacy. It is how intimacy becomes better fitted to the actual human being in the room.

There is a deeper dignity in naming the support one wants without apologising for wanting it. "Could you listen for five minutes and then tell me you are with me?" does not grovel. It does not command. It does not perform independence. It lets the need take a clear shape. The person asking remains responsible for the request; the person receiving remains free to answer truthfully. That is what makes support feel like connection rather than rescue.

The forward test comes when distress is visible and the old wish appears: surely they should know what I need. Perhaps, sometimes, they will. But secure love does not depend on perfect guessing. It depends on making care easier to give and easier to receive. The question is whether the next need will be hidden inside mood, silence, and disappointment, or offered plainly enough to be met: listen first, hold me for a minute, help me decide, remind me you are with me. Clarity does not make support less romantic. It makes it real.

Chapter 12
Build Your Secure Script Kit

Why can a person remember every hurtful sentence ever spoken to them, yet forget the one sentence that would help them speak with dignity under pressure? The moment arrives, and the mind goes strangely bare. A late reply, a tense look, a request for space, a conflict that begins to climb. Somewhere, in calmer hours, the person knew what they wanted to say. They had language for closeness, reassurance, boundaries, repair. But the body is louder now. The old script reaches the mouth first.

That is why a secure script kit cannot be a warehouse of elegant phrases. Under stress, no one rummages calmly through a hundred options. The useful kit is smaller, plainer, and closer to the hand. One sentence for reaching. One sentence for waiting. One sentence for space. One sentence for repair. The aim is not to become rehearsed in a lifeless way. The aim is to have a few trustworthy words available when instinct would otherwise choose accusation, pursuit, collapse, or silence.

The right sentence must sound like the person using it. Borrowed language can open a door, but it cannot live in the mouth if it feels false. Some people need warmth in their scripts. Some need brevity. Some need directness because softness makes them evasive. Some need gentleness because directness, under pressure, becomes too sharp. A phrase that works beautifully for one relationship may sound theatrical, stiff, or even manipulative in another. Secure language is not copied. It is fitted.

The central tension is that scripts must be practised enough to become reachable, yet honest enough not to become performance. A phrase is not secure because it is polished. It is secure because it tells the truth without causing unnecessary harm. "I am getting activated, and I want to slow down" has value only if the person means to slow down. "I need space, and I will come back" has value only if return is real. "I am sorry I raised my voice" has value only if the voice becomes part of the work. The sentence is a doorway, not a disguise.

This matters because relationships are shaped less by occasional insight than by repeated moves under pressure. A person may understand attachment, recognise a pursue-withdraw loop, and believe deeply in honest communication, yet still send the protest text when fear rises. Knowledge is not always available to the nervous system at the moment it is needed. Practice makes language less dependent on ideal conditions. The phrase moves from page to body, from theory to reflex, from aspiration to rhythm.

There is humility in practice. Many adults dislike rehearsing relational language because it feels artificial, as though love should produce the right words naturally. But the words that arrive naturally are often the ones learned in fear. The cold "fine", the sharp "you always", the apologetic collapse, the silence that punishes, the overlong explanation, the apology that begs to be forgiven before it has owned impact: these are rehearsed too. They have simply been rehearsed unconsciously. A secure script kit is the decision to practise something kinder on purpose.

The kit must also leave room for reality. Scripts can reduce confusion, but they cannot make an unsafe relationship safe, a dismissive person responsive, or a chronically evasive pattern trustworthy. There are moments when better wording reveals the limit rather than fixes the problem. If care is repeatedly mocked, boundaries repeatedly pushed, apologies repeatedly emptied of change, or vulnerability repeatedly used against the person offering it, the next step may require firmer protection, outside support where appropriate and accessible, or a sober reassessment of what the relationship can truly hold. Language is powerful. It is not omnipotent.

The movement now narrows the whole book into a usable set of defaults, then widens again into practice and discernment. A personal shortlist gives the reader phrases for the recurring pressure points: closeness, reassurance, boundaries, repair, and activation. Low-stakes rehearsal makes those phrases less awkward before a crisis demands them. The final test is not whether the scripts sound beautiful, but whether the relationship can receive truth with respect when the scripts are spoken.

The unresolved question is practical and revealing: when the next hard moment comes, what sentence will be closest to the hand? Not the cleverest sentence, not the most impressive, not the one that would sound best on a page. The one that can be spoken while the chest is tight, the phone is silent, the room is tense, or the old pattern has begun to move. A secure script kit is small because the crucial moment is small: the breath before the old words return, and the choice to reach instead for a sentence that keeps love honest.

Your personal script shortlist

Why does the perfect phrase vanish at the exact moment it is needed? The conversation has begun to tilt. A reply came late, a tone sounded flat, a boundary was set too quickly, a familiar fear stirred under the ribs. In calmer hours, the person knew the better sentence. They had language for reassurance, closeness, repair, and space. But now the body has taken over the desk. The page is blank. The old words are already reaching for the mouth.

This is why a personal script shortlist matters. Under stress, the mind does not behave like a well-organised library. It behaves more like a drawer opened in the dark. What comes to hand is usually what has been used most often: the protest text, the cold "fine", the over-apology, the sharp "you never", the retreat into silence, the explanation that arrives too soon. A hundred beautiful phrases are useless if none of them can be found when the nervous system is already moving. The kit must be small.

A secure script is not a borrowed line recited with polished calm. It is a sentence that still sounds like the speaker while giving their frightened self a better route. The language must fit the person's voice, values, and relationship. Someone plain-spoken may need, "I am getting activated; I want to slow down." Someone warmer may need, "I care about us, and I need a minute before I speak badly." Someone who tends to disappear may need, "I am overwhelmed and quiet, but I am still here." A phrase that feels false will not survive pressure. It will be discarded by the body before it reaches the tongue.

George A. Miller's 1956 paper, "The Magical Number Seven, Plus or Minus Two", is often invoked too loosely, but the larger point about limits on immediate mental capacity remains helpful. People cannot hold endless options in working memory, especially when emotion narrows attention. Conflict makes that narrowing sharper. A person trying to choose from dozens of possible scripts while hurt, embarrassed, or afraid is likely to default to the most familiar sentence, not the most secure one. The shortlist respects human limits instead of pretending insight alone will override them.

The first default belongs to closeness. It should be simple enough to say without drama and clear enough that the other person is not made to guess. "Can we sit together for a few minutes? I miss you." "I feel far away from you and would like a small moment of closeness." "Could we have a quick cup of tea before we go back to everything else?" The exact wording matters less than the structure: the wish is named, the request is specific, and the answer is allowed to be real. The sentence should not smuggle in blame. It should open a door, not begin a trial.

The second default belongs to reassurance. This is the sentence for the moment when the mind wants to cross-examine love. "Could you tell me something you appreciate about us right now?" "I am feeling unsure; could you reassure me once?" "Your quietness is landing as distance for me - are you tired or upset?" A good reassurance script is present-tense and bounded. It asks for one signal rather than an unlimited guarantee. It helps the anxious body find ground without making the other person responsible for abolishing every doubt that has ever appeared.

The third default belongs to boundaries. This is the sentence that keeps care from becoming depletion. "I care, and I cannot keep doing this by text; can we talk at seven?" "I need thirty minutes to decompress, then I want to reconnect." "I have answered; I am not discussing this further tonight." Boundary scripts must be especially well fitted to the person using them because fear often distorts their tone. A boundary that sounds apologetic may invite negotiation. A boundary that sounds contemptuous may injure the bond. The strongest version is usually plain: care, limit, return or alternative.

The fourth default belongs to repair. This is the sentence that returns after harm without hiding in shame or explanation. "I raised my voice; that was frightening and unfair. I am sorry." "I sent too many messages after you asked for space. I see how that pressured you." "I went quiet without saying what was happening. I understand how that could feel like withdrawal." Repair scripts should name behaviour before motive, impact before context, and change before grand promises. The apology does not need to be long to be serious. It needs to be exact.

The fifth default, often the most useful, is the activation sentence: the line one can always say when the body has started to move faster than judgement. "I am getting activated, and I want to slow down." "I am starting to get sharp; I am going to lower my voice and try again." "I want to answer, but I need a minute to find the right words." This sentence is the handrail. It does not solve the conflict. It prevents the conflict from being handed over to the least regulated version of the self. Every person needs at least one such line close to the hand.

The shortlist should be chosen by pressure point, not by aesthetic preference. A person who tends to chase does not need ten poetic closeness requests; they need one line that interrupts pursuit. A person who tends to shut down needs one line that communicates presence before silence is misread. A person who tends to over-explain needs one apology that stops before it becomes a defence. A person who tends to become sharp needs one reset sentence that can be spoken quickly. The script kit should answer the actual pattern, not an idealised version of the self.

John Bowlby's attachment work in London across the mid-twentieth century, including his 1951 World Health Organization report, helps explain why these defaults matter. Under perceived threat, people reach for access, space, protest, shutdown, or control not as abstract ideas but as bodily strategies. The secure script gives the attachment system a cleaner action. It does not argue the body out of fear. It gives fear a better sentence. That is why the wording must be brief enough to use while the body is still afraid.

Mary Ainsworth's Strange Situation research in Baltimore in the late 1960s and early 1970s made visible how patterns of seeking, avoiding, protesting, and settling can appear around separation and reunion. Adult relationships are not laboratory scenes, but they do contain recurring moments of disconnection and return. A shortlist gives those moments a predictable bridge. When the late reply comes, the script is ready. When space is needed, the script is ready. When repair is owed, the script is ready. Repetition does not make the language fake; it makes the language available.

A useful shortlist is not morally neutral. It should reflect values. If honesty matters, the scripts must not be manipulative. If tenderness matters, the scripts must not be punishing. If autonomy matters, the scripts must leave room for consent and capacity. If accountability matters, the scripts must not hide behind explanations. The sentence should sound like the person one is trying to become in love, not merely the person one becomes under threat. This is not performance. It is alignment.

There is a credible limitation. Scripts can become tools of control if they are used to sound secure while avoiding the substance of the moment. A person can say, "I need space and will return," yet fail to return. They can say, "I hear you," while refusing to change anything. They can apologise with beautiful precision and repeat the same behaviour. The script is not the repair. It is the entrance to repair. Its truth is measured by what follows: the kept return time, the changed message, the softened tone, the boundary honoured, the apology made visible in conduct.

The reconciliation is to treat scripts as defaults, not masks. A default reduces harm when stress is high; it does not replace judgement. There will be moments when the exact sentence needs adapting because the relationship, the context, or the other person's capacity has changed. There will be moments when a script reveals that the other person can respond with care. There will also be moments when the same clear sentence is ignored, mocked, or punished. The shortlist is not a guarantee of safety. It is a way to speak with self-respect while reality shows itself.

The best way to choose a script is to test it aloud. The mouth is a stern editor. A sentence that looks elegant on the page may feel stiff, theatrical, submissive, or too clinical when spoken. "I am experiencing relational insecurity" may be accurate and completely unusable in a kitchen at half past nine. "I feel wobbly and need reassurance" may be better. "I require emotional attunement" may be less useful than "Could you listen for a minute and tell me you are with me?" Secure language should be intelligent, but it should not require a seminar to understand.

The shortlist also benefits from being written somewhere visible before it is needed. A note on a phone. A card in a drawer. A page in a journal. The point is not dependence on the object; it is rehearsal through contact. The more often the eyes meet the sentence in calm moments, the more likely the body can reach for it in difficult ones. The everyday object becomes a small tool of return. Not dramatic. Useful.

The personal kit might include one line for each recurring state: when I want closeness, when I need reassurance, when I need space, when I am activated, when I have caused harm. Five sentences can change more than fifty admired and forgotten phrases. A person might choose: "Can we sit together for a few minutes? I miss you." "Could you reassure me once, then I will take a walk?" "I need thirty minutes, and I will come back." "I am getting activated; I want to slow down." "I raised my voice; that was unfair, and I am sorry." The power lies in availability, not abundance.

These defaults should also be relationally honest. A script that assumes a level of warmth the relationship does not have will feel false. A script that is too casual for a serious pattern will minimise the issue. A script that is too intense for a small moment will overload it. The sentence must meet the scale of the situation. "I miss you; can we have tea?" fits ordinary distance. "I need us to talk about the repeated pattern of disappearing after conflict" fits something heavier. A secure kit includes softness, but not vagueness.

It is useful to notice which scripts provoke resistance. A person who feels embarrassed by "I need reassurance" may be encountering shame about need. A person who dislikes "I am sorry I raised my voice" may be encountering fear that accountability will make them powerless. A person who struggles with "I need space and will return" may be encountering a habit of disappearing without contact. Resistance is information. The sentence may need revising, or the pattern may need more courage than the person expected. Either way, the discomfort should be read rather than dismissed.

The script should also be repeatable without escalation. A sentence that becomes harsher each time it is said is not yet secure. "I need a return time" can be repeated calmly. "Why do you always make me beg for basic decency?" cannot. "I am not discussing this further tonight" can remain steady. "How many times do I have to tell you?" escalates the conflict it is trying to end. The repeatability test is severe and useful: can this sentence hold its shape when the other person is disappointed, defensive, quiet, or slow to understand?

There is dignity in having a default. Many people fear that prepared phrases make love less spontaneous, as though sincerity must always arrive unrehearsed. But the most harmful lines in intimate life are often rehearsed too: rehearsed by history, fear, family patterns, past relationships, shame, and repeated conflict. The question is not whether a person will speak from rehearsal. The question is which rehearsal will have been practised. A secure script kit is simply conscious rehearsal in the service of less harm and more truth.

The quiet motif is the small card in the drawer. It does not solve the argument. It does not make anyone brave by itself. But it waits there, plain and reachable, holding the words the body may forget. The card represents a deeper commitment: when pressure rises, the old script will not be the only one available. Another sentence has been chosen in advance, not to control the other person, but to keep faith with the self.

The forward test comes when the next hard moment narrows the mind. Which sentence will be closest to the hand? If the answer is still "fine", "whatever", "you always", or silence without explanation, the old kit remains in charge. If the answer is one clear line for closeness, reassurance, boundary, activation, or repair, the relationship receives a different offering. Not perfection. Not guaranteed safety. A practised sentence with enough truth in it to keep the door from closing too quickly.

Practising without a crisis

In 1885, Hermann Ebbinghaus published *Memory: A Contribution to Experimental Psychology*, drawing on experiments he conducted largely on himself in Berlin. His work is remembered for a plain but inconvenient truth: what is not revisited is easily lost. The finding belongs to memory research, not romance, yet it has a sharp domestic application. A person may know the secure sentence in the morning and be unable to find it at night, when the voice tightens, the phone stays silent, and the old fear arrives before thought can put on its shoes.

The right words do not become available merely because they are correct. They become available because they have been handled before. Under stress, people do not usually invent their best language; they reach for what is familiar. If sarcasm is familiar, sarcasm appears. If silence is familiar, silence takes the room. If over-explaining has been practised for years, it will arrive faster than the clean request. Practice is not artificial. It is how the nervous system learns where the handle is.

Low-stakes rehearsal matters because crisis is a poor classroom. When a person is already activated, the body is narrowing options. The mind wants speed, protection, relief, victory, escape, or proof. It does not want subtlety. A calm moment, by contrast, gives language a chance to enter without the pressure of immediate repair. Saying "I am getting activated, and I want to slow down" while already calm may feel faintly awkward, but that awkwardness is useful. It allows the sentence to become less foreign before it is needed for real.

Anders Ericsson, Ralf Krampe, and Clemens Tesch-Romer's 1993 paper on deliberate practice, published in *Psychological Review,* focused on expertise rather than intimate communication. Still, its central insight travels carefully: skilled performance develops through focused repetition, feedback, and adjustment, not merely through desire. Secure speech is not a musical instrument or a sport, but it does have a performance element in the most human sense. A person must be able to produce the right action under pressure. The sentence must move from admirable idea to reachable behaviour.

The simplest practice begins with reading the shortlist aloud. Not silently. Aloud. The mouth has to know the phrase. A sentence that looks graceful on paper may feel too formal, too soft, too exposed, or too unlike the speaker when voiced. "I require reassurance" may be accurate and unusable. "I feel wobbly; could you reassure me?" may fit. "I am experiencing activation" may sound clinical. "I am getting worked up; I want to slow down" may work better. Rehearsal is not about memorising someone else's elegance. It is about finding language that can survive contact with one's real voice.

A weekly check-in is one low-stakes doorway. It need not become a ceremony. It can be as ordinary as tea at the table or a brief walk after dinner. The value lies in normalising direct questions before the relationship is under strain. "What helped you feel close this week?" "Was there a moment you needed reassurance and did not ask?" "Is there a boundary we should make clearer before it becomes a fight?" Such prompts make asking less dramatic. They turn directness into a shared rhythm rather than an emergency tool brought out only after damage has occurred.

The weekly rhythm should remain modest. If it becomes a full emotional audit every time, one or both people may begin to dread it. The practice should be light enough to repeat and serious enough to matter. One appreciation. One need. One request. One adjustment. The exact form can change, but the discipline is the same: speak before resentment has accumulated, listen before defensiveness has armed itself, and make one small agreement that can be kept. The small card in the drawer becomes a living conversation.

Individuals can practise without a partner present. A person can take one recurring trigger and write the old line beside the secure line. Old line: "Fine, forget it." Secure line: "I am disappointed, and I would still like to reconnect later." Old line: "Do you even care?" Secure line: "I am feeling unsure; could you reassure me once?" Old line: silence without explanation. Secure line: "I am overwhelmed and struggling to speak; I am still here." This is not mere word substitution. It is pattern recognition. The person learns to hear the first note of the old song before the whole song begins.

Couples can practise through tiny role rehearsals, but they must be handled gently. The point is not to stage a false argument or provoke old pain. It is to make one sentence less strange. One person might say, "Pretend I have gone quiet after a long day; I want to practise asking for context." Then the phrase is spoken: "Your quietness is landing as distance for me - are you tired or upset?" The other person can answer simply: "Tired, not upset." The exchange may take less than a minute. Its importance is not theatrical intensity; its importance is availability.

There is a credible limitation. Practice can become performative if it is used to sound secure while avoiding actual vulnerability. A person may learn the polished sentence but still use it to control, evade, or appear mature. "I need space and will return" means little if the return does not happen. "I hear your hurt" means little if no behaviour changes. "I want to slow down" means little if it is used to shut down every difficult subject. Practice strengthens what is sincere. It cannot make insincerity safe.

The reconciliation is to tie every practised line to a visible behaviour. If the script is about space, the behaviour is returning when promised. If the script is about reassurance, the behaviour is asking once and letting the answer count. If the script is about repair, the behaviour is changing the next action, not merely improving the apology. If the script is about boundaries, the behaviour is holding the line without contempt. The phrase is the entrance. The conduct is the proof.

Practice also needs feedback, but not the brutal kind. After a low-stakes attempt, the useful question is not "Did I do it perfectly?" but "Did that land closer to how I meant it?" A partner may say, "When you said it that way, I could hear the request without feeling blamed." Or, "The words were good, but your tone still sounded like you were bracing for a fight." Or, "I understood the boundary, but I needed a clearer return time." Such feedback is not criticism of the person. It is fitting the script more closely to the relationship.

For some people, the hardest practice is receiving a script without mocking it. When a partner tries new language, it may sound awkward at first. There may be pauses, self-consciousness, even laughter. The listener has a choice: punish the awkwardness or honour the attempt. "That sounded rehearsed" may be true, but it may also discourage the very change both people need. A kinder response is, "I can hear what you are trying to say. Try again." Secure language often begins in ungainly form. So does any new skill worth keeping.

A useful drill is the one-sentence reset. During calm time, a person chooses the line they will use when they notice escalation. They say it several times, slowly, until it no longer feels like a quotation. "I am getting sharp; I am going to lower my voice and start again." "I am getting overwhelmed; I need ten minutes and I will come back." "I want to understand this, and I am starting to defend." The sentence should be short enough to retrieve when pride, fear, or shame is already moving. Long scripts rarely survive heat.

Another practice is the support menu. In a calm moment, each person names what usually helps when distressed: listening, touch, practical help, reassurance, quiet company, a plan, a return time, or space without disappearance. The exercise prevents future guessing. "When I am anxious, reassurance helps before problem-solving." "When I am overwhelmed, touch does not help until I have had a few minutes." "When I am angry, a lower voice helps me stay present." These statements turn hidden needs into known options. The relationship stops treating distress as a mystery to solve from scratch.

Practice should include repair, because repair is harder when shame is high. A person can rehearse the structure before it is urgently needed: behaviour, impact, apology, next step. "I interrupted you; that made it harder for you to finish. I am sorry. I will slow down and let you complete the thought." Saying this in calm time may feel almost too formal. But when real repair is required, the form will be familiar. The hinge will move more easily.

It is equally important to practise endings. Many conversations fail not because people cannot begin, but because they do not know how to stop without abandonment or victory. A couple can practise sentences such as, "Let us pause here and come back after dinner," or, "I think we have done enough for tonight; I want us to end kindly," or, "We have not solved it, but I do not want to keep pushing." Ending well is not avoidance when there is a return or a shared acknowledgement. It is containment.

There is also a place for private rehearsal after a difficult moment. Not rumination. Rehearsal. Rumination replays the wound and gathers ammunition. Rehearsal asks, "What could I say next time that would be cleaner?" A person might review a conflict and notice, "I asked for reassurance by accusing." Then they choose a replacement: "Next time I will say, 'I feel unsure and need one reassuring sentence.'" This transforms regret into preparation. The past is not merely suffered; it is studied for the sake of a different future.

Practice must stay humane. No one should turn secure language into a perfection project. People will still speak badly, freeze, miss cues, over-explain, or send the wrong message sometimes. The point of rehearsal is not to eliminate human mess. It is to make repair more available and harm less automatic. A practised couple is not a couple that never gets activated. It is a couple with more ways back.

The small card returns as a symbol of this work. At first, the card sits in the drawer with sentences chosen in calm weather. Then the phrases are spoken aloud, tested in weekly check-ins, adjusted after feedback, used in small moments, repaired when they fail, and slowly made ordinary. The words stop being decorative. They become part of the household rhythm, like putting keys in the same bowl or turning off the light before sleep. Ordinary is the goal.

The forward test is whether the language exists only as insight or has become reachable under strain. When the next late reply, sharp tone, blank silence, or need for reassurance appears, the body will reach for what it knows. Practice decides what it knows. The old script may still be nearby, fluent and impatient. But another sentence can be closer to hand: one rehearsed without crisis, fitted to the voice, and strong enough to carry truth when the room begins to heat.

When scripts are not enough

Why can the right sentence fail in the wrong relationship? A person has done the work. They no longer send the sharp text. They ask for reassurance cleanly. They name the boundary without contempt. They apologise without collapsing. They say, "I need space, and I will come back," or, "I am feeling anxious; could you reassure me once?" The words are clear, measured, almost brave. Yet the response is the same cold wall, the same mocking laugh, the same vanishing act, the same refusal to care that anything has been said at all. The small card is in the hand. The door does not open.

This is the difficult truth at the edge of every communication book: language can improve the conditions for connection, but it cannot create mutuality where mutuality is repeatedly absent. A script can lower defensiveness, reduce ambiguity, interrupt protest, and offer a cleaner route towards repair. It cannot make another person listen. It cannot turn contempt into kindness by itself. It cannot convert chronic avoidance into reliable return, or make someone respect a boundary they are determined to cross. The sentence may be secure. The setting may not be.

The first sign that scripts are not enough is repetition without movement. One awkward exchange may need clearer wording. A recurring rupture may need practice. But when the same respectful request is dismissed again and again, the question changes. It is no longer, "How can I say this better?" It becomes, "What is the pattern showing me?" A person might ask for a return time after space and repeatedly receive silence. They might apologise clearly while the other person uses the apology as ammunition. They might name hurt without accusation and still be told they are dramatic, needy, impossible, or too sensitive. At that point, the problem is not vocabulary. It is relational responsiveness.

John Bowlby's attachment work in London across the mid-twentieth century gave enduring language to the human need for reliable emotional access. Yet reliability is not a mood. It is visible behaviour. Does the person come back after asking for space? Do they repair when they cause harm? Do they take a boundary seriously after it has been stated clearly? Do they respond to distress with some measure of care, even if imperfectly? Secure communication asks for evidence, not fantasy. If the evidence repeatedly points towards dismissal, evasion, contempt, or instability, no script should be used to argue against what is plainly happening.

Contempt is one of the clearest warning signals. John Gottman and Robert Levenson's observational work with couples, associated with the University of Washington in Seattle across the late twentieth century, placed contempt among the behaviours that corrode relational safety. Outside the laboratory, contempt is easy to recognise in the body before it is named in theory: the sneer, the eye-roll, the mocking imitation, the "here we go again," the deliberate use of a private vulnerability as a joke, the refusal to treat another person's pain as worthy of adult regard. A script may soften criticism. It cannot make contempt safe.

Dismissal can be quieter and more confusing. It may sound like "You are overthinking," "I am not doing this," "You always make everything emotional," or "I already said sorry, what more do you want?" Sometimes dismissal wears the costume of calm maturity. The dismissive person may appear reasonable because they are not visibly upset, while the person asking for care looks emotional and therefore easier to discredit. This imbalance can make the clearer speaker doubt themselves. They may keep refining the sentence, shrinking the need, polishing the tone, hoping that perfect delivery will finally earn a humane response. The small card becomes a plea.

Chronic unresponsiveness has its own signature. It is the unreturned conversation, the delayed repair that never happens, the "later" with no later, the boundary acknowledged and then ignored, the apology accepted but never reciprocated, the vulnerable request met with absence. One missed return may be human. Repeated failure to return is information. One clumsy response may reflect stress. A pattern of refusing emotional engagement reflects the structure of the relationship as it is being lived. To keep treating structure as a wording problem is to lose contact with reality.

The credible limitation is that nobody responds well all the time. A relationship should not be judged by one tired answer, one poor repair, one defensive evening, or one awkward attempt to offer support. People have bad days. They misread each other. They fail under pressure. They need time to learn. The question is not whether someone is flawless; it is whether there is good-faith movement. Does care return? Does behaviour change at least in small visible ways? Does the person show curiosity about impact? Can they tolerate hearing that something hurt without making the entire conversation about their own discomfort? Imperfection is workable. Refusal is different.

The reconciliation lies in measuring pattern, proportion, and repair. Pattern asks whether the same problem keeps returning in the same form. Proportion asks whether the response fits the moment or punishes the need. Repair asks whether both people can return to the rupture with enough honesty to make future harm less likely. If a person sometimes struggles but returns, listens, and adjusts, scripts may still have fertile ground. If they repeatedly mock, evade, punish, intimidate, or vanish, scripts may only help the clearer person see the limit more clearly.

Self-respect requires a shift from persuasion to boundary. Persuasion says, "How can I make you understand that this hurts?" Boundary says, "I have explained this clearly, and I will not keep participating in the same pattern without change." Persuasion may still have a place early in a misunderstanding. But after repeated dismissal, persuasion can become self-abandonment. The person keeps offering more evidence of their pain to someone who has already shown insufficient care with the evidence they had. A boundary does not need to be cruel. It needs to be real.

A boundary in this territory should be specific and behavioural. "I cannot keep having conversations where my feelings are mocked." "If you leave during conflict, I need a return time; otherwise I will not continue as though the issue is resolved." "I am willing to repair, but I am not willing to be insulted while we do it." "I need consistency around this, not another apology without change." These sentences do not diagnose the other person. They name the condition required for continued engagement. They bring the focus back to what can be observed.

There may also be a point at which support beyond the couple becomes necessary. Counselling support, where appropriate and accessible, can help when two people keep entering the same loop despite genuine effort, or when one person needs help recognising their own pattern without shame. The value of such support is not that a professional magically supplies the right sentence. It is that a safer, more structured space may reveal whether both people are willing to take responsibility. If only one person is willing to reflect, practise, and change, the limits of the relationship become harder to ignore.

It is important not to use counselling as a threat or a final performance of seriousness. "We need help with this pattern" is different from "Go to counselling or else." A steadier sentence might be, "I do not think our scripts are enough for this pattern. I would like us to seek support if we both want to keep working on it." The "both" matters. One person can seek individual support for clarity, grounding, and boundaries. Two people are required for relational change. No outside support can make mutual work mutual if one person refuses the premise.

Safety must remain a primary measure. Communication is unsafe when honest speech leads to humiliation, retaliation, intimidation, threats, coercive pressure, or the use of vulnerability as leverage. Dismissiveness is painful; fear is more serious. If a person begins editing every sentence not to be clearer but to avoid punishment, the script kit has entered the wrong job. It is no longer supporting intimacy. It is trying to manage danger. At that point, clarity should move towards protection: trusted support, careful boundaries, and decisions that prioritise wellbeing over preserving the appearance of connection.

There is grief in recognising that better language may not be enough. The grief deserves respect. A person may have hoped that if they became less reactive, less accusing, less avoidant, less sharp, the relationship would become safer. Sometimes it does. Sometimes one person's clearer language gives the other person enough room to soften, repair, and grow. But sometimes the cleaner language only reveals the other person's unwillingness to meet them there. That revelation hurts because it removes a comforting illusion: that if one could simply say it perfectly, love would finally respond.

The danger after such a revelation is self-blame. A person may think, "I should have known sooner," or, "Maybe I still did not say it well enough." Precision matters, but endless self-audit can become another way to avoid the harder truth. The question is not whether every sentence was flawless. No one speaks flawlessly under strain. The question is whether the other person responded to good-faith clarity with good-faith care. When the answer is repeatedly no, the failure does not belong solely to the speaker's wording.

The next step may be a firmer agreement, a pause in certain kinds of conversation, outside support, a change in contact expectations, or a boundary around what will happen if the pattern continues. Sometimes the next step may be private: writing down the pattern as it actually occurs, telling a trusted person the truth without minimising it, noticing the physical cost of staying in the same loop, or deciding what level of responsiveness is necessary for the relationship to remain emotionally safe. The focus is not dramatic ultimatums. It is sober self-respect.

A useful internal script here might be, "I can speak clearly, and I cannot do the listening for both of us." Or, "Their response is information." Or, "I do not have to keep making my need smaller to make this relationship seem workable." These sentences are not bitter. They are stabilising. They protect the person from confusing endurance with devotion. They also prevent the opposite error: turning one disappointment into a final verdict before the pattern has been seen with enough clarity.

The small card returns one last time. It has served well: closeness, reassurance, boundaries, repair, activation, space, support. It has helped the speaker stay honest without becoming harsh, open without becoming helpless. But a card is not a key to every door. Some doors do not open because the wrong words were used. Some do not open because the person on the other side is not willing to open them. Recognising that difference is not failure. It is maturity.

The forward test is no longer simply, "What should I say?" It is sharper: "What has happened when I have said it clearly, kindly, and more than once?" If the answer is movement, the scripts remain part of growth. If the answer is chronic dismissal, unsafe escalation, or absence dressed as complexity, the next secure sentence may not be another attempt to explain. It may be a boundary, a request for support, or the quiet admission that self-respect must now speak louder than the hope that perfect wording will finally be enough.

About the Author

Kaia Solander writes about the small moments that decide whether love feels steady or scary: the pause before a text, the breath before a hard sentence, the repair after a misstep. Her work is rooted in a simple belief that many relationship problems are not a shortage of care, but a shortage of usable language under stress. She is especially interested in the crossroads between tenderness and autonomy - how to ask for closeness without grabbing, and how to set limits without turning cold.

Across years of listening to friends, partners, and readers describe the same spirals in different accents, Kaia has focused on turning emotional insight into plain, speakable phrases. She has a practical, compassionate style: name what is true, ask for what would help, and keep your dignity while you do it. Her approach respects that people carry different histories, temperaments, and thresholds, and that "secure" is often built through repeated, ordinary repairs.

A quiet historical thread runs through her perspective: before instant messaging, connection often travelled by letter, with gaps of days or weeks that demanded patience, imagination, and trust. Kaia brings that sensibility into modern life - not romanticising the past, but remembering that uncertainty is not automatically danger, and that clarity can be an act of love.

www.ingramcontent.com/pod-product-compliance
Lightning Source LLC
LaVergne TN
LVHW100727061126
851857LV00011B/424
9789309332630